GODS & THRONES

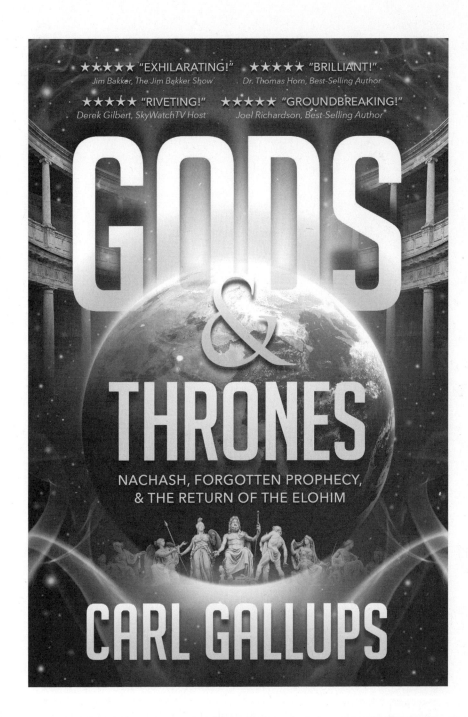

★★★★★ "EXHILARATING!" ★★★★★ "BRILLIANT!".
Jim Bakker, The Jim Bakker Show   Dr. Thomas Horn, Best-Selling Author

★★★★★ "RIVETING!" ★★★★★ "GROUNDBREAKING!"
Derek Gilbert, SkyWatchTV Host   Joel Richardson, Best-Selling Author

GODS & THRONES

NACHASH, FORGOTTEN PROPHECY, & THE RETURN OF THE ELOHIM

CARL GALLUPS

DEFENDER

CRANE, MO

GODS AND THRONES: Nachash, Forgotten Prophecy, and the Return of the Elohim
by Carl Gallups

Printed in the United States of America.

Unless otherwise noted, all Scripture references are from the New International Version.

Cover design by Jeffrey Mardis.
ISBN: 9780999189405

DEDICATION

≷

For Hannah and Parker.
Two of the richest treasures in my life.

Acknowledgments

THREE COUPLES HAVE been particularly instrumental in expanding the ministry field with which the Lord has blessed me. I consider them to be dear friends, and to them I am truly grateful. Those couples are: Joseph and Elizabeth Farah of WND and WND Books, Tom and Nita Horn of SkywatchTV and Defender Publishing, and Jim and Laurie Bakker of *The Jim Bakker Show*.

A special acknowledgment is due to Joseph and Elizabeth for believing in me enough to publish and promote what eventually became my first bestselling book, *The Magic Man in the Sky: Effectively Defending the Christian Faith*. They subsequently published the next four of my books, landing me on the Amazon Top-60 bestselling list.

I am grateful for the research assistance provided by my son, Brandon, who is cohost of our *Lion of Prophecy TV* video broadcasts and our *Freedom Friday with Carl Gallups* international radio broadcasts, which originate from the 1330 WEBY studio in Milton, Florida. My thanks to station manager, Mike Bates, for allowing me to have a microphone since 2002. Thanks also to Mike Shoesmith, a valued research assistant and the executive editor of the *PNN News and Ministry Internet Network* at www.ppsimmons.com.

Of course, the people and staff of Hickory Hammock Baptist Church in Milton, Florida, deserve a distinct word of gratitude for allowing me to be their pastor and ministry partner since March 1987. The Lord has given them an extra measure of patience and love. I love being your pastor, friend, and colaborer in Christ Jesus. Thank you for your continual encouragement.

Nothing I am able to do in life would be possible were it not for the grace of Jesus Christ, who has blessed me beyond my deepest desires. The greatest of those blessings has been my precious wife and childhood sweetheart, Pam—and the beautiful family that has come from our decades together. Thank you, Pam, for standing by me—even in the toughest of times.

A Note from the Author

WHILE OTHERS HAVE written about many of the topics in this book, I am not aware of any other book that deals with the specific theological subjects contained herein, and then so thoroughly connects them to everyday life, current geopolitical affairs, prophetic events of our time, and the eternal future of the born-again believer. In that way, I believe you will find this book uniquely helpful.

When I began teaching my church family what is now most of the content of this book, they couldn't stop talking about what they were discovering on our journey through the Word of God. Our study caused them to dig into the Word with more enthusiasm than I had ever seen, and greatly transformed their overall understanding of the contextual biblical message. I pray that you have a similar experience.

More than three dozen scholarly commentaries, as well as several theological publications, a number of books by renowned authors, more than two dozen biblical translations, the peer-reviewed writings of biblical language experts, and various encyclopedias and dictionaries have been referenced throughout this work in an attempt to ensure the most contextually accurate study possible.

The Scripture passages cited in this book are presented in three different formats. In shorter sections, where a particular biblical truth is simply being pointed out, the Scripture is represented in block-quote, or in a plain-sentence form. In the longer passages, those Scriptures are displayed verse by verse. Using the different formats makes for overall ease of reading and better clarity of the subject matter at hand.

This study demands referencing a sizable assortment of scholarly Bible translations. Each version is clearly noted. When a passage is left unreferenced, it is rendered in the New International Version.

For a more gratifying reading experience, the chapters average only seven pages in length. Enjoy the journey!

CONTENTS

PART FOUR

THE PURPOSE

PART ONE

⤝⤞

The Mystery

*Having made known unto us the mystery
of his will, according to his good pleasure
which he hath purposed in himself.*
—Ephesians 1:9, KJV

UNVEILING THE MYSTERIOUS

I saw thrones on which were seated those who had been given authority to judge.

—REVELATION 20:4

WARNING! THE TRUTHS you are about to discover will forever change the way you read your Bible. In fact, this might prove to be one of the most important books about the Word of God that you've ever read, especially as it directly correlates deep spiritual truths to your life and to present-day global concerns. If you're up for that—read on…

Have you ever wondered, "What in the world is *wrong* with us?" Don't worry, you really *are* seeing what you think you see. And billions around the planet share the same concerns. Without a firm grip on a biblical worldview, the matter can certainly be a perplexing one. Considering the magnitude of the grandeur of the creation in which we are immersed, and the indescribable pleasures consistently available to us, how can it be that almost everyone is making such a gigantic mess of *everything*?

After all, think of the typical news cycles with which we are daily pummeled: Nightmare scenarios of global nuclear annihilation, plagues, disease, natural disasters, genocide, Islamic terrorism, unimaginable butchery, unspeakable crimes against children, national borders collapsing, the Middle East imploding, world powers colliding, horrific cultural decay, massive government corruption, the rule of law collapsing, riots, cities burning, public gang rapes, police officers targeted and shot down in the street, pornography pandemic, vicious hate attacks, extreme left-wing philosophical lunacy, genetic mixing of animals and humans, massive political corruption, the polluting of marriage/gender/family, killer robots, killer drones, and sex robots. Not to mention the scourges of rampant pedophilia, bestiality, sex-slave markets, miniaturized spy drones, household appliances that listen to our conversations and record our living habits, political targeting of Christians in America, a worldwide epidemic of Christian persecution, computer banks filled with our identity information and personal habits, suicide and addiction scourges, sexually transmitted disease epidemics, and an entire generation growing up in a constant quest to find a "safe space"—*good grief!* Well, you get the idea.

The full list of our days' shameful exploits could fill several pages. I stopped with this relatively short list because I didn't want your head to explode. But you know it's true. And, practically everyone else in the world asks the same perplexing questions: Will the madness ever stop? Who will deliver us from the lunacy? How much longer can we continue like this?

I am often asked, "Why does everything seem as though it's falling apart?" My answer is that it is not "falling apart"; rather, everything is actually *coming together*—exactly as the Word of God said it would. Of course, some people don't like that answer. However, as you will soon see, it is the plain biblical truth.

THE PUZZLE OF LIFE

The revelations that await you are similar to a gigantic jigsaw puzzle lying on a table. All the pieces are there, but they aren't yet snapped together in their proper places. As you finger through the pile of colorful fragments, you get an idea of how certain portions of the picture might eventually look, but the completed concept still eludes you. However, as increasingly more pieces are fitted into their proper positions—you begin to see the image—and it finally makes sense. And that's when it hits you...

I must caution you: Some of what you will discover in the pages ahead might offend the ecclesiastical sensitivities so prevalent in our modern age. Sadly, American Christians have, by and large, scrubbed many of the foundational supernatural truths of God's Word from our scriptural interpretation, as well as from the clear proclamation of the Word of God. Yet, you will soon see the contextual attestations of what were previously veiled as *mysteries*. Most likely, you will frequently ask during this journey, "Why have I not been made aware of these biblical concepts before now?"

Albert Einstein once said, "The most beautiful thing we can experience is the Mysterious—the knowledge of the existence of something unfathomable to us, the manifestation of the most profound reason coupled with the most brilliant beauty."[1]

Prayerfully, you will uncover that kind of unfathomable knowledge, except, of course, you will have the advantage of discovering these delights through the revelation of God's divine *code book*—living words, eternal truths—veiled to the unbeliever, but made known to us by the Creator himself. Excited?

Thank you for picking up this book, and thank you for turning to the next page. May the Lord richly bless you as we take this journey together.

Now, let's get right to the puzzle before us. Those pieces lying on the table are begging to be placed in order.

1

DID YOU KNOW?

*Do you listen in on God's council? Do you limit wisdom to yourself?
What do you know that we do not know? What insights do you have
that we do not have?*

—JOB 15:8–9

DID YOU KNOW that God has two families?

As shocking as that declaration might sound, this is exactly what the Bible affirms. You'll soon discover that truth. You'll also learn how that fact ties the entire biblical message together, and how it fits directly into your present life as well as your eternal destiny.

But that's not all…

What if I told you that God has revealed to us precisely what life is really all about, and that the truth of the matter is vastly different than what the average believer even imagines?

Have you ever been shown in God's Word that a heavenly governing council has surrounded the throne of God since before God laid the foundations of the earth? Did you know that Heaven's divine ruling chamber is actively involved in the affairs of the nations—especially in the events of our own profoundly prophetic days?

Did you know that angels can die? Did you know that Yahweh proclaims that truth and Jesus affirms the fact? Did you know that a certain group of angels have already been judged by Yahweh and marked for the death sentence?

What if I could show you that a portion of Yahweh's heavenly chamber was involved in a profane primordial rebellion against God's authority, and that this fact sheds much understanding upon what you are watching unfold in today's headline news and among the nations of the world?

Were you aware that at least a portion of that ancient heavenly insurrection involves the mystery of the sixth chapter of Genesis and the mysterious days of the Nephilim just before the Flood of Noah's day? By the way, did you know that Jesus Himself warned us that something concerning the Genesis 6 mystery will be reenacted just before His Second Coming?

MORE SURPRISES

Have you ever heard of the goat-demons? What about the Watchers? How about a living, breathing idol? What do you know about Beelzebub? The Bible speaks of all these. Believe it or not, they are *each* being directly manifested in our own day. Some of their obvious display has been widely reported in the headlines of global news, yet most of the church is completely unaware because they simply do not understand the truths you are getting ready to discover.

Did you know that the very first Hebrew word in the Bible translated as "God" is also the most unique, controversial, and mysterious of all His names, carrying with it several highly contentious implications? The proper understanding of that word will open up whole new worlds of biblical comprehension. Trust me.

Have you ever noticed, especially in your reading of the Old Testament, that there is prolific use of the word "gods?" And, this particular word is not always utilized as a reference to mere idols—as you might think it would be. As a matter of fact, its most frequent use is that of describing something entirely different than an idol. What you will discover in this regard might very well rock your theological world.

Have you ever wondered how God could have ordered the Israelites to "kill them all!" in reference to the Canaanites and other tribal peoples who were living in proximity to God's newly formed nation? You are getting ready to discover the shocking answers to those questions.

Did you know that four different times in the Scripture, God appears to describe Himself as "us?" What in the world could *that* mean? You'll find the answer ahead, and it is probably not what you're thinking now.

Are you familiar with the modern scientific proof of the existence of multiple realities? The fact of the presence of multiple dimensions of physical existence was declared in the Bible thousands of years ago, but only in the last few decades has this truth hit the headlines of our scientific journals. As you will soon discover, this scientific and biblical truth directly impacts your daily life in several very important ways.

MORE BOMBSHELLS

Was the serpent in the Garden of Eden really a talking snake, or is that image actually an important metaphor for something much more diabolical than you have ever imagined? If the snake is a metaphor, then what about the trees in the garden, the fruit, or the eating of the fruit? Are they symbols as well? What exactly was the deadly "knowledge" imparted to Adam and Eve that caused a literal cosmic upheaval—and is directly linked to every form of evil that plagues us now? Why did God allow the temptation opportunity in the Garden in the first place? Did God "set up" Adam and Eve to fail? Get ready for some intense scrutiny of what the Scriptures might actually be communicating regarding this topic.

Have you ever wondered why the world is so infatuated with the possibility of UFO and alien visitations? How is it that even respected scientific organizations, NASA and U.S. military officials, powerful world leaders, and presidential candidates, as well as other leading government officials, seem to be immersed in the message that we may soon make "contact?" Could the world be in the throes of a demonic setup? Does the Bible have anything to say about this possibility?

Did you know that even internationally renowned scientists are warning the world of a high-tech doomsday scenario that might soon arise because of the wanton eruption of new and uncontrollable scientific discoveries that possess hideous dangers for mankind?

One more thing: Have you ever questioned the reason why Jesus "showed Himself alive" after the resurrection for a specific period of forty days? The answer to that mystery might astonish you. One seldom hears teaching on this amazing truth—yet the fact of it is right there in the Word of God.

Here's something perhaps even more astounding: Every single question and statement we have just laid forth directly links with each other through strong contextual connections. When examined in their related order and proper theological tie-ins, an amazing biblical message begins to unfold before our eyes. The disclosure of the bigger picture that develops in the pages ahead will prove to be a real game-changer in your daily walk with the Lord and in your understanding of the Word of God.

THE ENEMY KNOWS

Here's another secret: Satan knows the answers to everything we just asked. Furthermore, he desperately does not want you to know what you'll soon discover.

Satan also knows his time is short (Revelation 12:12). God's prophetic clock is winding down, and Satan is in a frenzy to defeat the *Throne of Heaven*. The evil one is stepping up his diabolical game plan.

His agenda is more appallingly dreadful than you can begin to imagine—and he's playing for keeps.

If you were not familiar with at least a few of the foregoing assertions, you are in for some astounding disclosures as we move forward. I predict you are going to have more than one "aha!" moment along the way.

How It Happens

One of the most important contextual considerations when it comes to properly interpreting the Word of God is the cultural framework in which the text was first created. Without a grasp of the life philosophy of the early biblical writers and its first audiences, our westernized worldviews often overlay their prejudices upon the original meaning of the biblical text. There's nothing like entrenched tradition, forced paraphrasing, political correctness, closely guarded sectarian creeds, and blindly accepted denominational dogma to conceal the truth of what God's Word actually intends to reveal.

Evidence

Would you like proof of these dramatic claims? Try this one on for size: The Pharisees of the New Testament days completely missed the coming of the Messiah for whom they had so urgently longed. And remember, they were the Bible *experts* of their day. They were the commentators, professors, preachers, and academic scholars of religious thought. They were the guardians of theological "truth."

But how could they have so badly botched their view of Jesus the Savior? Their mistaken biblical interpretation, their dogma, their prejudices, and their traditional teaching about Messiah—all of it—served to obscure the full revelation of Yahweh as He stood right before them in the flesh.

Because Israel's religious elite missed the prophetic signs that signaled His appearance, they accused Jesus of being demon-possessed and utterly delusional. Next, they pompously arranged for the unspeakably brutal beating and the ultimate crucifixion of the Heaven-sent Son of God. But it gets worse…

They carried out their wicked deed within a stone's throw of the temple of God. And, they did every bit of it right outside the gates of the city of God. Before proceeding with their plan, they had first convinced themselves that they were actually doing God a favor, and that they were carrying out their endeavor shielded by the high calling of "protecting the true word of God." Anyone who dared to question their deadly pursuit was rebuked and impugned. Even the temple guards and the respected Pharisee, Nicodemus, learned this lesson (John 7:45–52).

That's How We Miss It

And, that's how we fail to see what God intends for us to discover. Therefore, as we move forward, we will attempt to always let the Bible contextually interpret the Bible *first*. That means letting the biblical languages speak their foundational truths, and it means putting the words that make up those languages into their proper historical, grammatical, and cultural frameworks—regardless of our preconceived notions otherwise.

This is what the Pharisees neglected, or sometimes *refused,* to do. This is why they bungled their interpretation of the Scriptures that so clearly pointed to the true Messiah, and then summarily crucified the Son of God. And they did these things in their intense desire to hang on to their own importance and their long-held prejudices. Let us endeavor to not make similar mistakes.

First, we will lay down our theological foundation. Then we'll discover some amazing biblical connections, and finally, we'll bring direct biblical application of those connected truths to the world in which we live, as well as to our individual lives.

Now…are you ready for a *worldview* tune-up? Perhaps some biblical bombshells along the way as well?

If so, flip the page and let's continue!

2

THE SEEN AND THE UNSEEN

*For in him [Jesus] all things were created: things in heaven and on earth,
visible and invisible, whether thrones or powers or rulers or authorities;
all things have been created through him and for him.*

— COLOSSIANS 1:16

A LITTLE BOY once wrote Dr. Billy Graham and asked a question that
billions of others have pondered, even if the question is expressed in
slightly different words: "I'm eight years old and I'd like to ask you a
question. Where is heaven? Can I see it with a telescope?"

Dr. Graham's answer to the child began like this:

No, you can't see heaven with a telescope, because heaven exists
beyond anything we can see. In fact, it apparently exists in a
dimension entirely different from anything we know. But that
doesn't mean heaven isn't real–not at all. In fact, the Bible tells us
that someday all the things we see around us (including the stars
and galaxies in space) will pass away–but heaven will remain.

In other words, heaven is even more "real" than the earth and the stars.... You and I can barely imagine what that will be like, because it will be far greater than anything we will experience on earth.[2]

WITHOUT QUESTION?

Thus far, I have addressed the unseen realm as though the reality of it is without question. Admittedly, to the modern mind the concept does sound a bit ethereal and a little difficult to conceptualize. After all, our world is filled with the contemporary marvels of tangible technological wonders, and the larger part of the stuff of our lives is physically visible to us. To think of physical beings that exist in another dimension of reality is simply beyond our normal realm of logic.

However, when seriously considering the question of realms of reality that are primarily hidden from our earthly eyes, it really shouldn't be too difficult to concede. After all, our current knowledge of quantum physics understands the reality of the *unseeable*; invisible-to-the-eye realms consisting of the smallest known atomic particles, as well as the energy forces that hold those particles in their proper orbits. Yet, these invisible elements make up the stuff of everything in the universe that is perceptible.[3]

Researchers in the field of physics insist that multiple dimensions of reality actually do exist, and they believe they have recently presented the scientifically measured evidence to prove their postulations. A leading physics publication explains the matter in this way:

Little did Bill Poirier realize as he delved into the quantum mechanics of complex molecules that he would fall down the rabbit hole to discover evidence of other parallel worlds that might well be poking through into our own, showing up at the quantum level.

The Texas Tech University professor of chemistry and bio-chemistry said that quantum mechanics is a strange realm of reality. Particles at this atomic and subatomic level can appear to be in two places at once. Because the activity of these particles is so iffy, scientists can only describe what's happening mathematically by "drawing" the tiny landscape as a wave of probability.

Particles do occupy well-defined positions in any given world. However, these positions vary from world to world, explaining why they appear to be in several places at once. Likewise, quantum communication of faraway particles—something Albert Einstein called "spooky action at a distance"—is actually due to interaction of nearby worlds.[4,5]

Then there was this proclamation making its way into international headlines in May 2017: "Multiverse: have astronomers found evidence of parallel universes?" Following is an explanatory excerpt from that article:

> They call it the multiverse. It's a cosmos in which there are multiple universes. And by multiple, I mean an infinite number. These uncountable realms sit side by side in higher dimensions that our senses are incapable of perceiving directly.... Yet increasingly astronomers and cosmologists seem to be invoking the multiverse to explain puzzling observations.... *Each alternate universe carries its own different version of reality....* The latest piece of evidence that could favour a multiverse comes from the UK's Royal Astronomical Society.[6] (emphasis added)

One might argue, "Yes, but there's a big difference between atomic particles, energy forces, and parallel universes and that of the possibilities of physical/spiritual forces in the hands of literal but unseen beings." Good point! Let's consider that relevant argument.

The question really boils down to this: Is it possible for two intelligent and living physical entities to exist in the same plane (or even *multiple* planes) of reality without one reality being aware of the other?

UNSEEN REALITIES

Hydrothermal vents are openings in the earth's surface. Geothermally heated water gushes forth from these fissures, many of which are located miles beneath the ocean's surface. The deepest known hydrothermal vents exist in the Caribbean, at depths of over three miles.[7]

None of the biological organisms living at depths of more than three miles below the ocean's surface have ever witnessed the complexities of human life above the surface of the ocean—and they never will. In those depths below the sea's waves, there are deeply interconnected societies of sea life that have no idea that the rest of us—*billions of us*, much less the universe around us—even exists.

Imagine if one *hydrothermal-vent-shrimp* said to another one, "I know for a fact that no other worlds or realities exist beyond the location of our realm and beyond our physical limitations. How *could* they exist? That's ludicrous! That's absolutely impossible! I mean, all you have to do is look up! It is a scientific fact that all you see is blackness that goes on forever!"

Of course, that shrimp would be entirely incorrect in its pronouncements. But, the shrimp could have no way of knowing, or of even finding out if its theory was correct. That deep-water creature simply cannot exist outside of the domain for which it is physically equipped to live. Therefore, it could never imagine that anything else could exist beyond that realm of reality. Everything above the surface of the miles-deep ocean exists only in the unseen realm, relative to the realm of the hydrothermal-vent-shrimp's reality. However, what is an unseen realm to the shrimp is still a very real level of physical reality—"seen" by billions of other life forms.

Let's come up from the bottom of the ocean for a moment and consider another community, one a little closer to home. Imagine a large fish pond that exists in the middle of a several-thousand-acre tract of land in the middle of nowhere. Nothing but mountains and forest surround this particular body of water.

The fish living in the pond have never experienced a human being, nor can they conceive of one. Even if they did see some shadowy figure of a human just through the surface of the water, the fish would still have no comprehension of what that being actually was, or the complexities of how the human might function within the unseen realm of its own world.

In fact, the fish would have no real comprehension of the gigantic world around them or the universe in which that world is encompassed. Yet the physical domain of that very real world is just beyond the surface of the water above. More than seven billion humans live in that world! And, ultimately, the existence and future of those fish is in the hands of humans—unseen and intelligent beings that exist outside their world of reality.

Startling Implications

The point is that in both of these illustrations, we have demonstrated that one form of intelligent physical life can exist in the same plane of earthly existence as another. And it can do this unaware that anything else exists within that same dimension of reality.

However—and this is a very important consideration: Humans are able to penetrate both of these dimensions of life. Not only are we able to interact in these dimensions; we can actually effect changes within both realms. We can go in and out of their realities, but they cannot enter our reality. Think of the spiritual implications of these truths!

TIME TRAVEL

Also consider the matter of time travel. Wait! Please don't close the book! I'm serious. So is science. And, so is the Bible.

How else do we explain David being taken to the foot of Jesus' cross one thousand years before it happened (Psalm 22:15–18), Isaiah seeing Jesus' trial and death more than six hundred years before it happened (Isaiah 53), or Daniel experiencing the court of heaven, the Antichrist, and Jesus—over twenty-five hundred years into his future (Daniel 7)? Of course, we can't leave out Paul, who was caught up to paradise and transported into the very last days (2 Corinthians 12:2–4) or John, who, thirty years after Paul, had a similar experience, which gave us the book of Revelation (Revelation 4:1). Both Paul and John had to have been taken at least two thousand years into their future, right up to our very own time and beyond.

We might call these experiences dreams, revelations, or visions, but the fact remains that, regardless of how God did it, He took these people to a time far into their futures. They truly were time travelers. The biblical fact of the matter cannot be denied; neither can the scientific facts. There is so much about life, alternate dimensions, and quantum physics that we simply do not yet comprehend, yet Yahweh is the inventor of them all!

Modern science also recognizes the potentiality of time travel. In May 2017, *Newsweek* published an article titled, "Time Travel Is Mathematically Possible with New Mind-Boggling Model." The synopsis of the subject was stated as:

> Traditionally, we think of the universe as being made up of three spatial dimensions, and a fourth dimension representing time. But mathematician Ben Tippett at the University of British Columbia, Canada, says this is wrong. He believes time should not be separated from other three spatial dimensions—instead all four run together, simultaneously.... Working with David

Tsang, an astrophysicist from the University of Maryland, he has worked out a way to use this principle to make time travel possible. Their findings have now been published in the journal Classical and Quantum Gravity.[8]

GOD'S UNSEEN REALM

We are not equipped to see God's realm in our day-to-day human existence. Yet, we are assured by His Word that the unseen realm does exist, and it is very real. We are also assured that beings from that realm do interact with our world, especially interacting among the powers, thrones, and principalities that make up our planet's network of intelligent life (Ephesians 6:10ff, Psalm 82).

Consider a couple of biblical declarations of what we have just learned:

The Son is the image of the invisible God, the firstborn over all creation. For in him all things were created: things in heaven and on earth, visible and invisible, whether thrones or powers or rulers or authorities; all things have been created through him and for him. He is before all things, and in him all things hold together. And he is the head of the body, the church; he is the beginning and the firstborn from among the dead, so that in everything he might have the supremacy. For God was pleased to have all his fullness dwell in him, and through him to reconcile to himself all things, whether things on earth or things in heaven, by making peace through his blood, shed on the cross. (Colossians 1:15–20)

For our struggle is not against flesh and blood, but against the rulers, against the authorities, against the powers of this dark world and against the spiritual forces of evil in the heavenly realms. (Ephesians 6:12)

CONTEMPLATION

There are two realms of physical existence—the seen and the unseen—the visible and the invisible. Both were created by Yahweh/Jesus, and they were created with an eternal purpose. They are both very physical realities, merely operating within different dimensions. The dimensions of time, space, and matter do not limit God or the directions He might give to those entities within the hidden realm—the Bible is bursting of this truth. The human realm has very little knowledge of the complete depths of the invisible dimension. Yet, that realm knows virtually everything about the human realm.

To cite Dr. Graham again, "You and I can barely imagine what that will be like, because it will be far greater than anything we will experience on earth."[9]

The apostle Paul, who witnessed first-hand the unseen realm, declared, "But as it is written, eye hath not seen, nor ear heard, neither have entered into the heart of man, the things which God hath prepared for them that love him." (1 Corinthians 2:9 KJV)

You will never again read Scripture in quite the same way after completing the journey you are about to undertake. I promise.

Now, let me introduce you to some amazing revelations regarding God's unseen dimension and how all of this impacts *your* life…

3

MEET THE RELATIVES

No, we declare God's wisdom, a mystery that has been hidden and that God destined for our glory before time began. None of the rulers of this age understood it, for if they had, they would not have crucified the Lord of glory.

—1 CORINTHIANS 2:7–8

LET'S BEGIN OUR journey by unpacking the *two-family* declaration. That claim was set forth in the very first sentence of the opening chapter. Once we nail down this puzzle piece, at least a portion of the overall picture will be well on its way.

Our theological excursion commences in the book of Ephesians. The apostle Paul, who had previously been caught up to paradise (2 Corinthians 12), had no doubt been exposed to the following truth with his own eyes. He uses the certainty of that revelation to declare one of the greatest biblical mysteries regarding the reality of Yahweh's kingdom domain:

For this reason I bow my knees before the Father, from whom every family in heaven and on earth derives its name. I pray that out of the riches of His glory, He may strengthen you with power through His Spirit in your inner being. (Ephesians 3:14–16)

Did you see it? God says He has a family in Heaven, and He also has a family on earth. All of those creatures that are truly a part of His gloriously combined household, whether the portion in Heaven or the one on earth, get their name from Him. Using the word "name" in this sense signifies that both of these families owe their very existence to God Himself. He is Creator and Father of *both* families.

The Greek word translated "family" in this text is *patria* (Strong's #3965). This particular word is used only three times in the entire New Testament: Luke 2:4; Acts 3:25; and Ephesians 3:15.[10]

Of the twenty-five top academic Bible translations, all but two use the English rendition "family" for Ephesians 3:15. The two that use other interpretations choose "paternity" and "fatherhood." These interpretation choices are not as contextually plain as family, but they carry a similar perspective.[11]

So then, we are on very safe biblical ground to declare what most translations plainly present regarding this passage: Yahweh has two distinct groups—families—of intelligent, free-willed, created beings—one in Heaven and one on earth. God is Father of each of the families. Both families are under His name, meaning that each is a special representative of His divine image and glory.

However, there are ongoing debates as to exactly *who* makes up these two families. Some commentators insist that Paul was speaking only of humans: redeemed humans who have already died and are now in Heaven, and those redeemed humans who are still alive on earth.

Other scholars suggest there is something much deeper to be understood, something that involves what the Bible's first audiences knew as fact. Once you understand the phraseology of Ephesians 3:15 as the ancient Jewish mind understood it, your perception of many other Scriptures will pop off the pages of your Bible with brand-new life and clarity.

THE HEBREW MINDSET

Practically the entire Bible was written first for a Jewish audience. Even the New Testament church was predominately Hebrew in its makeup for at least the first couple of decades. It would take that long before the apostle Paul would begin his gospel outreach to the Gentiles and then finally convince the early church, under Peter's leadership, to do the same.

The *Cambridge Bible for Schools and Colleges* commentary gives unmistakable clarity in the matter of the word "family" in the Ephesians 3 passage:

> It is worth observing that the word "family" was used by the Rabbis in a sense somewhat akin to the sense (thus explained) of this passage. With them "the upper family" and "the lower family" meant, respectively, the Angels and Israel. Wetstein here quotes a Rabbinic comment on Jeremiah 30:6: "All faces; even the faces of the upper and lower family; of the angels and of Israel." And again; "God does nothing without counsel taken with His upper family."[12]

The Jewish understanding of the two families, upper and lower, is undeniable. You will discover later in our study that the Old Testament, the first "Bible" of the early New Testament church, abounds with that particular revelation. The Jews were aware of this truth precisely because it was the model that had been revealed to them by Yahweh Himself.

MEANING OF "FAMILY"

It is also important to clarify that the word "family" does not necessarily suggest our typical understanding of it, as in the relational unit consisting of a mother, father, and children living together in a house. Rather, the meaning here is better defined as the concept of a *type-class* that is comprised of specific beings.

Another way to look at it is like this: A *family* of living creatures is living at the deepest levels of the ocean floor, in the watery realm. Another *family* of living creatures lives beyond the surface of the ocean, in the dimension of the earthly realm.

The academically respected *Jamieson, Fausset, and Brown Commentary* addresses the matter of Ephesians 3:15 in the following manner:

> Scripture views angels and men, the saints militant [born-again believers] and those with God [those who have already died in Christ], as one holy family joined under the one Father in Christ, the Mediator between heaven and earth (Ephesians 1:10; Philippians 2:10). Hence, angels are our "brethren" (Revelation 19:10), and "sons of God" by creation, as we by adoption (Job 38:7).
>
> The Church is part of the grand family, which comprehends, besides men, the spiritual world, where the archetype, to the realization of which redeemed man is now tending, is already realized.
>
> This universal idea of the "kingdom" of God as one divine community is presented to us in the Lord's Prayer. By sin men were estranged, not only from God, but from that higher world in which the kingdom of God is already realized.[13] (emphasis added)

Before moving to the next chapter, let's examine another scholarly work concerning the meaning of the word *patria*. The explanation ends with a particularly astonishing punch. This lesson is found in the *Elli-cott's Commentary for English Readers:*

> The original word (patria) here rendered "family" is literally derived from the word "father" (pater). It has been proposed to render it fatherhood, and translate, from whom all fatherhood whatever derives its name—all lower fatherhood being, in fact, a shadow and derivative from the Fatherhood of God. The translation is tempting, yielding a grand sense, and one thoroughly accordant with the treatment of the earthly relationship below (Ephesians 6:1–4).
>
> But the usage of the word is clearly against it; and we must render it every family—that is, every body of rational beings in earth or heaven united under one common fatherhood, and bearing the name (as in a family or clan) of the common ances-tor. Such bodies are certainly the first germs or units of human society; what their heavenly counterparts may be, who can tell?[14] (emphasis added)

Yes, indeed, who can tell what those heavenly counterparts may be?

But hang on; you will soon discover the fuller answer to that ques-tion, as well as several other equally astounding biblical realities.

Are you still with me? I can assure you, we have barely scratched the surface thus far.

4

RESTORING PARADISE

No eye has seen, no ear has heard, no mind has conceived what God has prepared for those who love him—but God has revealed it to us by his Spirit. The Spirit searches all things, even the deep things of God.

—1 CORINTHIANS 2:9–10

WE ARE BORN. We live for seventy to ninety years if we are blessed. Then, somewhere in the mix of it all, we die. But then what?

A Christian might answer, "Then we go to Heaven! *Right?*"

But, what does "going to Heaven" mean? I don't know about you, but I'm not really wild about sitting on a cloud playing a harp for ten gazillion years. A day or two maybe, but not eternity.

Try entering these age-old questions into your favorite Internet search engine:

- What's the meaning of life?
- What will we do in eternity?

- If God created the earth for an eternal and glorious purpose, why did He allow it to get so messed up in the first place? Could He not simply have stopped the madness in its tracks from the beginning?

Be prepared to spend hours going through the endless kaleidoscope of metaphysical musings regarding these questions. But be warned, unless you happen to land upon an extremely solid biblical site, you won't even come close to the truth of the matter. And what a shame that is, because the true answer, as we pull together the entire mosaic of the revealed biblical mystery, is nothing short of astounding.

THE NEXT PIECE OF THE PUZZLE

The apostle Paul insists that the solution to the mystery of humanity's existence has been made known to us through the revelation of God's Word. Paul addresses the subject within the first few verses of his letter to the church at Ephesus:

> Having *made known* unto us *the mystery of his will*, according to his good pleasure which he *hath purposed* in himself: That in the dispensation of the fullness of times he might gather together in one *all things* in Christ, *both which are in heaven, and which are on earth*; even in him. (Ephesians 1:9–10, KJV emphasis added)

There it is again: Things in Heaven and things on earth. Once more, we observe the concept of the two families. Yahweh is going to bring both families together under the eventual kingdom reign of Jesus Christ. But, is that it? Is that what life is all about? Well, it is at least the beginning of a much larger picture.

Here is one thing we are beginning to discover, though: This experience we know as the entire history of mankind has, all along, been one giant boot camp experience. It is the proving ground for eternity. The brief journey we call *life* is actually the divine test of the eons.

THE HEAVENLY STRATEGY

The crux of the cosmic test is this: Will the divinely created heavenly realm serve Yahweh and love Him by their own free will? Or, will that particular domain of creation reject His love and rebel against His rule and authority, even though they were in the very presence of Yahweh since before the earthly realm was formed? After all, the angelic beings were not created as robots or puppets on strings. Nor do they have a button on their backs that God pushes to invoke preprogrammed actions. Angels were created with "free will." They are therefore eternally accountable for their choices.

The test is similar for God's human creation. What portion of the lower family (Psalm 8:5; Hebrews 2:7) will freely choose to receive God's offer of salvation in Jesus Christ, then ultimately partake in His magnificent eternal purpose through spiritual adoption into His family?

Every twinkling of what is occurring in the world at this very moment, as well as all that has transpired in ages past, is being gloriously employed to bring about Yahweh's endgame. Even Satan and his minions are being *used* by the Lord for His own grand purpose. In every evil thing—and every wicked person—God is maneuvering it all within the entirety of His cosmic plan. Yahweh is filtering out the good fruit from the bad, the obedient from the rebellious, and the self-centered from the Kingdom-centered. And, *your* life is right in the middle of the test. How are you doing thus far?

Never doubt: Yahweh *is* allowing us to freely choose the side we prefer. However, nothing can stop the ultimate *mystery of His will* from being fulfilled. Our choice in the matter is to pick the team with whom we will align ourselves (Joshua 24:15).

To confirm what we have thus far asserted, let's examine the *Jamieson, Fausset, and Brown Commentary* (JFB) on Ephesians 1:10:

Gather together in one, [anakephalaioosasthai]—"sum up again (in their original unity) for Himself under one head;" "recapitulate." The "good pleasure which He purposed" was "to sum up *all things* [ta panta: "the *whole range* of things"] in Christ" [to Christoo: "the Christ"].

God sums up the **whole creation** in Christ, the **Head of angels, with whom He is linked by His invisible nature; and of men,** with whom He is linked by His humanity; of Jews and Gentiles; of the living and the dead (Ephesians 3:15); of animate and inanimate creation. Sin has disarranged the creature's relation of subordination to God. God gathers up all in Christ. (Colossians 1:20; emphasis added)[15]

UNITING JEW AND GENTILE

Did you notice that the *JFB Commentary* entry for Ephesians 1:10 also highlights the bringing together of Jew and Gentile into a united earthly group? This declaration is an important part of the biblical-family concept as well. The point is that, as far as God is concerned, among humankind's redeemed there are two distinct groups within the totality of that converted household. The two groups are Yahweh's initially chosen instruments—the Jews—as well as the Gentiles, or non-Jews.

God is in the process of bringing together both of these earthly groups in Jesus Christ as one great family, a family also known as the Church, the *called-out ones*. God is bringing them together from among the ranks of humanity into one new humanity (Romans 11, Ephesians 2–3).

The joining of Jew and Gentile into one household is yet another *mystery revealed*. Paul explains the mystery:

His purpose was to create in himself one new humanity out of the two, thus making peace, and in one body to reconcile both of them to God through the cross, by which he put to death their hostility. (Ephesians 2:15–16)

We see the truth of this mystery emphasized again in Ephesians 3:

Surely you have heard about the administration of God's grace that was given to me for you, that is, **the mystery** made known to me by revelation, as I have already written briefly.

In reading this, then, you will be able to understand my insight into the **mystery of Christ,** which was not made known to men in other generations as it has now been revealed by the Spirit to God's holy apostles and prophets.

This mystery is that through the gospel the Gentiles are heirs together with Israel, members together of one body, and **sharers together in the promise in Christ Jesus.** (Ephesians 3:2–6, emphasis added)

Not only will Yahweh eventually bring together the upper family of Heaven with the lower family of the earthly realm, He will first heal the division between Jew and Gentile through the blood sacrifice of Jesus Christ.

Once the divine plan of uniting the redeemed Jews with the redeemed Gentiles is completed (Romans 11), God will then bring together His faithful beings in Heaven with the salvation-purchased beings of earth. But it is not just the created beings that Yahweh will restore; His plan is even larger than that.

TOTAL UNITY

Barnes' Notes on the Bible interprets the startling message of Ephesians 1:9–10 like this:

The reference is to the unity which will hereafter exist in the kingdom of God, when all his friends on earth and in heaven shall be united, and all shall have a common head. Now there is alienation. The earth has been separated from other worlds [the heavenly realm] by rebellion. It has gone off into apostasy and sin. It refuses to acknowledge the Great Head to which other worlds are subject, and the object is to restore it to its proper place, so that there shall be one great and united kingdom.

All things—[Greek] ta panta. It is remarkable that Paul has used here a word which is in the neuter gender. It is not all "persons," all angels, or all human beings, or all the elect, but all "things."…

Everything is, therefore, put under the Lord Jesus, and all things are to be brought under his control, so as to constitute one vast harmonious empire.[16]

An empire that encompasses all things. Now there's a thought! A united realm, under the kingship of Jesus Christ—and we, the earthly redeemed, are declared to be co-heirs of that domain:

Now if we are children, then we are heirs—heirs of God and co-heirs with Christ, if indeed we share in his sufferings in order that we may also share in his glory. (Romans 8:17)

This thing called the meaning of life is beginning to sound a bit more involved than just an eventual ticket to heaven. Would you agree? But hang on. There's so much more to come…

THE PICTURE BEGINS TO UNFOLD

Yahweh is not only going to unite the two families; He will also restore the totality of the elements of the fallen creation, both mind and matter.

He will restore the sum total of everything to its original condition: the complete restoration of all things under the headship of Jesus Christ. This understanding makes you want to burst into a song of praise, doesn't it?

> Praise God, from whom all blessings flow;
> Praise Him, all creatures here below;
> Praise Him above, ye heavenly host;
> Praise Father, Son, and Holy Ghost. Amen.[17]

And get this: Everything we have thus far discovered is still not the totality of what lies ahead for the redeemed part of God's family called humankind. There are still many more surprises to come. We have only pulled together the first few pieces of the puzzle.

In order to fully understand the interactions between the two dimensions of God's creation, we have to wade into some deep and eternally significant territory. We will next unveil what the Bible really says about the beings of the heavenly dimension and their divinely appointed thrones.

Aren't mysteries fun? Ready for more?

PART TWO

THE THRONES

As I looked, "thrones were set in place,
and the Ancient of Days took his seat."

—DANIEL 7:9

5

ELOHIM

I said, "You are 'gods'; you are all sons of the Most High."

—PSALM 82:6

THIS IS WHERE the test of translation sincerity really begins. Will we truly allow the Bible to faithfully and contextually interpret itself—*first?* Or, will we permit accepted traditions and relatively modern cultural sensibilities to overrule what the Scripture intends to convey? As you will soon discover, prohibiting those overrides is not always an easy task. The Pharisees in Jesus' day certainly faced, and often failed to overcome, those difficulties.

To begin this study, let's have some fun with a few peculiar English words. This exercise will help to recognize the significance of similar oddities within the Hebrew language, and that understanding will be vital in our overall pursuit of several important biblical truths.

TRICKY WORDS

See if you can determine what the following words have in common: deer, bass, trout, moose, offspring, cod, bison, aircraft, spacecraft, buffalo, sheep, fowl, quail, furniture, luggage, rice, wheat, gold, silver, bronze, barley, blood, wildlife, knowledge, spinach, chili, spaghetti, macaroni, sunshine, and camouflage. There is one linguistic feature that each of these words share. Do you see it?

Each of the nouns in the list is spelled and pronounced the very same way regardless of whether it is used in the singular or in the plural. Go ahead, try and put an "-s" or an "-es" on the end of any of these nouns. Funny stuff, huh?

When any of these particular words is left unattended by qualifying words, we have no idea if the word is meant to be understood as singular or plural. For example, if I exclaim "Buffalo!" do you think of a stampeding herd of buffalo or a lone buffalo standing in the middle of a grassy plain?

In addition, there are English words that actually do end with an "-s" that can either be plural or singular, depending upon the context, such as species and series. The way in which those words are properly interpreted depends upon context and accompanying qualifiers.

To make this exercise even more complex, there are also a few English terms that end with the letter "-s" or "-es" but, surprisingly, are not plural. Those words can only be used in the singular sense when left with no other qualifiers. A few nouns in this category are billiards, news, binoculars, mumps, measles, shingles (the disease), glasses (the eyewear), and diabetes.

Hebrew grammar often presents the same types of linguistic nuances. One such Hebrew word, *Elohim,* is the subject of our next level of study. It is by far the most prevalent of the words translated as "God" that are found in the Hebrew version of the Old Testament. And, through the ages, that singular Hebraic expression has presented more than a few translation difficulties.

ELOHIM

In the Hebrew Bible four words are translated as the English word "God." Those words are: *El, Elah, Elo'ah,* and *Elohim.*

1. The oldest Semitic word meaning "God" is El. Hebrew scholars believe its meaning is strength or power. El occurs 238 times and is first used in Genesis 14:18 in the expression "God Most High" [El Elyon].

2. Elah is the Aramaic word for the one true God. It is used in the Aramaic portions of Daniel and Ezra. It is also used in one verse in Jeremiah (10:11). The word is found less than two dozen times in the scriptures. Its plural form Elahin is used at least once for the one true God (Daniel 5:23).

3. The word Elo'ah is used almost sixty times, mostly in the book of Job. Many scholars believe it to be the ancient singular form related to the word Elohim.

THE FOCUS OF OUR STUDY

4. The fourth word for God is the most contentious of them all. The generic term elohim refers to the one true God. In that sense, it is found over 2,500 times. But it also can be rendered as gods, divine beings, angels, idols, and things which are divine or mighty. In total, elohim occurs 2,602 times in the Hebrew version of the Old Testament. Obviously, this is a very complex Hebrew word requiring careful contextual consideration when translating.

When used of the one true God, elohim is thought to denote what is often termed by Hebrew language scholars as a plural intensification of majesty, honor, or fullness. That is, He is God/Creator in the fullest sense of the word; He is "God of gods" or literally, "Elohim of elohim" (Deuteronomy 10:17; Psalm 136:2).[18]

Elohim is the very first name of God to which we are introduced in the Scriptures. In Genesis 1:1, the text reads, "In the beginning, God (*Elohim*) created the heavens and the earth."

GOD OR "GODS?"

Elohim is exactly like the English word "buffalo" in that it can be used either in the singular or plural depending upon context and the linguistic qualifiers that surround it. However, it is spelled the same regardless of the use.

But, it is also like the word "series" because it ends in the distinctive Hebrew *-im*, the equivalent of the normally plural sense of English words that end in "-s" or "-es."

And, at the same time, *elohim* is like the English word "glasses." When we find *elohim* in the Hebrew text, we have to determine if that passage is speaking of common eyewear (singular—one type of object), or something completely different, like glasses used for drinking (plural—another type of object altogether). These are two different concepts entirely, yet both words are spelled and pronounced the same. In the same way the word "glasses" can be varyingly defined in English, the word *elohim* can also mean several very different things in the Hebrew language, depending upon context.

These considerations are important, because even though *elohim* is most often translated as "God," it can, for example, also be properly translated in the plural, as "gods." Clearly—and here begins the problem—there is a universe of difference between these two translation possibilities of the very same word.

But, there is even further complexity to the matter of translating the word *elohim*. Even when the word is translated as "gods," it can either mean inanimate gods—idols—or supernatural spirits—angels or demons—presenting themselves as false gods. *Elohim* can also mean "divine beings" in general. You will soon see that every one of these translation renderings is used at certain places in the Scriptures for the Hebrew word *elohim*.[19]

DID "GODS" CREATE?

When Genesis opens with the declaration, "In the beginning Elohim created…," we have to ask: Is this a declaration that only one God created everything, or was it a pantheon of Gods that did the creating? Verses 1–25 tell us plainly, by numerous declarations of the singular Hebrew verb, "He called," that the entirety of the creation account was the work of only the one true God. Of course, we know from numerous other Scriptures that this is the case as well, and we also know that the Bible doesn't even come close to teaching that there exists an assemblage of equal and sovereign "gods."

So, when we find the word *elohim*, how exactly is that word to be properly translated? The answer: *It depends* upon the context of the passage and which specific verbs and qualifiers accompany the word. Sounds easy enough, right? Oh, if it were really that simple…

GODS OR JUDGES?

There is yet another tricky area of translation regarding the word *elohim*. The difficulty occurs in those extremely rare instances when the context might call for the rendering to take on a more human understanding. In some cases, the translation choice is fairly clear. But, in other cases, the matter is not so definite. That's where the interjection of interpretation biases and cultural norms can come into play.

The fact is that in less than .5 percent of the total of 2,600 times *elohim* is used do we find the word translated as anything besides God Himself, much less human leaders. Thus, in only extremely rare instances is the word rendered as "kings," "judges," or "rulers." These are the translation choices that give scholars, commentators, and Bible students the most anxiety regarding the word *elohim.*[20]

For example, while some Bible translators might use the human definition of "judge" or "ruler" in a certain passage, other translators may determine the word to mean God Himself in that very same passage. How in the world can that be? Obviously, both can't be correct. Consider the different translation examples of Exodus 21:6 in this regard:

> ...then his master must take him before **the judges**. He shall take him to the door or the doorpost and pierce his ear with an awl. Then he will be his servant for life. (emphasis added)

In addition to the NIV, other versions that translate *elohim* as human "judges" in this verse include: KJV, HCSB, the Jubilee Bible 2000, NET Bible, King James 2000 Bible, Darby Bible, Webster's Bible, and the ISV.

However, not all translators see the word as a mere human judge. Observe how the English Standard Version translates the same verse:

> ...then his master shall bring him to God, and he shall bring him to the door or the doorpost. And his master shall bore his ear through with an awl, and he shall be his slave forever. (ESV; emphasis added)

A number of other versions also translate *elohim* in Exodus 21:6 as God Himself. Examples include the: NLT, NASB, NAS 1977, ASV, ERV, Word English Bible, and Young's Literal Interpretation Bible. And, to make the matter a tad more difficult, the Douay-Rheims Bible translates *elohim* in this same passage as "the gods" (divine beings, but not Yahweh).

So, which is it? We now have three different choices in the same passage for the rendering of the Hebrew word *elohim*. We have it translated as:

- God: Yahweh;
- the gods: divine beings
- the judges: mere human dignitaries.

Aren't you glad you don't have to make a living as a Bible translator?

LESSONS

We can glean three major takeaways from the rather involved exercise we have just completed.

First, in more than 99 percent of the instances of translating *elohim*, the word is correctly rendered as "the one true God," or as some other type of divine being—yet, a being that was created by Yahweh. One of these two possibilities must then always be our starting point for translation unless the clear and complete context absolutely demands another choice.

Second, when we speak of the upper family of divine beings, we are certainly not talking about a pantheon of Gods. There is no such teaching anywhere in the Word of God. However, there is a very clear biblical understanding of God's *created* upper family over which He is supreme. Those created beings God calls *elohim*, angels, the heavenly host, or sons of God; sometimes they are simply called "gods."

Third, in most instances where the word *elohim* is occasionally translated as a human ruler, there is still quite a disparity among scholars regarding the precise use of that particular representation. The humanistic rendition is simply not the predominant go-to translation to represent the word *elohim*. In order to justify the translation of the word in that way, the context must literally scream for only that depiction to be used.

READY FOR MORE?

By now, our study has, hopefully, enlightened you to see what you might have been missing regarding some very important biblical truths. Because, if you were not aware of these great truths, then you have truly missed out on the astounding grandeur of what lies ahead for those who are born again in Christ Jesus.

On top of that, you may also have been missing out on what is really going on in our quickly changing and highly prophetic world. And failure to benefit from those revealed mysteries would be an absolute shame.

We have just completed perhaps the most complex chapter in this book. If you need to, please go over it again. The truths we learned here will be vital for your understanding of contextual Scripture connections from this point forward.

Now, if you are ready to continue, take a deep breath and turn the page. What comes next might surprise you.

6

THE HEAVENLY COUNCIL

And he said, Hear you therefore the word of the LORD: I saw the LORD sitting on his throne, and all the host of heaven standing by him on his right hand and on his left.

—1 KINGS 22:19

THIS IS ONE of my favorite subjects to help students of the Word of God to understand, especially those who are discovering it for the very first time.

Yahweh created a court-like assembly of divine beings (*elohim*) through which He directed the original affairs of His kingdom work. And, according to both the Old and New Testaments, He *continues* to administer His kingdom relationships through this divine structure.[21]

Various Bible translations render the name of the "council of the *elohim*" as: "the great assembly," "heaven's court," "the divine council," and "the assembly of El." The heavenly council is also rendered in English translations as: "His own congregation," "the congregation of the mighty," "the assembly of God," "the assembly of the angels," "the hosts of heaven," "the heavenly host," or "the company of God."

Regardless of the particular words and phrases chosen by interpreters, the implication is the same. *Elohim* surrounds Himself with a court or a council that is made up of the *elohim*. They are His created and divine beings—His upper family.[22]

The attestation of this heavenly council has been copiously confirmed by renowned biblical language experts, as well as a variety of scholars and Bible translators. The only real question among interpreters appears to be which passages speak of a divine council and which ones speak of a mere human assembly. We'll examine this matter in more detail later.[23]

A PEEK AT PSALM 82

As an example of the truth of the divine council of Yahweh, the *New International Version* renders Psalm 82:1 as: "God presides in the great assembly; he renders judgment among the 'gods'."

Another translation of Psalm 82:1 is rendered in the *English Standard Version:* "God has taken his place in the divine council; in the midst of the gods he holds judgment."

Regardless of the way one might wish to interpret the matter, it's clear that Yahweh's purpose for being in the midst of the gods is to pass judgment; He is holding court. This truth could not be made any plainer than how it is written in the original Hebrew and how it is rendered in most English translations.

This particular biblical revelation does not mean that God *needs* angelic assistance or that without the *elohim* He would not be able to properly carry out the functions of His kingdom or even render a proper judgment. On the contrary, the Lord *permits* their presence at His throne, because this is why He created them! This is much the same as it is with us. God does not *need* us in order to advance His kingdom work on earth or even to preach His gospel of salvation, yet He allows us to assist in His eternal plan. He does this out of His love for us and

His desire to fellowship with us and to joyfully include us in His divine purposes. It would be as if I founded and directed a highly successful multinational corporation, then staffed the corporate offices with my children and grandchildren. I could have used anyone in the world I desired, or I could have simply chosen to run the business by myself. Yet, I chose to include my children to represent me and to assist in running my business affairs—because I love them and delight in sharing my *kingdom* work with them.

In the same way, the *elohim* are Yahweh's heavenly representatives; they are His celestial ambassadors. They also serve as God's witnesses as He brings forth His will, whether in the heavenly realm or on earth.

THE BOOK OF JOB

We observe the first obvious Old Testament example of the divine council in the opening words of the first chapter of Job, one of the oldest books in the Bible. But this time, in the original Hebrew text, the court members are called the "sons of God" rather than *elohim*. That Hebrew phrase in Job is interpreted as "angels" in the NIV, the "heavenly court" in the NLT, and as "divine beings" in the ISV:

> [6] One day the angels [sons of God] came to present themselves before the Lord, and Satan also came with them. [7] The Lord said to Satan, "Where have you come from?" Satan answered the Lord, "From roaming through the earth and going back and forth in it." [8] Then the Lord said to Satan, "Have you considered my servant Job? There is no one on earth like him; he is blameless and upright, a man who fears God and shuns evil." [9] "Does Job fear God for nothing?" Satan replied. [10] "Have you not put a hedge around him and his household and everything he has? You have blessed the work of his hands, so that his flocks and herds are spread throughout the land. [11] "But stretch out your

hand and strike everything he has, and he will surely curse you to your face." [12] The Lord said to Satan, "Very well, then, everything he has is in your hands, but on the man himself do not lay a finger." Then Satan went out from the presence of the Lord. (Job 1:6–12)

Once again, in Job 2:1–7, we observe the same divine assembly as they are in the process of rendering yet another judgment in the case of Job. Of course, the final declaration is always decreed by God Himself—the ultimate *Elohim*—creator of all the other *elohim*.

One final time, in Job 38:4–7, we hear the words of God attesting to the fact that the sons of God, the upper family, were present with Him at the forming of the world, and before humanity itself was created:

[4] Where were you when I laid the foundation of the earth? Tell me, if you have understanding, [5] Who set its measurements? Since you know. Or who stretched the line on it? [6] On what were its bases sunk? Or who laid its cornerstone, [7] When the morning stars sang together and all the sons of God shouted for joy? (Job 38:4–7, NAS)

The term "sons of God" is expressed in the Hebrew words *bene elohim*. And now we discover that this phrase can be properly translated as simply the "sons of God" or also as "angels," "the heavenly court," or "divine beings." In other words, the sons of God are *elohim*. This will be a very important fact to remember in several remaining chapters of this book. [24]

There are still a few other passages where we find the phrase *bene elohim* or its clear equivalent. In these cases, the phrase is also translated as heavenly/divine beings. For example, in Psalm 29:1, the Hebrew expression is most often translated as "heavenly beings." In Psalm 89:6, the phrase is rendered by various translations as "heavenly beings," "angels," "divine beings," "sons of the mighty," or simply the "sons of God." [25]

Ascribe to the Lord, you heavenly beings, ascribe to the Lord glory and strength. (Psalm 29:1)

For who in the skies above can compare with the Lord? Who is like the Lord among the heavenly beings? (Psalm 89:6)

What do the commentaries declare concerning this divine assembly of Job, and who makes up this council? Observe the following three examples:[26]

The Pulpit Commentary:

By "the sons of God" it is generally admitted that, in this place, the angels are meant (so again in Job 38:7).

Barnes' Notes on the Bible:

The sons of God—Angels; compare Job 38:7. The whole narrative supposes that they were celestial beings. Came to present themselves— As having returned from their embassy, and to give an account of what they had observed and done.

Cambridge Bible for Schools and Colleges:

...sons of the Elohîm, i. e. angels. The word Elohîm usually means God, but this is scarcely its meaning here.... The name Elohim or sons (i. e. members of the race) of the Elohim is a name given directly to angels in contrast with men. The word means probably "powers," "mights," and the name is given to God and angels in common; He is the Elohim preeminently, they are Elohim in an inferior sense.

There really is no way around the fact that the *lesser elohim*—as opposed to the ultimate *Elohim,* Yahweh—are also presented in the

Scripture as sons of God, angels, heavenly beings, *gods*, or divine beings. These *elohim* make up God's divine council.

THE COUNCIL OF THE HOLY ONES

The entirety of the passage Psalm 89:5–8 also presents a clear confirmation of the biblical reality of God's divine council:

> [5] The heavens praise your wonders, Lord, Your faithfulness too, in the assembly of the holy ones. [6] For who in the skies above can compare with the Lord? Who is like the Lord among the heavenly beings? [7] In the council of the holy ones God is greatly feared; He is more awesome than all who surround him. [8] Who is like you, Lord God Almighty? You, Lord, are mighty, and your faithfulness surrounds you.

The vast majority of commentaries concede that this passage is a direct reference to God's divine council, which is made up of the angelic realm. *Matthew Poole's Commentary* states the matter succinctly: "In the assembly of the saints; to the whole society of angels, called saints, as Psalm 89:5. Them that are about him; the angels, which are always in his presence, and encompass his throne."[27]

THE ANGELIC REALM

We also know from the Scriptures that even the angelic beings are subdivided into classes. We read of the seraphim (Isaiah 6), the cherubim (Genesis 3:24), and the archangel Michael—*one* (apparently of others) of the chief princes (Daniel 10:13, 1 Thessalonians 4:16), and Gabriel—the announcing angel (Luke 1).

We are familiar with Lucifer, the prince of the fallen ones (Isaiah

14:12), also known as Satan (Matthew 12:22–24; 2 Corinthians 11:14). We are told of the fallen *elohim*, the demonic realm (Deuteronomy 32:17, Matthew 25:40–41, Revelation 12:3), as well as the exotic living creatures surrounding the throne of God (Ezekiel 1:5 and Revelation 5).

The Bible reveals that angels appear as mortals (Genesis 18, Daniel 10). Sometimes they appeared in such glory that humans could barely remain standing in their presence; humans are sometimes prone to worship them (Colossians 2:18, Revelation 19:10).

Never doubt: Angels are not fat little baby-like beings with halos over their heads, floating on clouds and playing harps. That false idea comes straight out of Greek mythology. Rather, angels are often revealed as fierce warriors (Daniel 10), the very opposite of fat babies. They can appear in terrifyingly powerful legions (2 Kings 6:8–23). They are also able to singlehandedly destroy throngs of human warriors (Isaiah 37:36).

Angel-*elohim* are likewise known as "watchers" (Daniel 4:13, 17, 23). That translation comes from a specific Aramaic word *iyr* (Strong's 5894), meaning "a watching angel, or guardian angel."[28]

Consider an example from the book of Daniel concerning the use of the word "watchers." Notice the indication of their divine council nature:

This matter is by the decree of the watchers, and the demand by the word of the holy ones: to the intent that the living may know that the most High ruleth in the kingdom of men, and giveth it to whomsoever he will, and setteth up over it the basest of men. (Daniel 4:17, KJV)

The *Cambridge Bible for Schools and Colleges* offers a clear analysis of Daniel 4:17 that basically attests to everything else laid forth in this chapter:

God is represented in the O.T. as surrounded by an assembly of angels (1 Kings 22:19), who form almost a kind of heavenly council, Job 1:6; Job 2:1; Job 15:8, Jeremiah 23:18, Psalm 89:7; and it seems that in Daniel the decree is regarded as possessing the joint authority of God and of His council. By the later Jews this assembly of angels was called God's "court of judgement" (דין בית), or His "family" (פמליא); and He was represented as taking counsel with it, or communicating to it His purposes.[29]

At other times, angels are identified as "fellow servants" among the members of the redeemed humanity, and divinely appointed partners and protectors in the Kingdom work (2 Kings 6:17; Psalm 91:11; Revelation 19:10, 22:9).

The Bible offers another striking revelation about this subject. We are told that a certain group of horrifically rebellious angels are currently held in "prison" for the Great Day of Judgment at the end of the ages (Jude 1:6; 1 Peter 3:19; 2 Peter 2:4). We'll explore this startling revelation in much more detail in later pages of this book. However, we are also told that many other rebellious *elohim* are still very active among our earthly powers and thrones. They are under the leadership of Satan himself (Ephesians 6:10ff; Matthew 25: 41; Luke 11:15; Revelation 16:14, 20:8).

Every bit of what has been presented in this chapter is what the Bible clearly portrays as spiritual truth—cultural prejudices, "enlightened" thinking, and personal preferences notwithstanding.

I tried to warn you, didn't I?

7

THE THRONE, THE LAW,
AND THE SCROLL

Whether thrones or powers or rulers or authorities; all things were
created by Him and for Him.

—COLOSSIANS 1:16

IN DANIEL CHAPTER 7, we are treated to a startling glimpse of the
Throne Room of Yahweh—the majestic divine council. In this revelation, we are shown the days of the Antichrist—the very last days before
the return of the Lord Jesus Christ:

> [9] As I looked, thrones were set in place, and the Ancient of Days
> took his seat. His clothing was as white as snow; the hair of his
> head was white like wool. His throne was flaming with fire, and
> its wheels were all ablaze. [10] A river of fire was flowing, coming
> out from before him. Thousands upon thousands attended him;
> ten thousand times ten thousand stood before him. The court
> was seated, and the books were opened. (Daniel 7:9–10)

Notice that thrones, multiple, were set into place around the *one throne* of Yahweh. The ten thousand times ten thousand that stood before Him are obviously divine beings, and perhaps redeemed saints were among them as well (Revelation 7 and 14).

Heaven's court is in session. God is on His Throne, and the *elohim*—gods, angels, divine ones, sons of God, etc.—surround Him. They are seated on their assigned thrones and standing by the tens of millions in His presence.

The entry for this passage from the *Pulpit Commentary* illuminates the scene:

The symbol here is of a royal court, only the numbers are vaster than any earthly court could show. The angels of God are present to carry out the decisions of the judgment.... We are, however, not to regard this as the final judgment. Daniel is rather admitted into the presence of God in the heavens, and sees his judgment continually being prepared against the wicked.[30]

Barnes' Notes on the Bible has this commentary on Daniel's vision:

The use of the plural here [thrones] would seem to imply, at least, that the reference is not to the throne of God, but to some other throne. [Bible scholars] Maurer and Lengerke suppose that the allusion is to the thrones on which the celestial beings sat in the solemn judgment that was to be pronounced—the throne of God, and the thrones or seats of the attending inhabitants of heaven, coming with him to the solemn judgment.[31]

The *Cambridge Bible for Schools and Colleges* records its assessment of Daniel's vision in this manner:

Thrones are set for the heavenly powers, the assessors of the Judge: the Almighty Himself appears in the likeness of an aged man, seated on a throne of flame: angels in countless myriads stand in attendance around Him: and the books recording the deeds of the Gentile rulers are opened.[32]

THE LAW

We also find the divine council of Yahweh involved in another pivotal point in biblical/world history—*at the giving of the Law*. In the book of Deuteronomy, we are confronted with a majestic scene of Yahweh visiting the earth at Mt. Sinai. In that scene God, is once again accompanied by the divine council. The original text does not use the word *elohim*, but rather it uses the Hebrew words that literally translate to the "holy ones." But as you will see, the holy ones and the *elohim* are one in the same. And both of these terms are often interchangeably translated as "angels."

The following narrative recounts the giving of the Law at Sinai, just before the children of Israel would finally enter the Promised Land under the leadership of Joshua:

> [2] [Moses] said, "The LORD came from Sinai, And dawned on them from Seir; He shone forth from Mount Paran, And He came from the midst of ten thousand holy ones; At His right hand there was flashing lightning for them. [3] "Indeed, He loves the people; All Your holy ones are in Your hand, and they followed in Your steps; Everyone receives of Your words. [4] "Moses charged us with a law, a possession for the assembly of Jacob." (Deuteronomy 33:2–4, NASB)

Here we observe Scripture affirming that when Yahweh descended upon Mt. Sinai to give the Law to Moses and Israel, He was accompanied by, and came from the midst of, a myriad of holy ones—or *elohim*. Yahweh was not going to dispense the Law to His chosen people without the witness of His divine council. On that day, the law was literally put into effect, through the heavenly court.

NEW TESTAMENT CONFIRMATION

How do we know these *holy ones* were divine beings? We know it because other portions of God's Word confirm that fact for us. Once again, let us allow the Bible to interpret the Bible—*first*. Observe the following passages from the New Testament:

> What, then, was the purpose of the law? It was added because of transgressions until the Seed to whom the promise referred had come. The law was put into effect through angels by a mediator. (Galatians 3:19)

The *Jamieson, Fausset, and Brown Commentary* illuminates this passage from Galatians 3:

> Of a mediator—namely, Moses. Deut 5:5, "I stood between the Lord and you." Hence, the phrase, "By the hand of Moses." In giving the law, the "angels" represented God; Moses, as mediator, represented the people: a double mediation.[33]

This same truth is affirmed in the book of Acts, chapter 7. Stephen is preaching to the crowd of Jewish elders who, only a moment later, stoned him to death. Stephen is telling them that the Law of God, which they were presently breaking, was put into effect by angels. Observe Stephen's declaration:

> Was there ever a prophet your fathers did not persecute? They even killed those who predicted the coming of the Righteous One. And now you have betrayed and murdered him—you who

have received the law that was put into effect through angels but have not obeyed it. (Acts 7:52–53)

Stephen was appealing to the fact that the giving of the Law was witnessed by the *elohim* of God's heavenly court; therefore, the rulers who were about to illegally execute him were without excuse. They would be held accountable before God and His divine council.

Now observe the *Jamieson, Fausset, and Brown* Commentary interpretation of Stephen's assertion:

[Stephen's declaration in Acts 7:53] is explicitly stated (*as if it had been a known fact*) in Gal. 3:19, and Heb. 2:2); the general doctrine of Scripture regarding the ministry of angels, especially in all the higher operations of providence and grace, is quite in accordance with it; and Josephus and Philo both speak of it *as a recognized fact*.[34] (emphasis added)

Ellicot's Commentary for English Readers affirms the context of Acts 7:

The phrase expressed the current Jewish belief that angels were the intermediate agents through whom Israel received the Law; that it was their voice that was heard on Sinai.[35]

The *Meyer's New Testament Commentary* understands the text in a literal sense as well:

So that the arrangements made by angels (the direct servants of God), which accompanied the promulgation of the law, made you perceive the obligation to recognize and observe the received law.[36]

Ellicott's Commentary for English Readers ties together the Deuteronomy 33:2–4 passage with those New Testament passages, as well as the divine council passage in Daniel chapter 7:

The law itself was "ordained by angels in the hand of a mediator" (Galatians 3:19). It is called "the word spoken by angels" in
Hebrews 2:2. The language of Daniel 7:10 also provides a complete parallel. A fiery stream issued and came forth from before
Him: thousand thousands ministered unto Him" —The fiery
law came from the ten thousands on "His right hand;" or from
them, and from His right hand. This construction is by far the
most simple, and agrees with what we read elsewhere.[37]

John Saw Heaven's Court

Now that we understand these great truths of God's divine council, how
can we miss, ever again, the true splendor of the throne room scene in
the book of Revelation 4–5? In those passages John gives us an amazing
depiction revealing the majesty that surrounds the throne of God and
His heavenly court.

Who and what is present there? John's rapturous recounting describes
the Lamb that was slain, flashes of lightning and peals of thunder, burning lamps, and a sea of glass. But also there were the winged living creatures, multiple thrones, elders, and ten thousand times ten thousand
angels shouting, praising, and singing: "Worthy is the Lamb, who was
slain, to receive power and wealth and wisdom and strength and honor
and glory and praise!"

Oh yes, let's not forget that in Jesus' hand is the scroll, bound by
seven seals—the complete revelation of all that is to come. The heavenly
council is again in session, the *sons of God* surround the throne of Yah-
weh/Yeshua, and John was there to witness it.

From Genesis to Revelation, we see biblical attestation of the divine
council: a clear and central truth of God's Word. Understanding this
reality will shed a much brighter light on the entire biblical message.

The bigger picture is already becoming clearer, isn't it? But there's
still more—*much* more—to come.

8

I Said, "You Are 'gods'..."

God takes his stand in the divine assembly; among the divine beings he renders judgment.

—Psalm 82:1

If the last chapters proved to hold amazing revelations for you, you'll love what's coming next.

Our study now progresses by taking a deeper look at Psalm 82. Consisting of only eight short verses, it is titled "A Psalm of Asaph." The passage is loaded with amazing spiritual insight, as one might expect from the highly esteemed prophet Asaph. In fact, this is the same psalm Jesus quoted as He was standing in front of the Jewish elite when He went up to the Temple to preach a few months before Passion Week (John 10:33). Those particular Jewish elders accused Jesus of claiming to be God, though in their eyes He was but a *mere man*. Jesus quoted Psalm 82 to His accusers as a biblical attestation of His deity and to directly challenge their claim that He was only a mere man.[38]

Asaph was a renowned Levite singer and prophet who served in King David's court and was the son of Berachiah of the tribe of Levi (1 Chronicles 6:39, 15:17, 15:19, 16:4–7; 2 Chronicles 29:30). He is described as the chief Levite chosen to minister before the Ark of the Lord (1 Chronicles 16:4–7). This psalm reflects the important depth of insight given to Asaph from the Lord.[39]

PSALM 82—THE DIVINE ASSEMBLY

Apply what you have learned in the last chapters and read Psalm 82 through the filter of that contextual knowledge. I have emphasized certain words that should, by now, automatically catch your attention.

1 God takes his stand in the **divine** assembly;
among the **divine beings** he renders judgment:
2 "How long will you judge partially
by showing favor on the wicked?
3 "Defend the poor and the fatherless.
Vindicate the afflicted and the poor.
4 "Rescue the poor and the needy,
delivering them from the power of the wicked.
5 "They neither know nor understand;
they walk about in the dark
while all the foundations of the earth are shaken.
6 "Indeed I said, '**You are gods,**
and all of you are sons of the Most High.'
7 **However,** as all human beings do, you will die,
and like other rulers, **you will fall.**'
8 Arise, God, to judge the earth,
for all nations belong to you.
(Psalm 82, ISV, emphasis added)

Here again we see God's heavenly court. The scene is similar to what we saw in Job 1 and Daniel 7. The first verse of Psalm 82 plainly confirms that this is God's divine court.

As you might have guessed, the Hebrew word in this passage rendered as "divine beings" is *elohim*. In verse 6, we read the words of Yahweh as He reiterates the high position of these divine beings. He reminds them they are gods, *elohim*, also called "sons of the Most High," equivalent to *bene elohim*. God insists the *elohim* hold special places of authority within the heavenly realm, and He holds them accountable for the authority they exert upon earthly powers and thrones, as well as the human actions emanating from their divine influence.

God also reminds His *elohim* that a large part of their responsibility (vv. 4–5) is to assist humanity in their struggle against the dark powers of the fallen *elohim* (Hebrews 1:7, 14). They are reminded that humanity walks in darkness while earth's foundations are in spiritual turmoil. These *elohim* that refuse to faithfully uphold their God-assigned responsibilities will be punished. And what a great punishment it will be, as you shall soon see.

THE POWERS BEHIND THE THRONES

In light of what we have covered in previous chapters, one would think the interpretation of Psalm 82 would be fairly straightforward. But, that is not the case. A number of translators give the passage a human court rendering, rather than that of the divine court.

So what do those who disagree with our premise do with this particular passage in Psalm 82? They simply translate the second *elohim* in the first verse to something like, "He judges in the midst of the *rulers*." Several prominent translations do this very thing. This then gives the interpretive slant that God is speaking to mere human rulers rather than divine beings of His heavenly court.

The greater contextual problem is that there simply is no passage in the Bible where God is ever presented as standing in the midst of a human assembly of national rulers, and having a discussion with them. That idea is a foreign concept to scriptural truth and thus must be considered a foreign interpretation of Psalm 82.

A handful of Bible translations use the word "rulers" in Psalm 82:1, but no less than nineteen prominent versions, including the KJV, NIV, and ISV, use the words "divine beings," "angels," "the gods," or "heavenly beings" to denote exactly who it is that Yahweh is addressing.[40]

THE PROBLEM OF PSALM 82:7

In fairness, it must be pointed out that those who believe God is speaking to mere human rulers in this passage will often utilize Psalm 82:7 as the justification for their interpretation. God declares in that verse, "However, as all human beings do, you will die, and like other rulers, you will fall."

The critics will frequently assert something along the lines of, "Since divine beings don't die, God must be speaking directly to human rulers rather than to heavenly beings." I understand their argument and will admit that, upon first reading, the verse could be viewed in that manner.

However, there are major contextual problems with this hasty dismissal. The fact that God is addressing His divine assembly is clearly identified in the first verse. Therefore, the *elohim* of this entire psalm are identified by the fact that they are in the divine council. In other words, the overwhelming context of the entire passage cannot be negated by one seemingly difficult verse in the passage.

THE CORRECT CONTEXT OF VERSE 7

The purest contextual understanding of Psalm 82 is that the misuse of *elohim* authority involves the influencing of the human powers/thrones/

institutions of the earth, inclining them towards injustice and wickedness. Psalm 82:7 clearly records the judgment rendered by *Elohim*/Yahweh upon the *elohim*/gods—those who have disobeyed His commands and have misused their authority.

The declaration of "you will die as humans do," or, as some translations have it, "you will die *like* mere mortals" (NIV, NLT, NET Bible), is a judgment upon divine beings who otherwise would have been immortal. And what a horrible judgment that would be! They will ultimately receive the curse that humanity itself received at the Garden Fall: death, rather than eternal life.

NEW TESTAMENT ATTESTATION

Furthermore, the judgment pronounced in Psalm 82:7 is entirely consistent with similar New Testament declarations. Those particular New Testament attestations speak of the certainty of the *death sentence* that will befall Satan and his angels at the final judgment (Matthew 25:41; Revelation 20:10–15). They will be thrown into the lake of fire, which the Bible calls the second *death*. They will ultimately "die like mere men," just as Psalm 82:7 declares.

We even read in Jude 1:6 and in 2 Peter 2:4 that a number of fallen *elohim* are already in prison, awaiting the Day of Judgment. Every being that must appear before that terrible throne of final sentencing will suffer the death penalty—even the fallen *elohim*, which is exactly what Psalm 82:7 asserts.

Think of this important point as well: How would dying like men be considered a terrible judgment upon mere human judges, who were surely going to eventually die in the same way all humans die? No, Psalm 82:7 is not a judgment upon mere mortal rulers.

Dr. Michael S. Heiser holds a Ph.D. in Hebrew Bible and Semitic languages. He is also a scholar-in-rsidence at Faithlife, the maker of Logos Bible Software. He states of Psalm 82:7:

Although Yahweh told these *elohim* that they would die like men (Psa. 82:6-8)—that he would strip them of their immortality—there is no indication that the threat tempered opposition to Yahweh. The New Testament makes it clear that, once the powers of darkness understood that they had been duped by the crucifixion and resurrection, there was a sense that the timetable of their judgment had been set in motion (Rev. 12:12).[41]

The biblical concept of Yahweh as having removed rebellious angelic powers from their thrones in eons past might also find support in the New Testament passage of Luke 1:52:

He has brought down rulers from their thrones but has lifted up the humble.

Gill's Exposition of the Entire Bible interprets Luke's potential double-meaning of the passage like this:

As mighty kings and emperors from their thrones...or the mighty angels, from their seats...in heaven; who rebelling against God...were cast down to hell; and are reserved in chains of darkness, to the judgment of the great day.[42]

SATAN'S DEMISE

Additionally, as we will thoroughly examine in a later chapter, the progression of Ezekiel 28 ultimately winds up presenting a vivid description of Satan himself. This characterization begins in Ezekiel 28:14 and ends with verse 19.

Since we know Satan is the chief prince of the rebellious *elohim* (Matthew 9:34, 12:24, 25:41; Ephesians 2:2; and Revelation 12), verses 18 and 19 of Ezekiel 28 clearly support what we have observed as the judgment of Psalm 82:7. Observe what God says to Satan regarding his ultimate demise:

> By your many sins and dishonest trade you have desecrated your sanctuaries. So I made a fire come out from you, and it consumed you, and I reduced you to ashes on the ground in the sight of all who were watching. All the nations who knew you are appalled at you; you have come to a horrible end and will be no more. (Ezekiel 28:18–19)

Satan will be no more. He will be reduced to ashes, perhaps an allusion to his final destination in the lake of fire (Revelation 20:10). Satan is a divinely created *elohim* being who will ultimately *die like a mere man* (Malachi 4:3; Ecclesiastes 12:7; Genesis 18:27) and will finally wind up being the "Lord" of nothing.

Taking the foregoing biblical explanations regarding Psalm 82:7 and the totality of what we have learned thus far, the message becomes much clearer: God is pronouncing divine judgment upon disobedient *elohim*. They are using their heavenly power to influence earthly thrones in rebellious and appalling ways. They are the wicked powers behind the thrones. And these "gods" continue to manipulate earthly thrones even today (Ephesians 6:10–13; Revelation 16:14, 20:8). We'll explore this truth in much more detail a little later on.

Now, let's move to the next chapter to discover what biblical scholars and language experts have to say about Psalm 82 and the *elohim* thrones. We'll also discover some more surprising New Testament connections to our study as well.

I assure you, the following chapters will prove to be increasingly enlightening.

9

MALEVOLENT THRONES

I will shake the heavens and the earth. I will overturn royal thrones and shatter the power of the foreign kingdoms.

—HAGGAI 2:21–22

WHAT DO ACADEMIC sources say about the proper translation of Psalm 82? Admittedly, some biblical researchers choose the explanation of "earthly rulers" as the rendering for *elohim* in this particular Psalm. But, not all respected scholars take that view. Observe the following as examples from among those who do not:

The *Pulpit Commentary,* a favorite among many Bible expositors, states the matter as:

> God standeth in the congregation of the mighty; or, "in the congregation of God"–"the Divine assembly" (see Job 1:6; Job 2:1; Isaiah 6:1, 2, etc.). *El,* in the singular, can scarcely mean the "mighty ones of earth." He judgeth among the gods. He "holds a court of judgment in heaven, surrounded by the Divine ministers, who will execute his behests."[43]

There is also this contextual explanation from *Gill's Exposition of the Entire Bible:*

> God standeth in the congregation of the mighty.… The Syriac version renders it, "in the congregation of angels"; they are mighty, and excel in strength, and there is a large company of them, even an innumerable one, and who surround the throne of the Majesty on high. Christ, who is God over all, was among those on Mount Sinai, and when he ascended to heaven; and with these he will descend when he comes a second time, Psalm 68:17.[44]

The *Cambridge Bible for Schools and Colleges* weighs in on this controversial passage as well. Although this particular commentary would rather hold the view that the Psalm 82 *elohim* are earthly rulers, it does have to finally admit that the Syriac version of the Bible understands the matter quite differently:

> It might indeed be supposed that the [writer] intended to represent God as holding His court surrounded by angels, like an earthly king in the midst of his courtiers (cp. 1 Kings 22:19; Job 1:2); and so probably the Syriac translator understood the verse: "God standeth in the assembly of the angels, and in the midst of the angels will He judge."[45]

Notice that both *Gill's Exposition of the Entire Bible* and *Cambridge Bible for Schools and Colleges* appeal to the Syriac Bible translation as a potential translation source. Here is the reason, as explained by Bible scholar Dr. Bruce Metzger: "Syria was the country in which the Greek language intersected with the Syriac, which was closely related to the Aramaic dialect used by Jesus and the Apostles. That is why Syriac versions are highly esteemed by textual critics."[46]

Biblical language expert, Dr. Michael S. Heiser, explains the translation of Psalm 82 in the following synopsis:

The sons of God/the Most High here are clearly called elohim, as the pronoun "you" in verse 6 is a plural form in the Hebrew. The idea of elohim ruling the nations under God's authority is a biblical concept that is described in other passages…the sons of God are divine beings under the authority of the God of Israel.… There's no need to camouflage what the Hebrew text says. People shouldn't be protected from the Bible. The biblical writers weren't polytheists.

[Furthermore] God's divine council is an assembly in the heavens, not on earth. The language is unmistakable. This is precisely what we'd expect if we understand the elohim to be divine beings. It is utter nonsense to think of them as humans.[47]

OLD TESTAMENT AFFIRMATION

But, is there really any other *scriptural support* for the theme of Psalm 82 in regard to spiritual powers of wickedness being behind earthly thrones? Consider this significant passage from Daniel chapter 10. The important words have been highlighted:

Again the one who **looked like a man** touched me and gave me strength. "Do not be afraid, O man highly esteemed," he said. "Peace! Be strong now; be strong."

When he spoke to me, I was strengthened and said, "Speak, my lord, since you have given me strength."

So he said, "Do you know why I have come to you? Soon I will return to fight against the **prince of Persia**, and when I go, the **prince of Greece** will come; but first I will tell you what is written in the Book of Truth." (No one supports me against them except **Michael, your prince**.) (Daniel 10:18–21, emphasis added)

Daniel is visited by an angel who has come to give him the answer to an earlier prayer. We are told that this particular *elohim* looked like a man, but it turns out he was not a mere human, he was a divine being. We discover that he first had to do battle against two fallen *elohim* princes, one who is behind the throne of Persia and the other is the influencer of the throne of Greece.

Michael is presented here as an obedient *elohim prince*—one who is doing the proper bidding of the Lord, sent from the divine council. Michael is fulfilling the praise of Psalm 103:

> Praise the Lord, you his angels, you mighty ones who do his bidding, who obey his word. Praise the Lord, all his heavenly hosts, you his servants who do his will. (Psalm 103:20–21)

The *Bible Exposition Commentary: Old Testament* further expands the understanding of this truth. The citation comes from a commentary portion on Isaiah 14. But the truth of Daniel 10 is also mentioned in that particular assessment:

> The prophet saw in this event something far deeper than the defeat of an empire. In the fall of the king of Babylon, he saw the defeat of Satan, the "prince of this world," who seeks to energize and motivate the leaders of nations (John 12:31; Eph 2:1–3). Dan 10:20 indicates that Satan has assigned "princes" (fallen angels) to the various nations so that he can influence leaders to act contrary to the will of God.[48]

NEW TESTAMENT AFFIRMATION

The apostle Paul, who wrote the letter to the church at Ephesus, was also the man caught up to paradise and saw the truth of what was really happening behind the veil of the unseen dimensions (2 Corinthians

12:4). Apparently, Paul clearly understood the messages of Psalm 82 and Daniel 10:

> For our struggle is not against flesh and blood, but against the rulers, against the authorities, against the powers of this dark world and against the spiritual forces of evil in the heavenly realms. (Ephesians 6:12)

Notice that Paul speaks of these particular matters of wickedness as being operated from within the divine and unseen realms. Ephesians 6 is, therefore, a precise match with Psalm 82 and Daniel 10—a perfect contextual alignment of clear biblical truths.

DEMONIC PERVERSION OF TRUTH

We also know that demonic influence is behind the persistent attempt to pervert the Word of God among humanity and to wickedly influence the nations. Several passages of Scripture come to mind that attest to these truths:

> The Spirit clearly says that in later times some will abandon the faith and follow deceiving spirits and things taught by demons. (1 Timothy 4:1)

> And no wonder, for Satan himself masquerades as an angel of light. (2 Corinthians 11:14)

> …in order that Satan might not outwit us. For we are not unaware of his schemes. (2 Corinthians 2:11)

> Be alert and of sober mind. Your enemy the devil prowls around like a roaring lion looking for someone to devour. (1 Peter 5:8)

They are demonic spirits that perform signs, and they go out to the kings of the whole world, to gather them for the battle on the great day of God Almighty. (Revelation 16:14)

But even if we or an angel from heaven should preach a gospel other than the one we preached to you, let them be under God's curse! (Galatians 1:8)

Did you notice in Galatians 1:8 the particular declaration of judgment that is leveled upon the *elohim* that pervert the gospel of Jesus Christ? They will be "under God's curse." Do you know of a particular curse of God that has been pronounced upon rebellious *elohim*? Sure you do! It's found in Psalm 82:7: "You will die like mere men." Both the Old and New Testaments agree in this solemn matter, and so should we.

THE THRONE OF ULTIMATE EVIL

Before we move to the next chapter, let us also consider this remarkable passage found in Revelation 2:12–13:

These are the words of him who has the sharp, double-edged sword. I know where you live—**where Satan has his throne**. Yet you remain true to my name. You did not renounce your faith in me, even in the days of Antipas, my faithful witness, who was put to death in your city—**where Satan lives**. (emphasis added)

Twice we are told in the very last book of the Bible that Satan has an earthly residence and that he has a throne that is situated in a certain geographical location. And from everything else we have learned, we can deduce that Satan has set himself up as an *elohim* prince of that principality, or region. And what is that region? It is modern-day Turkey—the center of what used to be the ancient Islamic caliphate of the brutal and bloody Ottoman Empire.

Turkey is the epicenter of today's attempt to revive that same Islamic caliphate. Turkey is also a key player in all that is happening regarding the 2011 Arab Spring's implosion of the Middle East. That monumental event ultimately gave rise to the Islamic State of Iraq and Syria (ISIS).

Each of the foregoing factors has served to intensify the abject hatred towards the prophetically returned Israel. The last-days hatred of Israel was foretold in the Scriptures (Zechariah 12:3; Ezekiel 38–39; Luke 21:20), and that international animosity towards Israel is being diabolically directed and inspired by the rebellious *elohim*—under Satan's direct orders. This is why they are under God's curse and judgment.

TODAY

Do you discern overtones of Psalm 82, Daniel 10, and Ephesians 6 in any of today's geopolitical affairs—especially in the Middle East, and especially in the vitriolic hatred leveled against the revenant nation of Israel? Can you recognize more clearly now the fact that rebellious *elohim* are actually influencing the thrones and affairs of today's world? Do you also discern why the United States, the largest "Christian nation" the planet has ever known, is also under Satan's direct and vicious assault?

Even though the rebellion of the nations is ultimately influenced in the unseen realm, in reality, it is also right before our eyes, hiding in plain sight—just like Ephesians 6 said it would be. But we must have spiritual eyes and a proper understanding of important passages of Scripture in order to properly recognize what is happening.

Now that we have settled these amazing biblical truths, let's go to the foot of Mt. Sinai. It is there that we run into several more monumental theological truths—truths that often touch our own lives and frequently appear in international headlines.

10

NO OTHER GODS

You shall have no other gods before me.

—EXODUS 20:3

IT REALLY IS a simple matter: God explicitly forbids the practice of idol worship, especially among His own people. But, what is an idol, and why is the worship of a mere human-crafted, lifeless object so dangerous?

As ridiculous as idol worship might sound in our first-world culture, it must have been a particularly important concern to Yahweh. There is something in the fallen human soul that is especially vulnerable to this degenerate act. We know this because the first two of the Ten Commandments address the matter head on. Observe those ominous decrees in Exodus 20:1–6:

First Commandment:

[1] And God spoke all these words: [2] "I am the Lord your God, who brought you out of Egypt, out of the land of slavery. [3] You shall have no other gods before me."

Second Commandment:

[4] "You shall not make for yourself an idol in the form of anything in heaven above or on the earth beneath or in the waters below. [5] You shall not bow down to them or worship them; for I, the Lord your God, am a jealous God, punishing the children for the sin of the fathers to the third and fourth generation of those who hate me, [6] but showing love to a thousand [generations] of those who love me and keep my commandments."

These two commandments should now be rich with fresh meaning. Recognizing the significance of what we know about the word *elohim*, it is clear that Yahweh declared Himself to be the supreme Elohim, the creator of all that exists. Then He explicitly warned His people not to worship the sons of Gods, the divine beings, the principalities, or the angels; for if an *elohim* did allow humankind's worship, that *elohim* was proving to be a fallen one (demon).

And, as we discovered three chapters back, the Law itself was delivered in the presence of, and *through*, the faithful *elohim* who served as witnesses to the truthfulness of Yahweh's commands (Galatians 3:19). The *elohim* to which God refers are divine entities with which the people would have been, at least, indirectly familiar and perhaps entities to whom they might have been tempted to offer their worship and allegiance. Thus, God's first commandment to His newly formed nation was this: "I'm warning you right up front: Do not do this detestable thing. If you do, I will break fellowship with you and you will forfeit my divine protection from those *fallen ones* who seek to manipulate you and destroy you. So, for your own safety, you must stay faithful to me alone."

COMMANDMENT NUMBER TWO

Yahweh's second commandment is similar, but with a slightly different nuance of importance. God tells His people: "In fact, do not even carve out a figurine or statue (Old English, 'graven image') and then call it an *elohim*. "You shall not make for yourself an idol."

You see the connection now, don't you? If God's people were familiar with the real *elohim*—and they were—wouldn't they be tempted to try to craft the *likeness* of one into the form of some sort of statue or figurine, hoping perhaps to lure that divine source of intermediary power into their midst? Yes, they certainly were susceptible to such a temptation, and they had succumbed to it in the past. So, in effect, God said: "This practice is very dangerous business. I'm warning you: Do not do it!"

Clearly the idols were not mere nothings. Even though they were often declared worthless compared to the absolute power and sovereignty of the one true Elohim, they were still subject to being used in abjectly evil ways.

Even to manufacture an idol-image then ascribe to it power and a name was an affront to the unique majesty of Yahweh. After all, it would be through these people whom God would eventually bring forth His Word, His prophecies, His Christ, the gospel of salvation, His redeemed Church…and the ultimate sign of the soon return of Christ, the resurrected Israel in the last days. No, these people simply could not engage in idolatry—not without severe consequences.

A COSTLY WORSHIP SERVICE

Moses had barely received the commandments from Yahweh before many of the people who had been left waiting at the foot of Mt. Sinai had joined with Aaron in fashioning an idol in the form of a golden calf. On that day, three thousand people were put to death for their act of contempt, in spite of Yahweh's very recent deliverance of them from the clutches of Pharaoh's brutality (Exodus 32:27).

This was the day God was breathing life into His new nation. Israel would be born at the giving of the Law, on Pentecost. Even today, the majority of orthodox Jews celebrate Pentecost as the day Yahweh's Law was given through the witness of angels and by the human mediator Moses—directly from the midst of the divine council and God's throne.[49]

That brings me to yet another biblical nugget. It would also be on Pentecost, fifteen hundred years into the future, when the Church would be born through the giving of the Holy Spirit. On the day the Church was born, three thousand people were *restored* through the preaching of the gospel of Jesus (Acts 2:40). It seems Yahweh keeps accurate and balanced books, wouldn't you say? The divine symbolism of the two events taken together is hard to miss.

WHY A GOLDEN CALF?

Have you ever wondered why the people fashioned a golden calf as their object of worship? Many assume the image had something to do with the practices of pagan Egypt; that may be true to some degree. But, why a calf? And, why a *golden calf?* The simple fact is that, in the divine realm, there exists a similar *elohim* who is a direct intermediary before the throne of Yahweh.

According to John's vision of the throne room of God in Revelation 4–5, countless *elohim* are in His presence. But, immediately encompassing God's throne are positioned four living creatures. These are four very splendorous and radiant *elohim* who are continually proclaiming God's holiness. They are guardians of the Throne of Glory. They are intercessors between the throne of Yahweh and every creature that approaches it.

Of all things, one of those four *elohim* has the face of a…well, read it for yourself in Revelation 4:7:

The first creature was like a lion, and **the second creature like a calf**, and the third creature had a face like that of a man, and the fourth creature was like a flying eagle. (NASB, emphasis added)

Six of the top twenty-five most popular modern Bible translations interpret the second living creature to have the face of an "ox." The other nineteen versions translate the word in the most literal sense as "calf."[50]

The Greek word in question is Strongs' #3448, *moschos,* which accurately translates to "a young bullock"—or a "calf of the oxen breed."[51]

The rendering in some translations as "face of an ox" is technically correct; either way it is translated, the creature being represented is the same. It would be the same thing as if you were visiting a dairy farm and pointed to a young cow, or calf, and said, "Oh, look at that cow!" The most accurate way to have stated your exclamation would have been to say, "Look at that calf," but "Look at that cow" is also technically correct.

We see the same description of the four living creatures in Ezekiel 1:10, where the face of an ox is described as one of the *elohim*—they are called the "living creatures." Again, we see the four living creatures in Ezekiel 10:14. But this time, the face of the ox is not mentioned. It is replaced by "the face of a cherub." Obviously, distinction is being given to this one face in particular—a living creature that has the face of an ox/calf/cherub. In a later chapter of this book you will discover an amazing revelation about the specific identification of that particular cherub.

However, the point we are making now is that the people panicked because Moses had been gone from their midst for such a long time. They wanted a physical platform from which to summon the power of Yahweh to go before them as protection from their enemies. They were hoping to attract another mediator, one directly from the throne of God. Apparently, they thought Moses could not be depended upon to return anytime soon—if ever. So, Aaron obliged their impatient desires:

When the people saw that Moses was so long in coming down from the mountain, they gathered around Aaron and said, "Come, make us gods [or a God] who will go before us. As for this fellow Moses who brought us up out of Egypt, we don't know what has happened to him."

Aaron answered them, "Take off the gold earrings that your wives, your sons and your daughters are wearing, and bring them to me." So all the people took off their earrings and brought them to Aaron. He took what they handed him and made it into an idol cast in the shape of a calf, fashioning it with a tool. Then they said, "These are your gods [or this is your God], O Israel, who brought you up out of Egypt."

When Aaron saw this, he built an altar in front of the calf and announced, "Tomorrow there will be a festival to the LORD [Hebrew, Yahweh]." So the next day the people rose early and sacrificed burnt offerings and presented fellowship offerings. Afterward they sat down to eat and drink and got up to indulge in revelry. (Exodus 32:1–6)

It is important to note that several translations render the words of verse 4 as "this is your God." By now, you know the reason for the translation variation: The word for God/gods is *elohim,* and the context of verse 5 appears to point to the use of "God" rather than "gods."

The *Pulpit Commentary* addresses the matter of this context:

"'These be thy gods, which have brought thee.' Rather, 'This is thy god, which has brought thee.' The plural must be regarded as merely one of dignity."

Ellicott's Commentary for English Readers as well as *Barnes' Notes on the Bible* also agree with the *Pulpit Commentary's* grammatical assessment of the Hebrew language and context.[52]

From this understanding, we can deduce that Aaron said something along the lines of, "Here is your *elohim* intermediary, O Israel! Tomorrow we will have a sacrifice to Yahweh—through this intercessor. Maybe now Yahweh will hear us and protect us from our enemies as we move forward."

So, they fashioned the image of an intermediary *elohim* in the shape of one that looked like the calf of an ox. As a matter of fact, the worship of an *elohim*-calf would show up again, generations later, in the time of the kings of Israel:

> They rejected his decrees and the covenant he had made with their ancestors and the statutes he had warned them to keep. They followed worthless idols and themselves became worthless. They imitated the nations around them although the Lord had ordered them, "Do not do as they do."
>
> They forsook all the commands of the Lord their God and made for themselves two idols cast in the shape of calves, and an Asherah pole. They bowed down to all the starry hosts, and they worshiped Baal. They sacrificed their sons and daughters in the fire. They practiced divination and sought omens and sold themselves to do evil in the eyes of the Lord, arousing his anger. (2 Kings 17:15–17).

Is there any wonder why, throughout ancient paganism, we continually see the imagery of a cow with horns, or a horned bull, or even the face of a calf consistently making their appearances in the construction of the idols?[53]

These were the efforts of idolatry that Yahweh had forbidden within the words of the first two commandments. He warned them not to make "platforms" (idols) through which they might attempt to contact Him or the *gods*. Yahweh made it clear that this practice was the same as divination and witchcraft, one upon which He would surely level His divine judgment (2 Chronicles 33:5–7).

SYMBOLS OF CONNECTION

The sad irony of that day is that within the giving of the Law at Mt. Sinai, Yahweh would indeed provide the platform of connection that His people desired to possess, but it would be a heaven-ordained symbol, in the form of the *Tabernacle*. Furthermore, Yahweh would eventually provide the ultimate divine intermediary the human race so desperately needed: *Jesus Christ.*

Moreover, the early New Testament church would later discover that the Tabernacle itself was nothing less than the symbolic image of Jesus Christ and His completed work of atonement on Calvary's cross. This was Yahweh's strategy from the beginning, before He laid the first foundation stone of His glorious creation plan (Hebrews 9:11).[54]

In the meantime, the anxious people at Sinai decided they knew best. So, with Aaron's help, they sidestepped Yahweh's perfect plan. They fashioned the image of an intercessor *elohim* and began to summon its presence to intervene for them before Yahweh, thus opening up a channel of demonic flow. And they did this evil thing in the name of Yahweh.[55]

Now we understand why Yahweh became so angered at Sinai, and why those three thousand founders of the profane golden calf movement had to be cleansed from the camp before the blasphemous infection spread like a cancer to the entire young nation. By engaging in the practices of pagan idolatry, they would open the portals of the dark and diabolical dimensions of rebellious *elohim*—demonic entities that sought the destruction of God's people, and the new nation they would eventually form: *Israel.*

Now, let's take a closer look at the direct connection between "worthless" idols and the demonic realm.

11

WORTHLESS IDOLS?

They...angered me with their worthless idols.

—DEUTERONOMY 32:21

THOUSANDS OF YEARS ago, the people of what are now primarily the Middle Eastern nations understood that their countries were ruled by various "gods." They understood the power of the gods to be very real indeed. Today, when we speak of idols, we are tempted to sanitize the idea and proclaim them to be simply ancient, religious relics of superstitious people groups. We have completely removed the supernatural element of the very real demonic danger of idol worship—even though the Word of God urges us to do just the opposite. This fact is to Satan's abject delight.

But, is there really solid scriptural backing for the notion that an idol, manufactured by mere humans, could actually be used as the calling card of demons? Examine the following words, given just a few chapters after the Ten Commandments are reiterated by Moses. The pronouncement is found in Deuteronomy 32:

> [16] They made [Yahweh] jealous with their foreign gods and angered him with their detestable idols. [17] They sacrificed to demons, which are not God—gods they had not known, gods that recently appeared, gods your fathers did not fear. [18] You deserted the Rock, who fathered you; you forgot the God who gave you birth. [19] The Lord saw this and rejected them because he was angered by his sons and daughters. [20] "I will hide my face from them," he said, "and see what their end will be; for they are a perverse generation, children who are unfaithful. [21] They made me jealous by what is no god and angered me with their worthless idols." (Deuteronomy 32:16–21)

Do not misunderstand the phrases "what is no god" or "worthless idols"—as they are found here and in similar Scriptures. When taken in context with the entirety of God's Word, it is clear what was actually taking place within the spiritual realm concerning idol worship.

From *Matthew Poole's Commentary*, observe the entry for Deuteronomy 32:17:

> Unto devils, i.e. unto idols, which the devils brought into the world in opposition to God, in and by which the devils oft-times manifested themselves unto men, and gave them answers, and received their worship...the devils which inspired them deluded the nations with false pretences that they were a sort of lower gods. Moses therefore takes off this mask, and shows the Israelites that these pretended gods were really devils, those great enemies of mankind, and therefore that it was the height of madness to honour or worship them. [56]

GOAT DEMONS

We also observe in Leviticus 17:7, at the giving of the Law at Mt. Sinai, that God's people were even prone to worshipping idols in the form of a goat-*elohim* (demon). Although there are various representations of the original Hebrew word in this verse (i.e., goat-idols, devils, he-goats, demons, satyrs), most translators render the word as *goat demons*. For example:

> They are no longer to slaughter their sacrifices to the goat demons, with whom they have been committing prostitution. This will be a perpetual statute for you throughout your generations. (ISV)

We are informed in 2 Chronicles 11:15 that Jeroboam, king of Israel, not only approved of this particularly repulsive form of demonic worship, but he also appointed his own personal priests to the goat-worship order. Along with the goat demon, undoubtedly a precursor to the satanic goat-image of *Baphomet*, Jeroboam appointed additional priests for services of worship that involved the image of the golden calf of Aaron's Mt. Sinai shame. Both of these images were brought out of Egypt by the people of God and continued to be a curse on the land of Israel for hundreds of years thereafter:

> Jeroboam appointed his own priests for the high places, the goat-demons, and the golden calves he had made. (2 Chronicles 11:15, HCSB)

Observe what *Ellicott's Commentary for English Readers* has to say about the goat demon practice of ancient Egypt and Israel:

> **And they shall no more offer their sacrifices unto devils.**—The word (sēirim) here translated "devils," literally denotes hairy or

shaggy goats, and then goat-like deities, or demons. The Egyptians, and other nations of antiquity, worshipped goats as gods.

Not only was there a celebrated temple in Thmuis, the capital of the Mendesian Nomos, in Lower Egypt, dedicated to the goat-image Pan, whom they called Mendes, and worshipped as the oracle, and as the fertilizing principle in nature, but they erected statues of him everywhere. Hence the Pan, Silenus, satyrs, fauns, and the woodland gods among the Greeks and Romans; and hence, too, **the goat-like form of the devil**, with a tail, horns, and cloven feet....

The terror which the devil, appearing in this Pan-like form, created among those who were thought to have seen him, has given rise to our expression **panic**. This is the form of idolatrous worship which the Jews brought with them from Egypt, and to which reference is continually made.[57]

In the *Benson Commentary,* note how our earlier claim of idols being manipulatively used by fallen *elohim* is once again upheld by scholarly assertion:

Leviticus 17:7. *Unto devils*—So they did, not directly or intentionally, but by construction and consequence, because the devil is the author of idolatry, and is eminently served and honored by it. And as the Egyptians were notorious for their idolatry, so the Israelites were infected with their leaven, Joshua 24:14; Ezekiel 20:7; Ezekiel 23:2–3. And some of them continued to practice the same in the wilderness, Amos 5:25–26.[58]

The *Jamieson-Fausset-Brown Bible Commentary* adds this revealing note to their commentary on the goat-demons of Leviticus 17:

Moreover, the ceremonies observed in this idolatrous worship were extremely licentious and obscene, and the gross impurity of the rites gives great point and significance to the expression of Moses, "they have gone a-whoring."[59]

Even the comparable satanic rituals of today's world utilizing the infamous Baphomet goat-demon imagery follow the same patterns of ancient Egypt's sexually perverse worship. If one understands what they are observing, it quickly becomes apparent that those particular demonic entities are in full operation even today.

MODERN GOAT DEMONS?

If you are inclined to dismiss goat-man or goat-demon worship as merely ancient and third-world occult activity, it might surprise you to learn that a striking likeness of this specific ceremony was employed to initiate the 2016 opening of the Gotthard Base Tunnel project through the Alps in Switzerland. With a route length of 35.5 miles, the celebrated project is the world's longest and deepest railway traffic tunnel—a modern marvel of underground construction.

Shockingly, the inauguration ceremony for the Gotthard Tunnel was not the standard ribbon-cutting ceremony one might expect. Rather, it was rife with women simulating sex with each other in front of a figure of a resurrected goat-man idol. Observe these words from a media report of that Swiss ceremony:

The opening ceremony of the Gotthard Base Tunnel in Switzerland featured a "goat-man" that dies, is resurrected, is worshipped and is crowned as "the king of the world."

The goat-man that played such a key role in this performance bore a striking resemblance to Baphomet, which in recent decades has become one of the key symbols used to represent Satan in the occult community. So could it be possible that this entire ceremony was actually an Illuminati ritual that was intended to honor Satan? Don't pass judgment until you see the videos.[60]

Really? A *goat-man-god* that wants to be king of the world and given a place of honor before Europe's dignitaries? Complete with simulated sex acts between women—taking place in front of the goat demon? And, in the year 2016? Hmmm. The same demons, the same profane rituals—just a different time—*our* time. But not much has changed, has it?

SATAN, WITCHES, AND DEMONS

Then there was this *LA Weekly* headline in February 2017, "Is a Trump Presidency the Satanic Temple's Chance to Go Mainstream?" The focal point of the article is encapsulated in this quote, "'We decided that Satan was the ultimate rebel, and we realized the power of that symbol,' says William Morrison, a co-founder of the Satanic Temple's L.A. chapter."[61]

In the same month, the *New York Daily News* reported, "Witches of the world will cast a mass spell on President Trump." The ringleader of the global digital-age convocation said:

> This I consider to be primarily a self-defense measure. So many of us are just overwhelmed with the assaults on civil liberties, immigrants, the environment…this felt like a way to reclaim our power and say, "We have power over you. You don't have power over us."[62]

Why would Satan be so out-front with these ancient ritualistic displays of goat-demon worship and witchcraft, even in the midst of our enlightened culture? The answer is simple: Because he can. And because he's up to something big. And because his tactics have never changed. Sadly, he has not been required to change them.

The Unthinkable Sacrifice

We discover from the Word of God the incredible depths of depravity to which the original people of God sank when they continued to engage in worship of the so-called "worthless" idols. Take a look at Psalm 106:36–38:

> And [they] served their idols, which became a snare to them. They even sacrificed their sons and their daughters to the demons, and shed innocent blood, the blood of their sons and their daughters, whom they sacrificed to the idols of Canaan; and the land was polluted with the blood. (NASB)

Gill's Exposition of the Entire Bible is written in older prose, but the words are striking. Consider the entry for Psalm 106:36–38:

> Yea, they sacrificed their sons and their daughters unto devils. Who have their name here given them from a word that signifies to waste and destroy, they being the destroyers of mankind.
> [The word here for demon is] from the Arabic word "to rule", for these demons were heroes, princes who ruled over others, and so were reckoned among the gods. As Satan, the head of them, was a murderer from the beginning, the cause of the ruin of our first parents, and of all their posterity....
> These the Israelites sacrificed...their sons and daughters; which they not only caused to pass through the fire to Moloch... but they sacrificed them to be devoured, and actually burned them; see Jeremiah 7:31.
> ...First, these Israelites mix themselves with the Heathens they spared, whom they should have destroyed; then they learn, by being among them, to do as they did, to walk in the vanity of their minds like them; and then they are enticed to serve their

idols, and at last to sacrifice their sons and daughters to devils; which was no other than murder, and that of the most heinous nature.[63]

MAKING IT PERSONAL

How is this unspeakable atrocity of the Israelites any different than that which we currently practice in our own nation? We might be a little more sophisticated than to worship an image of a "god" before sacrificing the child in our womb upon the altar of convenience; however, the overall process and the end result are the same. We've merely sanitized the process a bit.

But, an idol can also be a concept, desire, possession, or philosophy that vainly sets itself up in the temple of our mind and places itself above Yahweh and his word (2 Corinthians 10:5). The Bible tells us this kind of mental/emotional and spiritual activity, perpetrated by the fallen *elohim*, will actually increase as time grows closer to the return of the Lord Jesus:

Now the Spirit speaketh expressly, that in the latter times some shall depart from the faith, giving heed to seducing spirits, and doctrines [teachings and influences] of devils. (1 Timothy 4:1, KJV)

When Gill wrote his commentary, there was no 1973 *Roe v. Wade* Supreme Court decision. Neither, did Gill have to give undue consideration to an oppressive atmosphere of political correctness. To put his commentary into a more modern context, Gill said that for the Israelites to kill their children in the name of certain culturally accepted practices and conveniences was nothing less than: utter murder, a heinous act, and a "sacrifice" unto demons. How could our wanton abortion practices be considered any less, especially when measured against what we now know about the influence of the fallen *elohim* upon humanity and our governments?

But the goat-demon sexual perversions and infanticide connections become increasingly disconcerting when we consider the revelations we will uncover in the next chapter. There we will discover the association between all those demonic distortions as well as the most ancient stumbling-block idol of all: Baal, *Lord of the earth.*

And, that particular fallen *elohim* entity is also very active in today's world. Just like the goat-demon manifestation, this one was featured in very recent international headlines. Yet so few in today's refined and cultured church even noticed.

And we wonder what is wrong with our churches, our nation—and the world...

12

LORD OF THE FLIES

Why should God be so jealous of the wooden idols of the heathen? Could he not compete with Baal?

—ROBERT G. INGERSOLL[64]

NOT ONLY WAS the matter of Baal worship a big deal in Old Testament days, but, believe it or not, it still is. Even in our intellectual age of technological wonders, Baal is still among us, and much more publicly visible than you might imagine.

In the times of the Old Testament, against the explicit commands of the Lord, convocations were held in Baal's honor throughout the land of Israel. There was even an elaborate priesthood affiliated with the cult. We see this fact in the prophet Elisha's challenge to the four hundred and fifty priests of Baal on Mt.Carmel (1 Kings 18).

While over a dozen gods/goddesses can be found in the Old Testament, Baal is by far the most prevalent, appearing more than sixty times under slight name variations. Often found in conjunction with Baal worship was the female fertility goddess known as Asherah/Ashtoreth (1 Kings 16). As nature gods energized by demonic spirits, Baal and Ashtoreth were claimed to have evolved out of the primeval watery chaos. You will recognize this as the same demonic tale of human origins taught to our children in the public school systems of America. Of course, our progressive culture passes the demonically inspired story off as enlightened thinking and, even worse, as settled science.[65]

Baal was originally known as *Bel* by the ancient Babylonians and is believed by many archeologists and historians to be the earliest known, most honored of national pagan deities. In their pantheon of gods, Baal was known as the lord of the earth. The Hebrews most likely learned Baal worship from the ancient Canaanites.[66]

The Hebrew word "Baal," at its foundation means simply: "husband, master, or owner" (Strong's OT # 1166 and 1167). But when the name is applied to the god-idol, the meaning is synonymous with "Lord, master, and owner of all."[67]

We find the worship of Baal starting in the book of Numbers and continuing through the book of Zephaniah. In the New Testament, in Romans 11:4, we again read about Baal. We also find several more instances of Baal in the New Testament using another well-known variation of the idol's name—*Beelzebub*.

The first time the worship of Baal is mentioned in Scripture is in Numbers, chapter 25. The scene is a grim one:

> While Israel was staying in Shittim, the men began to indulge in sexual immorality with Moabite women, who invited them to the sacrifices to their gods. The people ate and bowed down before these gods. So Israel joined in worshiping the Baal of Peor. And the Lord's anger burned against them.
>
> The Lord said to Moses, "Take all the leaders of these people, kill them and expose them in broad daylight before the Lord, so that the Lord's fierce anger may turn away from Israel." So Moses said to Israel's judges, "Each of you must put to death

those of your men who have joined in worshiping the Baal of Peor." (Numbers 25:1–5)

We know that in addition to perverted sexual rituals, one of the principle sacrifices offered in the frenzy of the worship service was that of offering up their children to the fires of Baal.

They bowed down to all the starry hosts, and they worshiped Baal. They sacrificed their sons and daughters in the fire. They practiced divination and sought omens and sold themselves to do evil in the eyes of the Lord, arousing his anger. (2 Kings 17:15–17).

They have built the high places of Baal to burn their children in the fire as offerings to Baal. (Jeremiah 19:5)

They built high places for Baal in the Valley of Ben Hinnom to sacrifice their sons and daughters to Molek, though I never commanded—nor did it enter my mind—that they should do such a detestable thing and so make Judah sin. (Jeremiah 32:35)

Most likely, the killing of their own children was also included in the profane sacrifices offered to Baal in the Numbers 25 reference.

KILL THEM ALL!

We often hear people question the love of God when He instructed the armies of Israel to completely wipe out the Canaanites living in the land (Deuteronomy 7:1–5, 12:2, 20:16–18). Baal worship was rampant among the Canaanites as well as the six adjacent and similar cultures of the Hittites, Girgashites, Amorites, Perizzites, Hivites, and the Jebusites.

In addition to the sordid sexual perversion and horrific infant sacrifice associated with the worship of Baal, the utter renunciation of Yahweh was also required. Self-mutilation, drunkenness, and promises of wealth-for-allegiance were a part of the Baal allurement as well. Does any of this sound familiar as it relates to today's modern culture?

It is also historically alleged that a common practice among the Baal worshipping Canaanites was to bury the body of a sacrificed child in the foundation of a house or public building—particularly at the time of its construction. This horrific act was employed as a talisman of blessing and prosperity. The practice is known among archeological researchers as "foundation sacrifice."[68, 69]

As a result of these types of hideous, ritualistic elements, the apostasy of Baal worship was no small thing to Yahweh. It became a dismal step into the chasm of Satan's darkest demonic realm. Observe the lament of Psalm 106 regarding this miserable stain upon Israel's association with the Canaanites:

> [34] They did not destroy the peoples as the Lord had commanded them,
> [35] but they mingled with the nations and adopted their customs.
> [36] They worshiped their idols, which became a snare to them.
> [37] They sacrificed their sons and their daughters to demons.
> [38] They shed innocent blood, the blood of their sons and daughters, whom they sacrificed to the idols of Canaan, and the land was desecrated by their blood.
> [39] They defiled themselves by what they did; by their deeds they prostituted themselves. (Psalm 106:34–39)

Once again, we are reminded by Scripture that any worship practice outside of the biblical worship of Yahweh is nothing more than the worship of fallen *elohim*. It was because of the abysmal depths of this satanic worship that Yahweh ordered Israel to destroy the people of the surrounding nations. However, Israel was partially disobedient in God's command; they did not destroy them all (Joshua 23—Judges 3). As a result, Israel would suffer the consequences of that insubordination for the rest of their existence. It seems the fallen *elohim* were able to demonically influence the Israelites to disobey Yahweh *just a little*. Satan used the diabolical manipulation in an attempt to side-rail what God was planning to do through Israel. This is exactly the kind of activity for which Yahweh condemned the disobedient *elohim* to the *sentence of death* on judgment day (Psalm 82:7).

It might be offensive to our modern sensitivities to think that a loving God could order the destruction of entire people groups. However, when we put the matter in context of the larger story, much of it still to be unfolded in the following chapters, not only does it make sense, but it becomes apparent that His order was entirely justified. It amazes me that some of the same people who are offended by Yahweh's order to "kill them all" apparently forget there is coming a final day of judgment in which, perhaps, billions will be utterly destroyed, along with Satan and his angels. The bottom line is that this is Yahweh's creation. It is Yahweh's plan. It is Yahweh's righteous decree—whether we approve or not.

BEELZEBUB

"Beelzebub" is the Greek form of the Hebrew *Baal-zebub*. The name translates to "Baal—lord of the flies." Beelzebub was the Philistine god, primarily worshiped in the ancient city of Ekron during the Old Testament times (2 Kings 1:2).

However, we also find the name Beelzebub used seven times in the New Testament. It is there the idol is identified as none other than Satan himself. Some biblical scholars attest that Beelzebub was also known among the people as the *god of filth*.[70]

Beelzebub was a particularly loathsome deity to the spiritually sensitive, and for this reason the title "god of filth" was used by the Jews as a nickname for Satan, ruler of the fallen *elohim*. Since Jesus also pointedly identified Beelzebub as Satan, we have no choice but to make the same identification (Luke 11:18–19). In order to show their utter contempt for Jesus, the Jewish religious rulers even identified Him as Beelzebub! Or, at the very least, they accused Him of casting out demons by the power of Beelzebub (Matthew 9:34, 12:24; Mark 3:22; Luke 11:15).

BAAL WORSHIP TODAY?

As the world rushes into the profoundly prophetic times before us, a number of researchers find striking similarities between ancient Baal worship and its resurrection in our own day. Is it possible the world is being set up for the soon arrival of the counterfeit "Lord of the earth?" Many prophecy watchers believe this is exactly the case.

In November 2016, the *University of California Press* published an article titled, "The Return of Baal to the Holy Land: Canaanite Reconstructionism among Contemporary Israeli Pagans." The article begins with these words:

> This article focuses on the recent emergence of Canaanite Reconstructionism in Israel—a miniature movement within the country's small, but growing, Pagan community. The discourse of Israeli adherents of Canaanite Reconstructionism regarding its links to ancient Canaanite culture and the land—indeed the very soil—of modern-day Israel is highlighted.[71]

Matt Barber, a well-known author, columnist, cultural analyst, and attorney whose legal expertise is in constitutional law authored an article titled, "Today's Baal Worshippers." In that article, Mr. Barber contends there are striking similarities between today's progressives, and particularly what he called the child sacrificers. He sees the growing Baal spirit of our times as a real and present danger. Following is a telling citation from that piece:

Ritualistic Baal worship, in sum, looked a little like this: Adults would gather around the altar of Baal. Infants would then be burned alive as a sacrificial offering to the deity. Amid horrific screams and the stench of charred human flesh, congregants—men and women alike—would engage in bisexual orgies. The ritual of convenience was intended to produce economic prosperity by prompting Baal to bring rain for the fertility of "mother earth."

The natural consequences of such behavior—pregnancy and childbirth—and the associated financial burdens of "unplanned parenthood" were easily offset. One could either choose to engage in homosexual conduct or—with child sacrifice available on demand—could simply take part in another fertility ceremony to "terminate" the unwanted child....

The worship of "fertility" has been replaced with worship of "reproductive freedom" or "choice." Child sacrifice via burnt offering has been updated, ever so slightly, to become child sacrifice by way of abortion. The ritualistic promotion, practice and celebration of both heterosexual and homosexual immorality and promiscuity have been carefully whitewashed—yet wholeheartedly embraced—by the cults of radical feminism, militant "gay rights" and "comprehensive sex education." And, the pantheistic worship of "mother earth" has been substituted—in name only—for radical environmentalism.[72]

The *National Center for Family Integrated Churches* (NCFIC) published a similar article titled, "Modern Baal Worship in Theaters, Stadiums and Living Rooms." The author postulated that much of today's thoroughly secularized culture incorporates many of the same elements utilized in the ancient pagan ritual:

It is a mistake to think of Baal worship as some kind of other worldly practice that never happens today. On the contrary, it happens all the time in the form of cultural variations of the same general patterns that we see in 2 Kings 21:1–9 and 2 Kings 17:7–23....

Baal worship in reality corresponds exactly to activities that most people freely participate in today. They do so without really understanding the nature of idolatry, for idolatry is simply enjoyment of things raised up against Christ....

Anyone who questioned the activity ended up on the wrong side of public opinion, like Elijah. Ahab summarized the attitude people had toward Elijah.[73]

Back in 2003, when America was still claiming about 80 percent of its population to be adherents to Christianity, the renowned Barna Group religious research organization found the largest Christian nation on the planet, the United States, to be literally engulfed in the activities that would otherwise identify with the spirit of Baal.

Barna's research indicated that America's general population insisted the following activities were perfectly acceptable moral behaviors: cohabitation—60 percent; adultery—42 percent; sexual relations between homosexuals—30 percent; abortion—45 percent; pornography—38 percent; the use of profanity—36 percent; and gambling—61 percent.[74]

Immersion in sexual perversion, the sacrificing of children for the sake of convenience and prosperity, and the lust for financial gain were all predominant features of Baal worship. And they are all principle features of America's list of acceptable standards. But remember, that survey was in 2003. Today the number of people in America claiming to be Christian has dropped to only 70 percent.[75]

Then, in 2017, the Barna Group reported the results of their latest findings regarding the true spiritual nature of post-Christian America. That newest study revealed that only 17 percent of Americans identified themselves as holding to a firm "biblical worldview" of life. Barna also asserted, "This widespread influence upon Christian thinking is evident not only among competing worldviews, but even among competing religions."[76]

Sadly, many people of God who dare to stand against the current cultural spirit of Baal are met with the same challenges faced by Elijah in the days of Ahab and Jezebel. We are often accused of fanaticism and of being intolerant trouble makers (1 Kings 18:17). We become loathed by the worldly people around us, as well as some within the church, who don't have a clue how spiritually deceived they have become. Accordingly, for many Christians, their modesty-meter and attentiveness to the Holy Spirit is often crushed by the trampling feet of the throngs rushing to the altar of today's sanitized image of Baal—who is still the god of filth. Should we be surprised by any of this, knowing what we now know?

But the situation is even more prevalent than most imagine. Apparently, the fallen *elohim* council under the rulership of the prince of this world determined that 2016–2017 was the perfect time for Baal to make a symbolic and highly public appearance. Baal was going to make his presence known around the globe through specific, strategic points of unveiling.

And so, the demonically manipulated kings of the earth (Psalm 82), whether they knew it or not, paid homage to the diabolical influence behind their thrones...

13

Baal Takes a Victory Tour

Is there no intellectual liberty in heaven? Do the angels all discuss questions on the same side?

—Robert G. Ingersoll[77]

"Next month, the Temple of Baal will come to Times Square!"

Those were the shocking words in the headline in a March 2016 edition of the *New York Times*. Spiritually perceptive Christians were stunned by the announcement.[78]

The article went on to explain that what was actually being put on display was a reproduction of the fifty-foot arch that formed the *gateway* to the Baal temple entrance in the Syrian town of Palmyra. The original arch was a two thousand-year-old structure the Islamic State (ISIS) had destroyed in 2015. The arch replica was scheduled to be displayed in London, New York City, and Dubai as a tribute to Palmyra's Baal Temple.

In April 2016, the reproduction made its debut in London, the premier center of global banking and finance. And, believe it or not, the timing of its unveiling there was planned to coincide with Beltane, a major pagan festival designated for the worship of Baal. Beltane translates to "the fires of Baal." As we now know, those fires were the altars of horrific child sacrifices—talismans of prosperity offered to the flames of Baal, "the lord of the earth."[79, 80]

Five months later, by late September 2016, the eleven-ton Baal arch was unveiled in New York City, in the park directly outside of city hall. The memorial was given its location of honor in the heart of the city's financial district, very near the Ground Zero Memorial of September 11, 2001.

Then, in February 2017, the Baal memorial was displayed in Dubai, a major center of global governmental and financial affairs located in the heart of the Middle East. From there, it was ultimately scheduled to be returned to Syria.

While the New York City display of Baal's Palmyra arch was touted as only a mere archeological, artful, and historical presentation, a number of prophecy watchers suspected that something much more supernaturally originated was actually at work.

Why was the Baal display in New York City deemed to be so important? And why was the memorial displayed so close to the Ground Zero commemorative, almost fifteen years to the day of that globally unprecedented, horrific Islamic terrorist event? And why display the symbol of Baal in the city that just happens to host the United Nations, the undisputed think-tank for the globalist agenda's ideals?

After all, wasn't the ancient god of Baal described as the lord over the earth and nations—and considered the supreme *anti-Yahweh*? Furthermore, why was the NYC display being brought to the heart of the economic center of the world's largest Christian nation and the second-largest economic center of the world? For the spiritually discerning, these were certainly legitimate points of consideration.

And, what was the importance of Dubai to the Baal spectacle? As it turns out, there were deeply significant spiritual connections to Baal's arrival in Dubai as well. The unveiling was purposely planned to coincide with the opening of the February 2017 World Government Summit. Once again, "Baal—the god of the earth and nations" shows up in a location where one-world-government ideals are front and center. Dubai is also considered by leading international corporations to be the top business gateway between Europe and Africa.[81]

At the Dubai summit, over which the presence of Baal's memorial loomed, there were four thousand leaders from one hundred and thirty nations of the world. The conference featured more than one hundred internationally-known speakers, including U.N. Secretary General Antonio Guterres; Christine Lagarde, director of the International Monetary Fund; and Elon Musk, a globalist billionaire named by *Forbes* to as one of the "World's Most Powerful People."[82, 83]

At the official website of the World Government Summit, one is able to scan through the list of official partners. Some of the most prominent partners include: he United Nations, the International Monetary Fund, the World Economic Forum, and the World Bank, along with a host of Arabic/Muslim organizations, Reuters, CNN, the Landmark Group, Emirates, and the *Harvard Business Review.*[84]

Following is the description of the 2016 Summit's purpose, as stated by Mohammed Al Gergawi, minister of cabinet affairs and chairman of the organizing committee, "The World Government Summit has now transformed into the largest platform for the next generation of government leaders, and aims to prepare for the future and improve the lives of nearly seven billion people *by gathering the world under one umbrella.*"[85] (emphasis added)

The "Baal Tour" appeared to be a spiritual-realm indication that Satan was symbolically claiming dominion of practically the entire globe.

ISLAM AND BAAL

There were those among the orthodox Jewish community who saw something even more potentially sinister connected to the ominous convergences: "Rabbi Pinchas Winston identified another troubling connection.… He argues the erection of monuments to Baal, specifically one of Roman origin now being built in an Arab nation at a summit dedicated to world government, signifies an alliance against Israel."[86]

Pastor and bestselling author Bill Cloud also wrote about the disturbing coalitions of the 2017 World Government Summit in Dubai: "When you see Western nations aligning themselves with Muslim nations and talking about one-world government, then you know that this alliance is plotting something."[87]

The Tour Continues

Then, in April 2017, the Palmyra Arch was again erected in a strategic location just before another globalist event was held in May of that same year. Rabbi Daniel Assur, a respected member of Israel's newly resurrected Sanhedrin Council, gave an interview to *Breaking Israel News* concerning what he saw as the deeply spiritual significance of the event.

The BIN news piece was titled, "Arch of Ba'al, With Shadowy Ties to New World Order, May Be Messiah's End-of-Days Gateway: Rabbi." Observe the following excerpts from that article:

> The first modern reappearance of the Arch of Palmyra was in London's Trafalgar Square in April 2016, when it was erected for (UNESCO) World Heritage Week. The unveiling coincided with the beginning of a 13-day period known in the occult as "the Blood Sacrifice to the Beast", the most important holiday for those who worship the god Ba'al, celebrated with child sacrifice and bisexual orgies.
>
> The reproduction…was [again] erected in Florence, Italy, one month ago as part of the first-ever Cultural Summit of the G7. This meeting was a prelude to the annual summit that brings together the leaders of the world's seven major advanced economies.

Rabbi Assur explained that this connection to Ba'al was essential to the New World Order, and was therefore necessary to elements in the G7 seeking world domination.

"There is no question that the arch is the portal for a new world... If the New World Order succeeds, then they will rule, God forbid."[88]

ARE WE ANY DIFFERENT?

Indeed, even in our day, the spirit of Baal and everything the kingdom of the fallen *elohim* represents appears to be alive and well and still influencing the world's thrones and powers. From a goat-demon-Baphomet worship ritual used to initiate an underground rail tunnel in Switzerland to parading a replica of an archway to Baal's temple throughout the economic and globalist powers of the earth, Satan's last-days demonic outpouring is no longer hidden. The empire of the fallen *elohim* is feverishly influencing the thrones and nations of the earth.

Might all of these factors be the spiritual precursors to preparing the world for the arrival of the ultimate *lawless one*? Never doubt. He is coming. He wants to be *god of the nations*, and the Bible says he will actually accomplish that goal, for a few years.

Just wait until you see what happens with the idol erected in *his* honor...

14

THE LAWLESS ONE

Lawlessness is occurring from one ocean to the other. And we're seeing the fulfillment of the Book of Judges here in our own time, where every man is doing that which is right in his own eyes—in other words, anarchy.

—MICHELE BACHMANN[89]

IN 2 THESSALONIANS 2, the apostle Paul identifies the figure of the Antichrist by the title "man of lawlessness."

But that's not all. We are also told, in that section of Scripture, there will be some sort of a global rebellion that occurs, used to mark Antichrist's arrival on the world scene. And then we are warned in verse 4:

He will oppose and will exalt himself over everything that is called God or is worshiped, so that he sets himself up in God's temple, proclaiming himself to be God.

We are also cautioned that the lawless one will make his appearance by a shocking display of *elohim* supernatural powers, causing the world to stand in awe of him. He will eventually declare himself to be the one true Elohim. And the unredeemed peoples of the earth will oblige his deception; they will bow to him in worship. They will call him "God."

This passage tells us that Yahweh will finally allow the unrepentant people to be given over to the demonic delusion they were so anxious to believe and exalt. Undoubtedly, the earth is in for some excruciatingly wicked days ahead—perhaps very soon. Read the warnings of 2 Thessalonians for yourself:

Don't let anyone deceive you in any way, for that day will not come until the rebellion occurs and the man of lawlessness is revealed, the man doomed to destruction. He will oppose and will exalt himself over everything that is called God or is worshiped, so that he sets himself up in God's temple, proclaiming himself to be God.

Don't you remember that when I was with you I used to tell you these things? And now you know what is holding him back, so that he may be revealed at the proper time. For the secret power of lawlessness is already at work; but the one who now holds it back will continue to do so till he is taken out of the way.

And then the lawless one will be revealed, whom the Lord Jesus will overthrow with the breath of his mouth and destroy by the splendor of his coming. The coming of the lawless one will be in accordance with how Satan works. He will use all sorts of displays of power through signs and wonders that serve the lie, and all the ways that wickedness deceives those who are perishing. They perish because they refused to love the truth and so be saved. For this reason God sends them a powerful delusion so that they will believe the lie and so that all will be condemned who have not believed the truth but have delighted in wickedness. (2 Thessalonians 2:3–12)

AN IDOL THAT LIVES?

Observe the warnings of Revelation 9:20–21:

> The rest of mankind that were not killed by these plagues still did not repent of the work of their hands; they did not stop worshiping demons, and idols of gold, silver, bronze, stone and wood—idols that cannot see or hear or walk.

We are again confronted with the presence of prolific idol worship that will unquestionably involve demonic habitation and/or diabolical manipulation. But this isn't idol worship of the Old Testament days. It isn't even a phenomenon concerning the days of the New Testament writers. The context here is that of the *end of the ages*—perhaps close to our own days.

Depending upon which translation one uses, we discover the New Testament has almost two dozen warnings about idol worship—including the worship of angels (Colossians 2:18; Revelation 22:8-9). The direct connection of that activity with demonic persuasion and inhabitation is found throughout those warnings (1 Corinthians 10:21).

Revelation 13 records the days of the Antichrist. The blasphemy of those days will be capped off by the construction of an image that is described as being brought to life.[90]

Have a look for yourself:

> [11] Then I saw another beast, coming out of the earth. He had two horns like a lamb, but he spoke like a dragon. [12] He exercised all the authority of the first beast on his behalf, and made the earth and its inhabitants worship the first beast, whose fatal wound had been healed. [13] And he performed great and miraculous signs, even causing fire to come down from heaven to earth in full view of men. [14] Because of the signs he was given power to do on behalf of the first beast, he deceived the inhabitants of the

earth. He ordered them to set up an image in honor of the beast who was wounded by the sword and yet lived. [15] He was given power to give breath [life] to the image of the first beast, so that it could speak and cause all who refused to worship the image [statue] to be killed. (Revelation 13:11–16)

The NIV says the image (idol) was given power to "breathe." The KJV uses the words "to live." In either case, something happens with this statue/idol/image that is demonically empowered. It is such a potent delusion that it will cause the people of the earth to worship the beast. Apparently, this particular phenomenon will be something the world will have never before seen. With the holographic, robotic, genetic, artificial intelligence, and transhumanism technologies of today it is hard to imagine what could *wow* our world to that extent. But whatever it is, it's going to be the greatest trick Satan has ever manufactured (Matthew 24:24; 2 Thessalonians 2:11).

BY WHAT NAME?

Whether he is known and worshipped as Bel, Baal, a goat-demon, Baphomet, or ultimately the one the Bible knows as Antichrist, an *elohim* personified, Satan has no preference. He only wants to take the place of Yahweh. He wants to rule the nations. He wants the whole earth to worship him. And he wants to "mark" those who belong to him with a symbol of absolute servitude so that he can show himself superior above all gods and all thrones. This is the pride of the supreme *fallen one.*

15

THE COMING REBELLION

To me, Satan ultimately represents rebellion.
—MARILYN MANSON[91]

WHEN WE THINK of the Antichrist, most likely we first think of the New Testament book of Revelation. After all, it contains the most pointed discourse about the subject.

But, as most pupils of the Bible know, the first extensive passages giving us insight into that diabolic character are found in the Old Testament book of Daniel. Interestingly, this is where we first discover the Antichrist's goal is to set himself up as king of the world. And of all things, the Bible reveals that his goal is also to exalt himself above *all* the *elohim* of the divine realm. Observe the revelation of Daniel 11:36:

> The king will do as he pleases. He will exalt and magnify himself above every god and will say unheard-of things against the God of gods. He will be successful until the time of wrath is completed, for what has been determined must take place.

Most commentators agree that the first reading of this passage certainly possesses prophetic references to the ancient Greek ruler Antiochus, who was to come upon the scene in Israel's historical life at a later date. He would viciously torment the Jews and set himself up as a "god." But, numerous commentators see what is traditionally held to be the greater fulfillment of this Scripture: the passage ultimately speaks of the Antichrist who is to come at the end of days.

The *Jamieson, Fausset, and Brown Commentary* is an example of how a number of Bible scholars see this passage from Daniel:

> The willful king here, though primarily Antiochus, is antitypically and mainly Antichrist, the seventh head of the seven-headed and ten-horned beast of Rev 13, and the "beast" of Armageddon, who gathers together there the kings of the earth against the Lamb (Revelation 16:13,16; 19:19).[92]

Notice also the connection of the words of Daniel 11 with the words of Paul's second letter to the Thessalonians. That passage proclaims the very same truth about the Antichrist:

> He [the man of lawlessness] will oppose and will exalt himself over everything that is called God or is worshiped, so that he sets himself up in God's temple, proclaiming himself to be God. (2 Thessalonians 2:4)

In the passage from Daniel 11, observe the words, "He will exalt and magnify himself above *every god* and will say unheard-of things against the *God of gods.*" We know exactly what the Hebrew renderings of these words are: *elohim.*

The Antichrist will finally think he has gained his place as the Elohim above all the *elohim.* And then, he will begin to blaspheme the one true *Elohim.* In his supreme arrogance, Satan will assume he has finally won his throne through the revealing of his *man of lawlessness*. His goal is to rule both Heaven and earth, and nothing less.

THE SON OF SATAN

Will the Antichrist be a human being or an angel of light disguised as a human—a hybrid of sorts, perhaps a human/*elohim*? Either way, he will at least be demonically controlled by Satan himself. For it is Satan who ultimately desires to be king of the *elohim* and supreme ruler of the nations (Isaiah 14; Ezekiel 28). We know angels can appear as humans. We also know Satan can appear as an angel of light if he so desires (2 Corinthians 11:14).

Numerous biblical scholars are of the opinion that what *Satan/Beelzebub/the prince of the elohim* is actually going to pull off is a counterfeit Jesus Christ scenario. The Atichrist could easily be called the *Son of Satan*, a man, but inhabited by the presence of the supreme, fallen *elohim*—in a similar way that Jesus revealed himself as a *man*, yet was, at the same time, fully God among us, the Son of God (Matthew 1:24).[93]

Conversely, the Antichrist could turn out to be *elohim/*Satan that has taken on the personage of a human being. In either case, the lawless one will be a fake god, one who will present himself as the real Christ. And since Jesus came performing miracles as proof of His deity, the Antichrist will also perform signs and wonders in order to convince the nations that his power is divine. He will set up a one-world kingdom, but his reign will ultimately turn out to be temporary.

THE FINAL SOLUTION

In Revelation chapter 13, we read of a one-world marking system known in biblical studies as *the mark of the beast*. It is a mysterious and much-debated marking system that will, apparently, be employed to identify every human on the planet. If a person does not have the "mark," he or she cannot buy or sell. In other words, when this prophecy is ultimately employed, it will not take long before earth's citizens will either take the mark—or die.

When that prophecy was revealed by John the Revelator over two thousand years ago, his predictions sounded like unmitigated science fiction. In fact, until very recently, most of humanity still considered Revelation's predictions to be technological impossibilities. But that is no longer the case.

THE GLOBAL MARKING DREAM

There is an organization that has global human marking all figured out, and it is openly planning its instrumentation. The year for completion of the agenda to literally have all seven-plus billion human beings on the planet marked for identification purposes is 2030. And who is it that has undertaken and publicly announced the plan? Of all things, it is the United Nations, and the plot is buried in the middle of the avalanche of material that makes up its infamous U.N. Agenda 2030.[94]

Does Psalm 2 ring truer for you now?

Why do the nations conspire and the peoples plot in vain? The kings of the earth take their stand and the rulers gather together against the Lord and against his Anointed One. (Psalm 2:1–2)

Yes indeed, *why* do the nations plot and conspire?

Because of our study thus far, you know the answer. We have pulled back the mysterious veil of the unseen realm, and we have biblically and contextually exposed the plot of the fallen *elohim*.

THE FIRST GENERATION

If you want some idea of where we currently stand in the timeline of prophetic occurrences, consider the firsts of our historical generation. In the totality of six thousand-plus years of humanity's existence, it has been only a little over the last one hundred of those years that certain last-days prophecies have literally exploded upon the world scene. And many of those amazing biblical predictions have come about only in the last couple of decades.

In my previous book, *When the Lion Roars: Understanding the Implications of Ancient Prophecies for Our Time,* I elaborate upon these prophetic revelations and document my observations using reliable mainstream sources.[95]

Consider just a few of the assertions from that book:

Just a little more than one hundred years ago, we were still traveling by horse and buggy. Now we travel through space, under the sea, through the air, across the waters, and up and down interstate highway systems with such regularity we barely even think about any of it.

Additionally, we are the first historical generation to be called the generation of World Wars. We have already produced two of them—and a third appears to be realistically looming upon the horizon. The technologies that the current superpowers possess to wage war in our day are terrifying. The world has never seen such immensely destructive power. And the advancements in those war-waging technologies are multiplying in wanton fashion, even among rogue and terror prone nations.

We are the first generation to see the prophetically promised return of the nation of Israel. We have also witnessed the concurrent alignment of the Ezekiel 38 and Psalm 83 nations that were predicted to form coalitions to come against that resurrected nation of Israel in the last days.

We are the first to witness the presence of Russia and China in the Middle East joining their military forces, physically situated in the middle of an imploding nation of Syria (Isaiah 17:1). And all the while, Russia (Magog?) continues to strengthen its ever-deepening ties with Iran (Persia).

We are the first to experience the political collapsing of Middle Eastern nations—resulting in the Arab Spring, the rise of ISIS, the ongoing extinction of Christianity in the region, and the massive refugee crisis that emerged from the mess. That crisis has resulted in the breakdown in national border security across the European nations and in the United States as well.

Turkey, the area to which the seven letters to the seven churches of Revelation were originally written, is now in the throes of an Islamic caliphate resurrection. We are the first generation since the fall of the Ottoman Empire to see this happening. The Bible says that Turkey is where "Satan has his throne." Nothing prophetic to see so far—right? But wait, there's still more.

We are the first historic generation to witness:

- The invention of the Internet and the instrumentation of its ubiquitous presence throughout the globe. With it comes one-world communication and information exchange.
- An unprecedented and exponential growth-explosion in every field of technological advancements.
- Every single one of the technologies of end-time prophecy predictions currently in use, including the promise of Jesus in Matthew 24:14 that the end of days would be marked by the technological ability to take the gospel throughout all the nations.
- Transhumanism, genetic engineering/splicing, eternal-life technologies, and human/animal hybrid experimentation.
- The unrestrained genetic modification and engineering of human infants.

- Sex robots, killer robots, killer drones, and pervasive robotic workers.
- Artificial intelligence that is on the verge of "learning" direct human interaction, and "consciousness."
- An astronomical rise in abject evil because of the pervasive use of certain internet technologies: pornography, global sex-slave trafficking, worldwide terrorism recruitment, prolific spying and information collection, hate-targeting, mind-invasion of billions of children, and much more.
- The return of the "Tower of Babel" one-world-language capabilities. We now have instant language translation capability through our cell phones and an internet connection.
- The technologies necessary, and the plans in place, to bring about the one-world "marking" system of the beast of Revelation.
- Unprecedented persecution of Christians around the globe— and especially in the Middle East, Africa, and Asia. There has never been anything to come close to the total numbers of persecuted and murdered Christians since Christianity burst onto the scene over two thousand years ago.
- The codification of the "spirit of the days of Lot and the days of Noah" ushered in, throughout the nations, but particularly in the June 2015 Supreme Court gay marriage ruling, coming from the heart of the largest Christian nation the planet has ever known.
- A plethora of world leaders calling for a "one world government" at the expense of the unique sovereignty of the world's nation-states.

Many more *firsts* for our historical generation could be listed, but you get the point. We are living in the most profoundly prophetic times since the first coming of Jesus Christ.

Directly in the middle of our generation, the *elohim* are scrambling for their thrones and positioning themselves for power. They too know the time is drawing near. They also are aware that soon the beast will take his throne-of-thrones and rule the nations.

Now that we have set forth a clear understanding for the foundational elements we have laid in the first two sections of this book, let's go back in time and make some important links. Let us now connect all that we've learned through *The Story* of God's Word.

From the Creation to the Fall of humanity, from the Flood to the birth of the gospel, and from the rebirth of Israel to our own prophetic days, believe me, there is a story.

And now, knowing what we know about Yahweh's eternal plan of the ages, the *elohim*, and the divine council, that story makes so much more sense.

Prepare yourself. There are astounding biblical bombshells ahead.

PART THREE

≫≪

THE STORY

*For you, O Lord, are the Most High
over all the earth;*

You are exalted far above all gods.

—EPHESIANS 1:9, KJV

16

LET'S MAKE A MAN!

Elohim said, "Let us make mankind in our image."

—GENESIS 1:26

WE CANNOT GET past the first chapter of Genesis before we run into a couple of huge questions.

First, why does God seemingly refer to Himself in the plural in Genesis 1:26, using the words "us" and "our"? With whom is Yahweh speaking? We have already settled the fact that the Bible simply does not affirm a polytheistic understanding of the kingdom of God; there is no "Pantheon of Gods," as some critics are prone to suggest.

Perhaps Yahweh was talking to Himself (i.e., the Trinity) when He used those plural descriptions? Or, might it be that He was referring to His "multiplied majesty?" Or, could it actually be something so obvious that a number of Bible commentators have simply missed it altogether? Armed with what you have learned thus far, you should have no problem grasping what we will unfold next.

THE TRINITY?

It is often suggested that God must have been speaking of His triune nature when he said, "Let *us* make…". The presence of the *trinity-truth* is clearly evident in the Scriptures, and especially in the New Testament. Therefore, I have no problem understanding the concept of the triune nature of Yahweh, because this is how He presents His reality in the totality of His word.

It is a biblical fact that God is called "Father" (Matthew 6:9), the Holy Spirit is called God (Acts 5:1–4), and Jesus is called God (Matthew 1:23). And, if we arrive in glory and find out that Yahweh was addressing the fact of His triune nature in Genesis 1:26, I'll certainly have no problem with that explanation.

PLURALITY INTENSIFICATION OF MAJESTY AND POWER?

Some scholars believe that when *Elohim* is found in a specific text as the identification of His name, there is an implied expression of the plurality of His majesty that is being emphasized by its use.

I will consent to the fact of God's splendor being so awe-inspiring that it can only be expressed in multiplicities of power and grandeur. And there may be a touch of that meaning in this verse as well. But, again, I don't think this is what is being emphasized in Genesis 1:26. Even many commentators agree that this explanation is too much of a forced inference in this particular case—when, instead, there is a more natural, biblically contextual understanding of the *us* and *our* statements used in this verse.

THE HEAVENLY COUNCIL?

Could it be that *Elohim* is speaking to the lesser *elohim*? We have thoroughly settled the issue that God's preferred mode for carrying out His work on earth is usually expressed through His divine council/court. Even the giving of the Law unto Israel was conducted in this manner (Acts 7:53). We also know that this divine assembly of created *elohim* were present with Yahweh at the creation event (Job 38:7). And, that is, after all, the immediate context of the verse we are now examining.

You might ask, "Are you suggesting that the *elohim* actually helped God create humankind?" Of course not. Several times the Scripture reminds us that only God/Jesus is our creator (Isaiah 42:5, Genesis 1:1, Colossians 1:16–17, John. 1:1–3). We are never told in the Scripture—*anywhere*—that angels created, or even came close to physically assisting in creating humankind.

Rather, what we are looking at in Genesis 1:26 is the pure joy and graciousness of our Heavenly Father. His declaration "Let us make a man" was a moment of ecstasy, a moment of wonder and marvel, and an event of limited inclusiveness—and God wanted His heavenly council to share in it in order to be eternal witnesses of the glory of that day.

DIVINE INCLUSIVENESS

In that context, the phrase "let *us* make" would be akin to me driving a bus full of my church's teenagers somewhere and saying, "Hey! I've had an idea! Let's go and get everyone on the bus a hamburger meal!"

Those teens would understand that when I say "let *us* get hamburgers," what I mean is that "I" will be the one to purchase and provide the hamburgers—not them. Since the idea was mine, they would never assume I meant that *they* would be doing the actual purchasing of the hamburgers for everyone.

Furthermore, those teens would not only get free hamburgers, but they would also be able to enjoy the trip at my expense. I bought the bus, I drive the bus, I pay for the gas, I pay for the insurance, I take the responsibility for their safety, and…"I" buy the hamburgers. However, I began the journey of the hamburger delight by saying, "*Let us* go get some hamburgers!" It is my joy to do the actual buying—and it is their joy to do the participating, and to enjoy the fruits of the journey. They, at the same time, become witnesses of my love as well as my gracious nature.[96]

It really is that simple. The divine council would accompany Yahweh in the creation process, and they would cheer when He breathed life into His creation. But God alone would actually do the creating. The *elohim* would go along for the ride, watch, and…gasp in awe (Job 38:7). They would be God's witnesses of that day.

Let me show you a couple of scholarly affirmations of this thoroughly biblical possibility. And remember, this was also the view that the earliest biblical audience would have taken as well. Observe the Genesis 1:26 entry from the *Cambridge Bible for Schools and Colleges*:

[This passage involves the] Jewish explanation that God is here addressing the inhabitants of heaven. In the thought of the devout Israelite, God was One, but not isolated. He was surrounded by the heavenly host (1 Kings 22:19); attended by the Seraphim (Isaiah 6:1–6); holding His court with "the sons of God" (Job 1:6; Job 2:1).

We are told in a poetical account of the Creation, that when the foundations of the earth were laid, "all the sons of God shouted for joy," Job 38:7 (cf. Psalm 29:1; Psalm 89:7; Psalm 103:19–22). It is claimed that, at the climax of the work of Creation, when man is about to be formed, the Almighty admits into the confidence of his Divine Purpose the angelic beings whose nature, in part, man will be privileged to share (Psalm 8:4–5, cf. Hebrews 2:7)….

The picture which it suggests is in harmony with the religious thought of the Israelites; and…the work of creating man is neither delegated to, nor shared with, others. God "created man in his own image" (Genesis 1:27); but, before creating him, He had associated with Himself all those who, through participation in image and likeness with Himself, would henceforth be allied to man.[97]

While *Ellicott's Commentary for English Readers* does not come to a decisive conclusion in the interpretation of "us" in this passage (they merely present the several accepted possibilities), they also have to admit what we already know by this point: "The Jewish interpreters generally think that the angels are meant."[98]

The *International Standard Bible Encyclopedia* agrees that the passage in question is best interpreted in context as the divine council:

Genesis 1:26 has the plural "us,"…most probably to the angels or mighty ones which surrounded the throne of God as servants or counselors; compare Job 38:7.[99]

Our thesis is a solid one. The first readers of this text, the ancient Hebrews, understood that "let *us*" was Yahweh speaking to His divine council. God was not speaking to other equal Gods residing in a pantheon. Nor was He talking to His trinitarian self. Neither was He referring to Himself in the third person as English royalty might do. He wasn't even referring to the intensified plurality of His unique nature.

Yahweh was adjuring His royal court to join Him in the *creation of creations*—mankind. He was thrilled to include them in what He was about to accomplish. They were exhilarated and honored to have been included in what Yahweh was about to accomplish. They would worship Him in awe upon His completion of the feat.

But that day would not be the last time Yahweh would use the word "us"…

17

HEAVEN'S WITNESSES

And I said, "Here am I. Send me!"

—ISAIAH 6:8

DOES YAHWEH USE the description of "us" anywhere else in His Word, besides Genesis 1:26?

That particular identifier is, in fact, used in three additional places: Genesis 3:22 and 11:5–9, and Isaiah 6: 6–8. In light of what we have discovered thus far, let's have a look at those three declarations.

LIKE ONE OF US

The first of the remaining plural identifiers is found in Genesis 3:22, just after Adam and Eve had been duped by the serpent in the Garden of Eden:

And the Lord God said, "The man has now become like one of us, knowing good and evil. He must not be allowed to reach out his hand and take also from the tree of life and eat, and live forever."

Let's go back to the *Cambridge Bible for Schools and Colleges*. Following is its commentary entry for Genesis 3:22:

He speaks to the Heavenly Beings by whom the throne of God was believed to be surrounded. [As in] Genesis 1:26 and Genesis 3:5, Genesis 6:1, Genesis 11:7. "As one of us" will then mean, not "like unto Jehovah personally," but "like to the dwellers in Heaven," who are in the possession of "the knowledge of the distinction between good and evil."[100]

The higher prose of *Matthew Poole's Commentary* on this passage is rather melodramatic, but the point he makes is clear:

[It is as if God said] Behold! O all ye angels, and all the future generations of men, how the first man hath overreached and conquered us, and got the Divinity which he affected; and how happy he hath made himself by his rebellion![101]

Again, reference is made to God using "us" as speaking to the divine council or the sons of God—*the angels*. The word "conquered" is used by *Poole* in its most archaic form, meaning: "Man has now trespassed over into our domain of knowledge of certain divine things—a place where he does not belong." The "Divinity" to which Poole so dramatically refers, of course, is the divine knowledge Adam and Eve acquired at the wooing and manipulation of a particular fallen *elohim*—Satan himself.

Speaking of Satan, let's not forget that the immediate context of Genesis 3:22 is found back in Genesis 3:5. Because, it is in verse 5 where Satan states clearly what he was offering to Adam and Eve. Observe how several different translations render this passage. By now, what you will read will not shock you. I have highlighted the pertinent words:

> For God knows that when you eat from it your eyes will open and you will be like divine beings who know good and evil. (NET Bible)

More than a half-dozen other translations render the phrase as "ye shall be as gods," knowing good and evil. Still, a few other translations have the verse translated, "You will be *like God.*" But the idea is the same regardless of how the word *elohim* is translated. Adam and Eve were tempted with the notion of becoming like God/or the gods; they would know everything the divine council knew. We'll take a much deeper look at the power of this temptation in a later chapter that deals directly with the Garden sin and the ultimate fall.

"Let Us Go Down"

The second additional instance of the use of "us" is found in Genesis 11:5–9:

> [5] But the Lord came down to see the city and the tower that the men were building. [6] The Lord said, "If as one people speaking the same language they have begun to do this, then nothing they plan to do will be impossible for them. [7] Come, let us go down and confuse their language so they will not understand each other." [8] So **the Lord scattered** them from there over all the earth, and they stopped building the city. [9] That is why it was called Babel—because there the Lord confused the language of the whole world. From there **the Lord scattered** them over the face of the whole earth. (Genesis 11:5–9, emphasis added)

The context of the passage is in reference to the Tower of Babel. And it is here that God, for the first time, divides humanity into individual nations and sets their borders. (Some scholars and students of the Scriptures see weighty contextual support that it was also at Babel that Yahweh disinherited the nations by giving them over to the lesser *elohim*, and then reserving unto Himself the nation of Israel as His unique people.)[102]

The passage is clear that it was the Lord—not the angels—who actually scattered the people and confused the languages. But, the *elohim* were there with God, just as they were with Him at creation and at the giving of the Law—witnesses to His holy righteousness.

The *Cambridge Bible for Schools and Colleges* affirms this position: "Jehovah is represented probably as enthroned above the heaven…as addressing the powers of heaven, 'the sons of Elohim,' who attend Him and minister to Him (cf. Job 1:6)."[103]

"WHO WILL GO FOR US?"

The final time the word "us" is used as it is spoken out of the mouth of God is found in Isaiah chapter 6. Observe verses 6 through 8 of this passage:

> Then one of the seraphim flew to me with a live coal in his hand, which he had taken with tongs from the altar. With it he touched my mouth and said, "See, this has touched your lips; your guilt is taken away and your sin atoned for."
>
> Then I heard the voice of the Lord saying, "Whom shall I send? And who will go for us?"
>
> And I said, "Here am I. Send me!" (Isaiah 6:6–8)

Once again, the *Cambridge Bible for Schools and Colleges* hits the meaning right on the head: "The plural is not that of majesty, but includes the 'council of the holy ones' (Psalm 89:7), or the angelic 'hosts of heaven' (1 Kings 22:19 f.)."[104]

Ellicott's Commentary for English Readers puts forth the same understanding:

> Here, as elsewhere (1 Kings 22:19: Job 1:6; Job 2:1; and perhaps Genesis 1:26; Genesis 11:7), Jehovah is represented as a king in council. The question reveals to the prophet that there is a work to be done for Jehovah, that He needs an instrument for that work. It is implied that no angel out of the whole host, no man out of the whole nation, offers to undertake it.[105]

Barnes' Notes on the Bible, while struggling to determine the true meaning of the use of plurality in this verse, finally admits that the Trinity argument simply is not the correct one:

> Thus, Genesis 1:26: "And God said, Let us make man in our image;" Genesis 11:6–7: "And Jehovah said, Go to, let us go down, and there confound their language." Such a use of the name of God in the plural is very common, but it is not clear that there is a reference to the doctrine of the Trinity. In some cases, it is evident that it cannot have such a reference, and that no "argument" can be drawn from the use of that plural form in favor of such a doctrine.[106]

One can almost visualize the scene. As Yahweh is seated in the midst of the divine council, He enquires, "Whom shall I send?". The question is His alone. The desire is His. The plan is His.

But then, as God points to the divine council, He directs Isaiah's attention to the whole host of the heavenly assembly and asks again, "Who will go for *us*?" Now the question is inclusive of the entire heavenly host. The implication is too much for Isaiah. He sees the responsibility, and he feels the burning urgency of it. Isaiah exclaims, "Here am I. Send me!" God smiled. The *elohim* exploded into applause. And Isaiah was commissioned by heaven's court.

Based upon all we have encountered in our journey thus far, how could these "us" statements, which we have now examined, credibly mean anything else?

Now that we have settled what "us" means, we are confronted with our next question. What does "in our image" mean?

Let's find out...

18

IN OUR IMAGE

On the other hand, if one begins with the Bible's position that man is created by God and in the image of God, there is a basis for that person's dignity.

—FRANCIS SCHAEFFER[107]

THE KINDERGARTEN TEACHER walked around her classroom, nodding with approval as she surveyed the crayon-scribbled pictures her students were busily creating. One child, moving her tongue back and forth in her cheek as she worked, scrawled away so intently that the teacher felt compelled to stop at the child's desk and ask what she was drawing.

The little girl replied, "I'm drawing a picture of God." The teacher gently corrected her, "Oh, honey, nobody really knows for sure what God looks like." The little youngster, without looking up and madly scribbling her colors onto the paper, responded, "Well, they *will* in a just a minute!"

What does it mean to be created in the "image" of God? Does it suggest that we know exactly what God looks like or that we look precisely like God? No, the actual mystery of the matter is infinitely deeper than that.

WE HAVE SEEN HIS IMAGE

We do, in fact, know *something* of His image—at least as He has chosen to make Himself visible to fallen humanity. Have a look at several New Testament disclosures of this truth. I have highlighted the relevant portions:

> **The Son is the image of the invisible God**, the firstborn over all creation. For in Him all things were created, things in heaven and on earth, visible and invisible, whether thrones or dominions or rulers or authorities. (Colossians 1:15–16, emphasis added)

> In their case the god of this world has blinded the minds of the unbelievers, to keep them from seeing the light of the gospel of the glory of Christ, **who is the image of God.** (2 Corinthians 4:4, ESV, emphasis added)

> Jesus said to him, "Have I been with you so long, and you still do not know me, Philip? **Whoever has seen me has seen the Father.** How can you say, 'Show us the Father'? (John 14:9, ESV, emphasis added)

> In the past, God spoke to our ancestors through the prophets at many times and in various ways, but in these last days he has spoken to us by his Son, whom he appointed heir of all things, and through whom also he made the universe. The Son

is the radiance of God's glory **and the exact representation of his being**, sustaining all things by his powerful word. (Hebrews 1:1–3, emphasis added)

The New Testament emphatically states that Jesus Himself is the image of the invisible God. After a lengthy discourse on the possible meaning of Jesus' words as found in the Colossians 1:15 passage, *Ellicott's Commentary for English Readers* comes to the following conclusion:

The true key to this passage is in our Lord's own words in John 1:18, "No man hath seen God at any time, the only begotten Son" (here is the remarkable reading, "the only begotten God"), "who is in the bosom of the Father, He hath revealed Him." In anticipation of the future revelation of Godhead, Christ, even as pre-existent, is called "The image of the invisible God."[108]

The passage of John 1:18, to which Ellicott refers, is a striking declaration. The NIV states it as follows:

No one has ever seen God, but the one and only Son, *who is himself God* and is *in closest relationship* with the Father, has made him known. (emphasis added)

Several major translations present the verse similarly, emphasizing that Jesus is God's unique human representation of Himself to us. This is important as we examine what God says about how He fashioned the human being from the beginning. The verse in question is Genesis 1:26:

Then God said, "Let us make mankind in our image, in our likeness, so that they may rule over the fish in the sea and the birds in the sky, over the livestock and all the wild animals, and over all the creatures that move along the ground." (emphasis added)

Two important words we must compare to all other truths about God and His divine council are "image" and "likeness." We have already determined that when God used the plural terms of "us" and "our," He was referring to Himself and the heavenly court that accompanied Him.

But is the eternally existent One, the *Elohim* who is without beginning and end and the creator of all that exists, shaped like a human being, or even like an angel? I do not believe the answer is as simple as that. So, what did God mean when He said that humanity would somehow bear the "likeness" of the upper family, including *Elohim* Himself?

UNIQUE BEYOND MEASURE

First, we must admit that humankind is undeniably and distinctly different than all other life forms on the planet—and in myriad scientifically measurable ways. To say that we are in God's "image" begins with the understanding that we are more like Yahweh than anything else in earthly creation.

Think how profound this truth is. We are the only living creatures on earth that:

- speak in highly complex language systems (hundreds of them)
- possess the gift of generational transference of knowledge
- write, create art, and record our words and art in libraries
- invent complex technologies of communication and information exchange
- have a highly developed sense of conscious awareness
- have a highly developed sense of a moral conscience
- build temples, churches, and other special locations for the express purpose of worship
- develop extremely complex societies—complete with intricate rules, regulations, laws, enforcement of the laws, and prisons and punishments for those that break the laws

- build towns, villages, cities, and other multifaceted living environments, complete with complex infrastructure technologies to sustain those communities
- create fire, cook food, and make and wear diverse articles of intricate clothing—from head to foot
- build hospitals, convalescence centers, and rehabilitation centers, in order to care for the sick and dying
- invent and build technological systems of transportation, especially at multiple levels (land, over sea, underwater, through the air, into space, and beyond our own solar system and galaxy)
- have a complex system of personal interrelationships involving an extreme range of emotions and societal rules for exhibiting those emotions
- build zoos and farms in order to collect, exhibit, and raise other animals (no other creature does these things in order to collect humans)
- establish complex issues of government, trade, monetary exchange, schools, universities, militaries, intercontinental interaction, and constantly look for life on other planets—the other earthly life forms don't even know other planets exist!

Then there is this recent 2017 admission by Nicholas Epley, a behavioral science professor at the University of Chicago:

> *Anthropomorphising*—when a human gives humanlike tendencies to inanimate objects and animals—is "a natural byproduct of the tendency that makes humans uniquely smart on this planet. Recognizing the mind of another human being involves the same psychological processes as recognizing a mind in other animals, a god, or even a gadget. It is a reflection of our brain's greatest ability."[109]

Along this same vein, the BBC ran a piece titled "Is Your Toddler Really Smarter than a Chimpanzee?" The point of the article was to show that "the divide between infant chimpanzees and infant humans is often startlingly small." While this assertion may hold a certain degree of truth, the fact remains that, as the human infant grows, it leaves the entire realm of the chimpanzee kingdom in the dust—*exponentially*. Consequently, the article concludes with the following necessary admission:

> It was obvious from [the] experiment that being raised in a human environment could not give a chimpanzee a human mind. Although she was one of the first non-human apes to communicate with humans in the form of signed symbols, she did not ever truly acquire language. The question scientists still wrestle with today is what exactly is going on in the minds of toddlers that allows them to acquire and use language where chimpanzees fail? And how does this relate to the skills that define human intelligence, allowing us to create moon landers and chai lattes?[110]

Let's sum up the matter like this: To the rest of creation, humans are like miniature gods—even "science" admits this truth. We can subdue and control every other living thing on the planet. We are the master of all, if we choose to be. On the other hand, there is not one other single living thing on the planet that can subjugate the entire human race. Not one. We are "gods" of the planet—by Yahweh's decree (Genesis 1:26). Humans will continue to create mind-boggling communication, transportation, and information technologies. Monkeys will always swing from trees and eat bananas.

The *elohim* are the *gods* of the heavenly realm, under the command of Yahweh. And we are the *gods* (Genesis 1:26) of the earthly realm, also under the sovereign and ultimate command of Yahweh. All of the created god-like beings, in both realms, are created in His image and likeness. As the esteemed theologian Francis Schaeffer asserted, "If one begins with the Bible's position that man is created by God and in the image of God, there is a basis for that person's dignity."[111]

In these ways, at least, this is what God meant when He declared, "Let us make man in our image and in our likeness." Man was to be unique from everything else on earth in the same way Yahweh and His created *elohim* are unique from everything else in the heavenly realm.

EARTH'S AMBASSADORS

However, the ultimate way in which we are created in the image of the upper family is that we are Yahweh's agents of representation on earth. We are His earthly witnesses and ambassadors in the same manner in which the *elohim* are His heavenly witnesses and ambassadors.

Yahweh is so much *other* than we are. God is not a mere man who is somehow a little bigger and a little smarter than we are. No, it is as if we were a lowly microbe and God is the super-genius scientist looking at us under a microscope. There simply is no comparison between the two living organisms. If we possess any likeness to God at all, it is only because He chooses to share that part of His glory with us out of His immeasurable love for us.

Yet…when *Elohim* decided to communicate with us—as we are—He became as one of us, in the person of Jesus Christ. Jesus is the *exact representation* of God with us. Now that's awe-inspiring.

ANOTHER HEBREW LESSON

The two Hebrew words used in the text of Genesis 1:27 that are of particular interest to us are *tselem* ("image") and *demuwth* ("likeness").[112]

Tselem derives from an unused Hebrew root word meaning "to bear a resemblance;" in other words, a representative figure. This word can also be used to speak of an idol. The word *demuwth* also carries the meaning of a resemblance, and in particular, the representative shape of something else. In other words, there is something about the modeling and overall shape of the human body that reflects the glory of God as well as His family of the heavenly realm.

The bottom line is this: The *shape* of humanity was God's idea from the beginning. In the ways we have discussed that shape thus far, it represents that of the upper family's overall image and shape. But, the *image* is more than a description of the mere shape or form; it goes directly to the uniqueness of our station and responsibility as well, just like the *elohim* of the divine realm.

GOD'S IMAGE IN THE ANGELS?

Here is where we might ask, "Do the *elohim* bear the 'image' of God as well?" The simple answer to the question is, "It appears so." We really cannot be dogmatic about the answer because the Bible is silent upon the issue.

However, we know that *elohim* and humans are much more alike than not alike, as compared to any other living thing. And we have already determined that when God said, "Let *us* make a man in *our* image," He was referring to the image of the divine realm.

It would appear, from all we know, that the divine *image* in which we have been created by Yahweh is something we share with the angelic realm. Perhaps this is why the angel in the book of Revelation declared himself to be in the same category of service as *your brothers* (Revelation 19:10, 22:9). We know that Yahweh/Yeshua created all things, including all thrones and powers. That would certainly include the entire realm of the *elohim* (Colossians 1:16). [113]

IN CONCLUSION

We know from Scripture that angels always appear to humanity in the form and shape of a human. Sometimes they are entirely indistinguishable from the rest of humanity, and at other times they are bathed in a divine radiance and glory—but still in the shape of a human being.

We also know that when Yahweh wanted to display Himself to humanity in a manner in which He would best be understood by us, He appeared as a human being, in the image of a man. And the most perfect presentation of that offering of His presence to us was in the person of Jesus Christ (Hebrews 1:1–3). Of this we can be certain: Humans are deeply connected to the image of God Himself, as well as to His upper family. This truth is exactly what Genesis 1:27 communicates.

We know that God is infinitely "other" than us. Jesus told us that "God is spirit" (John 4:24) He also told us that "no man has 'seen' God" (John 1:18, 1, 4:12). Both of these passages indicate that in His ultimate being and glory, God does not exist in the form of a mere human. God, as He really exists, is beyond our comprehension. Yet, who was telling us these great truths? None other than "God with us," *as a man*! (Matthew 1:24).

When God appears to either His upper family or His lower family, He may choose to appear in a form that more closely resembles their form, but He is above all other forms of reality. His dimension of existence is not ours. He is infinitely multidimensional; we are not.

But, you may ask, "Did Yahweh ever appear as a human being in the Old Testament?" That's a great question. Thanks for asking.

Turn the page for another surprise.

19

THE ANGEL OF THE LORD

The Angel of the LORD encamps around those who fear him and he delivers them.

—PSALM 34:7

DURING THE OLD Testament days, did Yahweh ever present Himself to humanity in the form of a man?

A few scholars continue to haggle over the nuances of the details involved, but the preponderance of biblical scholarship agrees: Yes, on occasion, God presented Himself to humanity in distinctly human form during Old Testament times.

The Hebrew text most often identifies God's appearances in human form as *malak Yahweh*. The Hebrew word *malak* literally translates to "messenger" or "representative." Thus, while first appearing to be only a messenger (angel) of Yahweh, what we really are witnessing in these instances is "Yahweh who brings His own message, personally."

God's appearance in human form is known as a theophany. We see the theophany grammatically rendered as the angel of the Lord, the angel of the Covenant, messenger of the Covenant, or the angel of the Presence, depending upon which verse and translation you are reading.

I HAVE SEEN GOD!

The first appearance of the angel of the Lord as God in the flesh is found in Genesis 16. In this text, God appears to Hagar, Sarah's handmaiden. However, the text finally identifies that particular revelation as being the Lord Himself:

> Then the angel of the Lord told her, "Go back to your mistress and submit to her." The angel added, "I will so increase your descendants that they will be too numerous to count." (Genesis 16:9–10)

> She gave this name to the Lord who spoke to her: "You are the God who sees me," for she said, "I have now seen the One who sees me." (Genesis 16:13)

Barnes' Notes on the Bible says of Genesis 16:9–10:

> "I will multiply."—This language is proper only to the Lord Himself, because it claims a divine prerogative. The Lord is, therefore, in this angel.[114]

Concerning Genesis 16:13, *Ellicott's Commentary for English Readers* states the matter beautifully":

> Thou God seest me.—Heb., Thou art El Boi, that is, a God of seeing. [Or, stated more literally] "Thou art a God that permits

Himself to be seen...." Hagar plays upon the word "*roï*," but her meaning is plain: "Do I not see, and therefore am alive, and not even blinded, nor bereft of sense and reason, though I have seen God."[115]

And the *Cambridge Bible for Schools and Colleges* explains the meaning of the verse in this way:

[*The Lord that spake unto her*]. These words definitely identify the Angel with a manifestation of the Almighty; see Genesis 16:7."[116]

OTHER APPEARANCES

The angel of the Lord appeared to Abraham (Genesis 18:1, 22:12–15). The angel of the Lord also appeared several times to Jacob, and is always identified in the text as the Lord Himself (Genesis 32:30, 48:16).

And it is none other than the angel of the Lord, later in the text identified as Yahweh, who appears to Moses in the burning bush:

[2] Here the angel of the Lord appeared to him in flames of fire from within a bush. Moses saw that though the bush was on fire it did not burn up.

[3] So Moses thought, "I will go over and see this strange sight—why the bush does not burn up."

[4] When the Lord saw that he had gone over to look, God called to him from within the bush, "Moses! Moses!"

And Moses said, "Here I am."

[5] "Do not come any closer," God said. "Take off your sandals, for the place where you are standing is holy ground."

[6] Then he said, "I am the God of your father, the God of Abraham, the God of Isaac and the God of Jacob." At this,

Moses hid his face, because he was afraid to look at God.
(Exodus 3:2–6)

We further find the angel of the Lord appearing to Joshua (Joshua
5:13–15), to Gideon (Judges 6:22), and to Samson's parents (Judges
13:21–22). The context in all three instances explicitly identifies the
angel as *Yahweh* in human form.

In total, we discover that the "the angel of the Lord" is referred to
fifty-six different times within fifty-one unique verses in the Hebrew
Scriptures.

CONTEXTUAL EVIDENCE

We can determine from the text in question whether the angel of the
Lord is actually Yahweh Himself or merely a divine being sent from
Yahweh's court. If the appearance truly is Yahweh in human form, the
contextual giveaways are:

- The text clearly and directly identifies the angel as Yahweh
  (Genesis 16:13).
- The angel has the power to give life (Genesis 16:10).
- The angel has the authority to judge the earth (Genesis 18:25).
- The angel receives worship and sacrifice (Genesis 22:12).
- The angel is omniscient (Genesis 16:13, Exodus 3:7).

WAS THIS JESUS?

The next logical question should be, "Then, can the angel of the Lord
be viewed as the first appearances of Jesus?" *Ah.* We have hit upon a very
important question. This is one of the nuances of interpretation concerning the mystery of the angel of the Lord referred to earlier.

Dr. C. Fred Dickason, a thirty-four-year scholar with Moody Bible Institute, with most of those years spent as chair of theology, explains the matter in this way: "We can solve the mystery if we allow that Jehovah God exists as a composite unity, as a triune God. His identity is with Christ."[117]

Dr. Dickason goes on to explain this thesis in great detail in his book titled *Names of Angels*. I think you will find the following excerpt from his commentary on the subject to be helpful:

> Christ's essential nature is that of genuine and complete deity. This is the clear presentation of the New Testament (John 1:1–2; Col 2:9; 3:1). We see in Matt 28:18–19 that all persons of the Trinity—Father, Son, and Holy Spirit—have the same name or authority. Even the Old Testament implicitly presents this concept.
>
> If we allow this, then we can better understand and solve the mystery of the Angel of Jehovah being identified as Jehovah and yet being distinct from Jehovah. Furthermore, we can then recognize the Angel of Jehovah's true identity: He is the second person of the Trinity, the Son, the Lord Jesus Christ, appearing before He became a member of the human race.[118]

The Bible appears to make it very clear that people in the days of the Old Testament who saw God in the flesh—the angel of the Lord— really saw the preincarnate Jesus. God occasionally allowed Himself to be viewed by human beings in the form of an "angel" [*elohim*], but only as much as they could understand within their earthbound ability. The actual, eternally existing, *being* of Yahweh is beyond the realm of our comprehension.

> And the Lord said, "I will cause all my goodness to pass in front of you, and I will proclaim my name, the Lord, in your presence. I will have mercy on whom I will have mercy, and I will

have compassion on whom I will have compassion. But," he said, "you cannot see my face, for no one may see me and live." (Exodus 33:19–20)

No one has ever seen God, but God the One and Only, who is at the Father's side, has made him known. (John 1:18)

God, the blessed and only Ruler, the King of kings and Lord of lords, who alone is immortal and who lives in unapproachable light, whom no one has seen or can see. To him be honor and might forever. Amen. (1 Timothy 6:15–16)

We know that in the only times God chose to reveal Himself to humanity in human form, He allowed Himself to be called "the angel of the Lord" in the Old Testament, or "Jesus Christ" in the New Testament. After the incarnation event of the birth of Jesus Christ, we never again hear of the angel of the Lord being used in the context of a visitation of God in the flesh. From the moment God took on flesh and entered this world as a human infant, all of humanity beheld God in the flesh as none other than Jesus of Nazareth. In Jesus, the world beheld Yahweh in the most unique way ever.

THE ONLY BEGOTTEN

These truths bring a deeper perspective to the understanding of Jesus being labeled as the "only begotten Son" (John 3:16). Some have been tempted to think of the archaic English word "begotten" to strictly mean "to be born," or "to be created." This false assumption is where certain cultic understandings derive that Jesus is not truly a being of deity but, rather, a mere created divine being—a lesser *elohim*.

But that is not what "only begotten" means. He is the literal and human manifestation of Yahweh, first as the angel of the Lord and then as Jesus Christ, who has eternally been with, and in, Yahweh Himself.

This is why some of the more modern translations of John 3:16 choose to render the description of Jesus as God's "one and only Son," or as God's "unique Son." These representations more accurately capture the entire biblical truth.

When God put on flesh in the form of Jesus Christ, it was the *one and only* appearance He would ever make in this exact fashion. His arrival in Jesus Christ would be an *entirely unique* manifestation of Yahweh to humankind, having first arrived to the earthly realm born through the womb of a woman (Galatians 4:4).

EXPLAINING THE UNEXPLAINABLE

All of the foregoing revelations, taken together, also explain the truth of the first few verses of John:

> In the beginning was the Word, and the Word was with God, and the Word was God. He was with God in the beginning. Through him all things were made; without him nothing was made that has been made. In him was life, and that life was the light of men. The light shines in the darkness, but the darkness has not understood it. (John 1:1–5)

Jesus was God. Jesus is God. Jesus always has been, and always will be—*God*. He was with God, and in God—from the beginning (John 1:1–4). He is not an *elohim* of God, Jesus is Elohim—in the form of God with us.

He is not a created being, a son of the gods, or even "a" son of God. He is God—coming out of God, and coming into the world through the womb of a woman...*the* unique Son (or human manifestation) of God.

In the angel of the Lord, He is not a mere angel with a message; rather, He is Yahweh who has come to personally bring His own message.

Now we also understand John 8:56–59; a passage that has given Bible students fits for ages:

[56] [Jesus said to the Jews] "Your father Abraham rejoiced at the thought of seeing my day; he saw it and was glad."

[57] "You are not yet fifty years old," the Jews said to him, "and you have seen Abraham!"

[58] "I tell you the truth," Jesus answered, "before Abraham was born, I am!"

[59] At this, they picked up stones to stone him, but Jesus hid himself, slipping away from the temple grounds.

In John 8, we see the Great I Am standing before the Jews. The One who first appeared to Abraham as the Angel of the Lord was right there among them. The One who had first appeared to Moses in the burning bush was now speaking directly to them. The One who was in the Father and with the Father from the beginning—and who now had come *from* the Father, yet was still *one* with the Father—was looking them in the eyes.

How could these magnificent things be? Because Jesus is God in the flesh—from eternity—and forevermore. We can call Him the angel of the Lord, Jesus Christ, or Yahweh manifest as man, but He is still the same *Elohim*.

JESUS WITH THE ANGELS

Now we will let the Scriptures answer another important question: How does God present Himself to the upper family of *elohim*? Does He appear in human form or in some other manifestation?

We know with biblical certainty that Yahweh has appeared in

humanoid form while present in the court of the *elohim*. As one example, remember that the divine council of *elohim* was with Yahweh at the creation scene. Observe what the New Testament says about that scene:

> In the beginning was the Word, and the Word was with God, and the Word was God. He was with God in the beginning. Through him [Jesus] all things were made; without him nothing was made that has been made. (John 1:1–3)

> For by [Jesus] all things were created: things in heaven and on earth, visible and invisible, whether thrones or powers or rulers or authorities; all things were created by him and for him. (Colossians 1:16–17)

> In the past God spoke to our forefathers through the prophets at many times and in various ways, but in these last days he has spoken to us by his Son, whom he appointed heir of all things, and through whom he made the universe. (Hebrews 1:1–2, emphasis added)

Barnes' Notes on the Bible has this to say about the declaration of Colossians 1:

> There was a reference to himself in the work of creation.... The universe was built by the Greater to be his own property; to be the theater on which he would accomplish his purposes, and display his perfections. Particularly the earth was made by the Son of God to be the place where he would become incarnate, and exhibit the wonders of redeeming love.
>
> There could not be a more positive declaration than this, that the universe was created by Christ; and, if so, he is divine.... If, therefore, this passage be understood literally, it settles the question about the divinity of Christ.[119]

So, we know from the contextual connections of both the Old and New Testament attestations that Yahweh did His work of creating the universe and everything in it, witnessed by the divine *elohim* council. Consider again the words of God found in His address to Job:

[4] Where were you when I laid the earth's foundation? Tell me, if you understand. [5] Who marked off its dimensions? Surely you know! Who stretched a measuring line across it? [6] On what were its footings set, or who laid its cornerstone— [7] while the morning stars sang together and all the angels shouted for joy? (Job 38:4–7)

Now we also understand that Yahweh accomplished this act of creation while in the personage of the One we know to be Jesus Christ (John 1:1–3; Colossians 1:16–17). There can be little argument of this clear biblical revelation.

Didn't I tell you, from the opening pages of this book, that you would never read the Scriptures in quite the same way again?

Hang on. Believe it or not, there are still more nuggets of biblical gold to unearth.

Now, let's take a closer look at the *elohim* we call *Satan*.

20

I WILL SIT ENTHRONED

I will ascend above the tops of the clouds; I will make myself like the Most High.

—ISAIAH 14:14

THE VAST MAJORITY of reputable scholars agree that two of the most illustrative passages that expose the magnitude of Satan's evil are found in Isaiah 14 and Ezekiel 28. Let's now examine what Yahweh has to say about Satan, beginning in Isaiah 14.

The prophet is told to "take up a taunt" against the king of Babylon. The Hebrew word for "taunt" is *mashal* Strong's OT #4912. That Hebrew word literally means: "a proverb, or a metaphorical illustration—a parable."[120]

In other words, while some of this passage would most certainly apply directly to the description of the human king of Babylon, the stated purpose of the depiction was to metaphorically compare that earthly king to someone else, namely, a fallen *elohim* of the divine council of God, the apparent chief architect of the heavenly rebellion. It quickly becomes obvious that the human king of Babylon is a spiritual comparison to Satan. Observe the key portion:

[12] How you have fallen from heaven,
O morning star, son of the dawn!
You have been cast down to the earth,
you who once laid low the nations!
[13] You said in your heart,
"I will ascend to heaven;
"I will raise my throne
"above the stars of God;
"I will sit enthroned on the mount of assembly,
"on the utmost heights of the sacred mountain.
[14] "I will ascend above the tops of the clouds;
"I will make myself like the Most High."
[15] But you are brought down to the grave,
to the depths of the pit. (Isaiah 14:12–15)

Barnes' Notes on the Bible records the following words concerning Isaiah 14 while also tying the passage to New Testament declarations:

[I will be like the Most High] There is a remarkable resemblance between this language and that used in 2 Thess 2:4, in regard to antichrist: "He, as God, sitteth in the temple of God, showing himself that he is God." And this similarity is the more remarkable, because antichrist is represented, in Rev 17:4–5, as seated in Babylon—the spiritual seat of arrogance, oppression, and pride. Probably Paul had the passage in Isaiah in his eye when he penned the description of antichrist.[121]

The Bible Exposition Commentary: Old Testament further expands the understanding of Isaiah 14:

The prophet saw in this event something far deeper than the defeat of an empire. In the fall of the king of Babylon, he saw the defeat of Satan, the "prince of this world," who seeks to energize and motivate the leaders of nations (John 12:31; Eph 2:1–3)....

This highest of God's angels tried to usurp the throne of God and capture for himself the worship that belongs only to God (Matt 4:8–10). The name "Lucifer" ("morning star") indicates that Satan tries to imitate Jesus Christ, who is "the bright and morning star" (Rev 22:16). "I will be like the Most High" reveals his basic strategy, for he is an imitator (Isa 14:14; 2 Cor 11:13–15). Like the king of Babylon, Satan will one day be humiliated and defeated. He will be cast out of heaven (Rev 12) and finally cast into hell (20:10).[122]

In Isaiah 14, we again run into elements of the divine council as well as the pride-based rebellion within that assembly, and finally, the ultimate last days judgment upon that rebellious *elohim*—*death*. This passage follows the pattern of Psalm 82 to the letter. And in the commentary entry just examined, we are reminded of Satan's chief goal on earth: to energize and motivate the leaders of nations.

Don't forget, this picture of Satan and his fall from Heaven was couched in a derisive taunt against the king of Babylon of Isaiah's day. Isaiah basically called Babylon's king Satan personified, and at the same time gave inspired insight into what actually happened in the heart of that particular fallen *elohim*.

From *Delitzsch's Biblical Commentary on the Prophecies of Isaiah*, we read:

A retrospective glance is now cast at the self-deification of the king of Babylon, in which he was the antitype of the devil and the type of Antichrist. The passage transcends anything that can be said of an earthly king and has been understood from earliest times to also refer to Satan's fall as described in Luke 10:18.[123]

Satan's fall was the result of his pride. His "I will" statements are the illustrative epitome of the evil that is in his heart and mind. The bottom line is that Satan desperately wants to be in the place of Elohim Himself. He wants to be God, and he wants to be the sole ruler of all of Heaven's *elohim* as well as the nations, kingdoms, and peoples of the earth. And to achieve his ends, he is continually directing his fallen *elohim* host of *gods* in the art of manipulating kingdom thrones.

Understanding this truth leaves little doubt that the realm of earthly politics is also very deeply spiritual in nature; it is often influenced by the demonic realm. Is there any wonder why the secular world leaders consistently insist that churches and Christians "stay out of politics"? The demonic realm desires to be the overriding influence in the realms of governments and nations.

Certainly, this is at least part of what Jesus meant when He commanded that His followers be the "salt and light" in the world. In that same command, Jesus also said that if we "lose our saltiness," we would certainly be "trampled underfoot" (Matthew 5:13). True enough, wherever and whenever Christians wholeheartedly "check out" of being involved in the affairs of civic operations and societal ethics, they are ultimately trampled underfoot—just as Satan desires.

Now let's examine exactly what position Satan held on the divine council, before he fell from grace. The book of Ezekiel provides the biblical insight for the disclosure of that mystery.

I can promise you, he's not just any *elohim*. He is the epitome of everything that is corrupt and vile.

21

Beauty Beyond Compare

It is amazing how complete is the delusion that beauty is goodness.
—Leo Tolstoy, *The Kreutzer Sonata* [124]

Ezekiel 28 follows the same pattern of *compound-reference* as is found in Isaiah 14. Every attribute of Satan and his ultimate demise described in Ezekiel 28 is found elsewhere in Scripture.

Admittedly, the passage is at first veiled in the shroud of the opening announcement, but as we move through the verses, it becomes apparent that a seismic swing takes place. The word to the King of Tyre becomes a lament, and the compound reference begins to take shape right before our eyes.

Through the words of the mournful dirge that follow, we peer behind the veil of God's unseen dimension and stare right into the face of the supreme fallen *elohim*. I am convinced that God's people are given this insight so that we might know just who it is that we are really up against:

[12] Son of man, take up a lament concerning the king of Tyre and say to him: "This is what the Sovereign Lord says:

159

'You were the model of perfection, full of wisdom and perfect in beauty.

[13] 'You were in Eden, the garden of God; every precious stone adorned you: ruby, topaz and emerald, chrysolite, onyx and jasper, sapphire, turquoise and beryl. Your settings and mountings were made of gold; on the day you were created they were prepared.

[14] 'You were anointed as a guardian cherub, for so I ordained you. You were on the holy mount of God; you walked among the fiery stones.

[15] 'You were blameless in your ways from the day you were created till wickedness was found in you.

[16] 'Through your widespread trade you were filled with violence, and you sinned. So I drove you in disgrace from the mount of God, and I expelled you, O guardian cherub, from among the fiery stones.

[17] 'Your heart became proud on account of your beauty, and you corrupted your wisdom because of your splendor. So I threw you to the earth; I made a spectacle of you before kings.

[18] 'By your many sins and dishonest trade you have desecrated your sanctuaries. So I made a fire come out from you, and it consumed you, and I reduced you to ashes on the ground in the sight of all who were watching.

[19] 'All the nations who knew you are appalled at you; you have come to a horrible end and will be no more.'" (Ezekiel 28:12–19)

KING OF TYRE?

How can we be certain that Ezekiel 28 is not simply about the king of Tyre rather than about Satan? Besides the obvious facts—which are: 1) the human king of Tyre was not the model of perfection, either in wisdom or in beauty; 2) nor was he in "Eden, the garden of God;" 3) nor was he ever a guardian cherub of the throne of God—it is also a fact that the king of Tyre was not *created;* rather, he was *born,* like any other human.

It certainly is true that the king of Tyre was never seated in the divine assembly, the holy mount of God, nor was he ever without sin, *blameless* in his ways. And if he was never seated in the divine assembly, then obviously he was never expelled from there.

However, the fallen *elohim* Satan fits the description of every one of these attributes. He *was* in the Garden; he was a created *elohim;* he was perfect from the beginning; he was blameless from the start; and he was, in eons past, at the *holy mount of God* and actively engaged in that divine assembly.

Furthermore, Satan *was* driven from that divine court and is filled with violence and death. His wisdom has been corrupted, and he will be made a spectacle before the kings of the world—*and,* he will be utterly destroyed. How could this illustrative passage of *compound reference* be any clearer?

Bible scholar Dr. Merrill F. Unger held a Ph.D. from Johns Hopkins University and a Th.D. from Dallas Theological Seminary. He was a professor of Old Testament studies at Dallas Theological Seminary. Dr. Unger wrote *Unger's Bible Dictionary,* numerous books on theology, and several academic level commentaries.

Dr. Unger sums up the message of Ezekiel 28 and the lament against the king of Tyre, with these words: "That the career of Satan is here reflected under the person of the king of Tyre is true because of *eleven reasons*"[25] (emphasis added).

He then lists and expounds upon those reasons, most of which I have just drawn to your attention.

Thomas L. Constable, Th.D., senior professor emeritus of Bible exposition at Dallas Theological Seminary, explains the passage like this:

Eden, the garden of God, is probably a figurative way of describing the blessing that this ruler [King of Tyre] had enjoyed at

God's hand (cf31:9; Genesis 13:10). If we take the statement literally, this must refer to someone who was in the Garden of Eden, probably Satan.[126]

Dr. E. W. Bullinger states the obviousness of the Ezekiel 28:13 declaration with this pointed affirmation:

Here is no evidence of a "legend", but a reality. Satan, the *Nachash* or shining one, was there.... This is added to leave us in no doubt as to what is meant by Eden, and to show that it was no mere "summer residence" of the "prince" of Tyre, but, the "garden" of Genesis 2:8–15.[127]

The acclaimed work of Robert Jamieson, A. R. Fausset, and David Brown, *Commentary Critical and Explanatory on the Whole Bible*, explains Ezekiel 28 and its connection to Satan in this manner:

The language, though primarily here applied to the king of Tyre, as similar language is to the king of Babylon (Isaiah 14:13 Isaiah 14:14), yet has an ulterior and fuller accomplishment in Satan and his embodiment in Antichrist (Daniel 7:25, Daniel 11:36 Daniel 11:37, 2 Thessalonians 2:4, Revelation 13:6).[128]

Don Stewart, an official biblical commentator for the online Bible study site *Blue Letter Bible,* speaks of Ezekiel 28 and its connection to Satan like this:

Though in context, Ezekiel was first speaking about the historical king of Tyre, he seemingly moved into the dateless past with a description of the original fall of Satan.... [Satan] had a special place next to the throne of God. Because of his special place, and his extraordinary beauty, he was lifted up with pride. This caused him to rebel against God, and to be judged for his sin.[129]

THE SHOCKER

However, the most astounding revelation we discern from Ezekiel 28, one that we find in no other passage about Satan, is that before his fall from the divine court, he was a guardian *cherub,* a sentinel of the holiness of the throne of Yahweh. He was one of Yahweh's right-hand *elohim* (Ezekiel 28:14).

Furthermore, Ezekiel describes how the cherubim actually looked. If you have never seen this before, prepare yourself for a biblical bombshell:

> [4] I looked, and I saw a windstorm coming out of the north—an immense cloud with flashing lightning and surrounded by brilliant light. The center of the fire looked like glowing metal,
> [5] and in the fire was what looked like **four living creatures**. In appearance their form was that of a man,
> [6] but each of them had four faces and four wings.
> [7] Their legs were straight; their feet were like **those of a calf** and gleamed like burnished bronze.
> [8] Under their wings on their four sides they had the hands of a man. All four of them had faces and wings,
> [9] and their wings touched one another. Each one went straight ahead; they did not turn as they moved. (Ezekiel 1:4–9, emphasis added)

Now, compare that passage about the four living creatures to the following from Ezekiel 10:15:

> [15] When the cherubim rose upward. These were the living creatures I had seen by the Kebar River.

The prophet Isaiah further confirms the exalted place of the cherubim in the hierarchy of Yahweh's divine council:

O Lord Almighty, God of Israel, enthroned between the cherubim, you alone are God over all the kingdoms of the earth. You have made heaven and earth. (Isaiah 37:16–17)

Additionally, in Ezekiel's description of the living creatures, including their faces (Ezekiel 1:10), we discover the words "face of an ox," and "feet like a calf." We also discover, as we continue to read that verse, the brilliant nature of those creatures. They possess the bright, golden hue of a flaming fire, or torch. Do visions of a *golden calf* come to mind?

YAHWEH'S CHIEF ELOHIM

Here's what we can take away from this study: Satan was an exalted cherub, one of the top four cherubim around the throne of God. Satan was not a mere run-of-the-mill cherub; he was different from all others. According to Isaiah 14 and Ezekiel 28, his splendor surpassed all other creatures of the divine counsel. His beauty and wisdom were without comparison. He was the model of perfection.

Observe the comments of the *Jamieson-Fausset-Brown Bible Commentary*: "Satan before his fall may have been God's vicegerent [earthly representative of Yahweh], whence arises his subsequent connection with [earth] as first the Tempter, then 'the prince of this world.'"[130]

The *Keil and Delitzsch Biblical Commentary on the Old Testament* says this about Satan's exalted position as one of the cherubim, before his fall:

The Cherubim, however, are creatures of a higher world, which are represented as surrounding the throne of God as occupying the highest place as living beings in the realm of spirits, standing by the side of God as the heavenly King when He comes to judgment, and proclaiming the majesty of the Judge of the world.[131]

We see the four living creatures again fourteen different times in the book of Revelation. In those passages, they are always surrounding the throne of God as guardian cherubim (Revelation 4–8, 14–15, 19).

Regardless of our speculations regarding the *prince of this world*, there is one thing we now assert with confidence regarding Satan: He was not a literal snake slithering through the Garden of Eden carrying on conversations with Eve. Rather, he is a created and divine being who has the wisdom, deceptive beauty, knowledge, and supernatural powers that are sufficiently expansive enough to ultimately fool the population of the entire planet. Satan can even appear as an "angel of light," and there is little doubt in the mind of many students of God's Word that this is exactly what he will do in the last days (2 Corinthians 11:14; 2 Thessalonians 2:11).

Now we have to ask: What exactly was the *knowledge* which this "first Tempter" offered to the very first humans that so drastically changed history?

And so the story continues—*from the beginning…*

22

Evil in the Garden

You were in Eden, the garden of God; every precious stone adorned you.

—Ezekiel 28:13

LIKE SO MANY other things accepted as truth about the Bible, the popularized Garden account of Genesis possesses its share of misrepresentation of facts.

For example, we often hear that Adam and Eve were created in the Garden of Eden, but that is not correct. Adam was *placed* in the Garden after having been created elsewhere, likely nearby:

> The Lord God formed the man from the dust of the ground and breathed into his nostrils the breath of life, and the man became a living being. Now the Lord God had planted a garden in the east, in Eden; and there he put the man he had formed.... The Lord God took the man and put him in the Garden of Eden to work it and to take care of it. (Genesis 2:7–8, 15)[132]

However, we later discover that Eve was, in fact, created in the midst of Eden. According to Hebrew text, Yahweh "formed" her out of the "side" (Hebrew, *tsela*) of Adam (Genesis 2:22). Eve's creation occurred after Adam had been placed in the Garden and was living there.

The fact is that the Garden of Eden was created prior to man's creation, and the Garden is where God chose to walk with man (Genesis 3:8). And since we are told that God purposely placed Adam in Eden in order to carry out a daily fellowship with Him, this leads some biblical scholars to believe that Eden was at least one place where Yahweh and His divine council first established their headquarters within the earthly realm (Ezekiel 28:13–16). This is an interesting biblical consideration for which there exists a sizeable body of reliable hermeneutical evidence.[133]

Another misconception concerning the Garden narrative is that Eve was alone in the Garden when Satan tempted her, and she later went to Adam and seduced him to do the same thing she had done. Genesis 3:6 sets the matter straight:

> When the woman saw that the fruit of the tree was good for food and pleasing to the eye, and also desirable for gaining wisdom, she took some and ate it. She also gave some to her husband, who was with her, and he ate it. (emphasis added)

You are probably aware that no apple, nor any other specific kind of fruit, is mentioned as being a part of the temptation experience of Adam and Eve. The Bible says only that they ate of the "fruit" from the "tree of the knowledge of good and evil"—and that they ate of it *together*. Of course, what kind of fruit it was assumes that it was a piece of literal fruit rather than another likely scenario—a metaphor for something much more evil than "eating." We'll explore that consideration in the next chapters.

THE TALKING SNAKE

Let's also examine the "snake" that entered the Garden to tempt the first couple. As previously discovered, Ezekiel 28 tells us in no uncertain terms that the being in the Garden was Satan. We also discovered in that passage that Satan is one of the exalted cherubim. Several times in the Old Testament, a manipulative adversary is mentioned by the identification of *Satan* (Job 1 and 2; Zechariah 3), and at least nine times in the New Testament. In none of these references is there even a hint that he is a talking snake. Satan is, however, said to be a divinely cunning being with whom we must be extremely careful, so that he does not outwit us (2 Corinthians 2:11).

With the one possible exception found in Genesis 3, Satan is never described in the Bible as a snake that speaks human language. He is, however, *symbolically* represented in the New Testament as a "serpent" and a "dragon" (Revelation 20:2), and even as a "roaring lion" (1 Peter 5:8).

The Greek word for "serpent," used in the New Testament, is *ophis*, Strong's #3789. Not only can that word mean a literal snake, but the Strong's Greek dictionary says the word can also mean: "figuratively— (as a type of sly cunning) an artful malicious person, especially Satan."[134]

The same is true of the Hebrew word *nachash*. This is the word used to describe the serpent who shows up in the Garden to converse with Eve. The word is Strong's OT #5175, which literally translates as "snake" or "serpent." However, the Hebrew dictionary connects this word as having originated from Strong's Hebrew #5172 (also *nachash* with a slight variation of spelling in the Hebrew). That word is defined as: "A primitive root; properly, to hiss, i.e. whisper a (magic) spell; generally, to prognosticate. One who learns from intense observation—a diviner."[135]

This description of Satan's personality matches the symbolic characterization of Satan found in Genesis and Revelation as a snake or serpent. Even today, we use the word "snake" in the same manner when speaking of a person who has lied about us, or who is especially cunning and deceptive. For example, we might say, "That old snake in the grass has deceived me, and he even lied about me."

By now, the understanding of the matter should be clear: This was no talking snake addressing Eve in the Garden. This was *elohim* Satan. This was *nachash,* the chief among the divine council cherubim and also the most beautiful, perfect, wise being that Yahweh had ever created (Isaiah 14; Ezekiel 28; 2 Corinthians 11:14). He also became the most arrogantly prideful of anything God created (1 Timothy 3:6).

Satan desired to possess the Garden creation as his own. He wanted the newly created earth as well. And, he wanted to have Adam and Eve as his own. He also desired to possess the nations that were destined to come from their seed. Satan sought to be *elohim* above all *elohim*, ruler of the heavenly host. Above all, he wanted to be like the Most High (Isaiah 14). Furthermore, he was determined that he would kill, steal, and destroy whatever and whoever he had to, in order to seize what he desired (John 10:10).

DOOR NUMBER ONE OR DOOR NUMBER TWO?

Obviously, Adam and Eve had been given a free-will choice. It was a decision that possessed eternal consequences. This is the central point of the entire narrative of the Garden of Eden account. One choice, if followed, would secure their position in paradise; the other choice would assure that the process of death and all the heartache that goes with it would ensue. God allowed the sifting to take place. Remember, from the very first chapters of this book, we learned that the sifting process was always a part of Yahweh's eternal plan.

What kind of temptation was involved in Satan's offer, and what kind of enticement could have possessed such sway over Eve's choice? What was Satan really trying to accomplish with his deadly temptation?

These questions have kept Bible students busy speculating upon the Garden account for thousands of years. While the direct answers do not appear to be given in the plain text, there certainly are some powerful clues, especially in light of everything we have learned about the divine council.

WHAT HAPPENED IN THE GARDEN?

Could it be that Satan's desire to bring the first couple down a notch was wrapped around his jealousy of them? Could it be that Satan saw this brand-new creation of Yahweh's as immediate rivals to his exalted position of beauty and fellowship with God? Could it be that Satan recognized and feared their eternal potential?

It also appears that Satan was already looking into the future. In his divining-*nachash* nature, he was even then plotting to one day rule the human/earthly nations and take his place of glory above the Most High (Isaiah 14). The breach of trust that Satan would have to create needed to be so repugnant that there was no chance Yahweh would back away from His promise of humanity's eternal punishment. Satan's trick would have to be so profane, so obscene, that the consequence would mean corruption for the entire future of the human race.

THE TEMPTATION

However, to the first humans, Satan's proposal must have appeared to be a win-win offer. Through his offer, they could find out what Satan and the divine council knew, and they could gain that knowledge with a promise that there would be no consequences. In so participating, they were assured they could actually take a position among the *elohim*, perhaps even on the divine council itself. So far, this theory appears to match the biblical narrative of Genesis 3:4–5:

"You will not certainly die," the serpent said to the woman. For God doth know that in the day ye eat thereof, then your eyes shall be opened, and ye shall be as gods, knowing good and evil. (KJV)

Satan offered the couple, beginning with Eve, the ability to step up the ladder in their created pecking order—with no penalty involved. The fact that humanity was created "a little lower than the divine beings" is a clear biblical truth (Psalm 8). Certainly, by the time Satan was tempting them with an elevation of power and position within God's kingdom, Adam and Eve were aware of this truth.

The temptation was seemingly backed by Satan's divine ability and promised on the direct authority from the chief of the *elohim* council. Eve *ate* first—then Adam. Apparently, they were both standing right there as Satan unloaded his offer of "knowledge." At the eating of that "fruit" they forfeited their state of perfection and innocence.

But what was it that caused the fall of humanity? Just what act of disobedience did they commit? Was it really something as simple as eating a piece of fruit? Is that what the text literally means to convey as humanity's curse? Or was it something much more sinister than that?

Get ready for a shocking contextual possibility…

23

THE FORBIDDEN FRUIT

I am not sure that the best way to make a boy love the English poets might not be forbid him to read them and then make sure that he had plenty of opportunities to disobey you.

—C. S. LEWIS[136]

IF YOU WERE to ask a fellow church member why the world is filled with such unspeakable evil, wickedness that seemingly grows worse by the day, the answer you would receive, practically every time, would be something like: "It started with the fall of Adam and Eve in the Garden." That answer would be correct, because that is exactly where the Bible says the evil started. Even the New Testament affirms the fact (Romans 5:12; 1 Corinthians 15:21).

However, if you followed up with a question about what could possibly have *happened* in the Garden that would have so totally corrupted everything on the planet and brought the sentence of death to all humankind, you probably would get an answer something along the

173

lines of: "Well, the Bible says Adam and Eve disobeyed God and ate the fruit from the forbidden tree. They believed the lie of the serpent." Again, the Bible actually says this. But is that presentation what the Bible *means,* literally? Ahh…there is the million-dollar question, the one that has perplexed biblical scholars since written commentary on the text has existed.

METAPHORICALLY SPEAKING?

Students of biblical hermeneutics know that even a literal rendering of a passage allows for figurative language considerations when that possibility is plausible. As an example, consider that Jesus declared we must "eat His flesh" and "drink His blood" in order to follow Him (John 6:53). Is that assertion meant to be taken literally? Are we to be literal cannibals, or are we to be sold-out, all-in followers of Christ? The answer should be obvious.

Also, are we really to "hate" our mother, father, sisters, and brothers in order to follow Jesus? (Luke 14:26). Or does it mean that our first allegiance, even over family members who are antagonistic to our faith, should be to the Lordship of Jesus Christ? Again, the answer is obvious.

I often explain the matter to people like this: The Bible sometimes does not mean exactly what it *says* (as the preceding examples illustrate), but it always means what it *means.* The challenge regarding a difficult passage is in the discovery of its actual, intended meaning.

Here's another example: The very first woman ate a single piece of fruit offered to her by a talking snake. As a result, the whole world fell into perpetual decay and has come under the eternal judgment of God. Every person on the planet is now genetically destined to spend eternity in Hell because this one woman ate from a forbidden tree and then gave it to her husband as well.

So, is the answer to the question "What really happened in the Garden" obvious, or not? Some say, "Yes, it means exactly what it says."

Others say, "It clearly is speaking of something much more serious than that." There stands the core of the debate we are now examining.

Is there even a hint from the Scriptures as to exactly what might have been involved? A distinctly conservative biblical-answer website offers a potential clue:

> Adam and Eve were innocent until they disobeyed God, bring-ing sin and death into the world (Romans 5:12). This death affected their bodies and souls and those of all of their descen-dants. At the moment of Adam and Eve's sin, they lost their innocence, as they were immediately aware, and they hid in shame from God (Genesis 3:7-8). *The couple tried to cover their sin, which they somehow associated with their sex organs.*[137] (emphasis added)

The last sentence of that quoted commentary cannot be disputed. Somehow, the *eating of the fruit* caused their first recorded reaction to be that of covering up their genitals and then hiding from God. They didn't cover their faces or their mouths; they didn't cover their heads or their feet, or any other part of their bodies. Apparently, the only parts that were related to their immediate shame were their sexual organs. But, how could *that* be?

Augustine of Hippo, writing from the late fourth century, is often touted as one of the most important church fathers in western Christi-anity. He is well known for his outspoken view of what he thought was involved in the first sin:

> For it was not fit that his creature should blush at the work of his Creator. But by a just punishment, *the disobedience of their genitals was the retribution to the disobedience of the first man,* for which disobedience they blushed when they covered with fig-leaves *those shameful parts which previously were not shameful.*[138] (emphasis added)

The reaction of Adan and Eve covering their genitals is addressed in *Gill's Exposition of the Entire Bible* like this:

They must know before that they were naked in their bodies, but they did not perceive that their nakedness was at all uncomely, or any disadvantage to them; but now they were sensible of both, that whereas they could look upon it before, and not blush or feel any sinful emotions in them, *now they could not behold it without shame*, and *without finding evil concupiscence arising in them.* (emphasis added)[139]

Gill continues in his commentary by emphasizing what he considers to be a rather obvious conclusion to be drawn from the Genesis 3 account:

And they sewed fig leaves together, and made themselves aprons; not to cover their whole bodies, but only those parts which, ever since, mankind have been ashamed to expose to public view, and which they studiously conceal from sight: *the reason of which perhaps is, because by those members the original corruption of human nature has been from the beginning*, and still is propagated from parents to children. (emphasis added)[140]

The *Guzik Commentary* concerning Genesis 3:7 hints towards a similar assessment:

Obviously, they covered their genital areas. In virtually all cultures, adults cover their genital areas, even though other parts of the human body may be more or less exposed from culture to culture. This is not because there is something intrinsically "dirty" in our sexuality, but *because we have both received our fallenness and pass it on genetically through sexual reproduction.* (emphasis added)[141]

Let's explore this matter a little deeper by comparing other meta-phorical elements of the passage, as well as other potentially related Scriptures.

TREES

Understanding that the serpent in the Garden was not a literal talking snake, and that there is probably a metaphorical veiling of a greater truth embedded in this passage, how then do we interpret Eden's *trees, fruit, and eating*? Are we really supposed to assume that the serpent was the only symbol used in the entirety of the Garden narrative?

The commentary from the *Cambridge Bible for Schools and Colleges* presents the contextual possibility of the two central trees of the Garden scene as being symbolic:

> The expression "tree of life" was used as a common metaphor of health and fruitfulness in Hebrew language, cf. Proverbs 3:18, "She (Wisdom) is a tree of life"; Genesis 11:30, "the fruit of the righteous is a tree of life."[142]

The *Pulpit Commentary* suggests something similar in the interpre-tation of the tree motif in Genesis 2:

> Hence the conclusion seems to force itself upon our minds that the first man was possessed of both immortality and knowledge irrespective altogether of the trees, and that the tree character which belonged to these trees was symbolical or sacramental, suggestive of the conditions under which he was placed in Eden.[143]

Gill's Exposition of the Entire Bible, as well as *Matthew Poole's Com-mentary* and *Ellicott's Commentary for English Readers* also hold that the two trees are metaphors of a much greater reality being set forth in the Garden account.[144]

A quick glance through a Bible concordance reveals how often "trees" are used in a metaphorical sense. Isaiah used trees and forests as symbols of strength (Isaiah 10:18–19, 32:19). Isaiah 55:12 speaks of the trees clapping their hands, and Psalm 1 speaks of a tree as symbolism for a righteous man. Trees are pictured as talking to each other (Judges 9:12). Israel is called an olive tree (Romans 11, Jeremiah 11:16) and a fig tree (Hosea 9:10; Matthew 24:32).

Now we have weighty contextual evidence that the "serpent" was not a talking snake, and the "trees" were probably not literal trees either. So, where does that leave us with "eating the fruit?" Believe it or not, the Scripture also connects gardens, trees, fruit, and *eating of the fruit* in several symbolic ways.

TREES, FRUIT, AND EATING

In the Song of Solomon, there are a number of vivid descriptions of intimacy between a man and woman. Song of Solomon 2:3 presents a particularly striking scene, employing an interesting choice of words. Notice the imagery of an apple tree representing the man. Look what else is said of this garden/forest encounter:

> Like an apple tree among the trees of the forest is my beloved
> among the young men. I delight to sit in his shade, and his fruit
> is sweet to my taste. (Song of Solomon 2:3)

That particular verse, in its proper context, is not necessarily meant to be a direct commentary on the Garden of Eden. The passage is often represented as a metaphorical love relationship between Yahweh and Israel, or a husband and wife, and then ultimately between Christ and the church. In either of those cases, however, the Song of Solomon passage, complete with a tree, fruit, and eating, is obviously meant to be taken as a representation of a greater truth. Furthermore, that metaphor of trees, eating, and fruit is also meant to carry with it the unmistakable connotation of sensuality.

The point is that similar imagery is found in the Garden narrative: An encounter takes place in a garden-forest, a seductive conversation ensues, promises are made, and something happens that is represented as the eating of the sweet forbidden fruit of the tree.

We again find the Garden imagery in Song of Solomon 4:16. The contextual metaphor unmistakably speaks of sensual love between a husband and wife:

> Blow upon my garden, let its spices flow. Let my beloved come
> to his garden, and eat its choicest fruits. (ESV)

We also see potential Garden imagery in Proverbs 30:20, where a woman who is committing sexual sin is presented as shamelessly eating of the pleasure of her sin and then haughtily says, "I've done nothing wrong!"

> Such is the way of an adulterous woman; she eateth, and wipeth
> her mouth, and saith, I have done no wickedness. (KJV)

MORE EDEN IMAGERY

Still another passage alludes directly to the Garden scene of Genesis. In Ezekiel 31:9, we find these words:

> All the trees of Eden that were in the Garden of God envied him.

This passage, taken in its entire context, represents Eden's trees as nations, and, surprisingly, as *living* entities.

A woman's breasts are called "fruit" in Song of Solomon 7:4. Fruit is also used metaphorically as a child in the womb (Deuteronomy 7:13) or the activities and choices of our lives (Psalm 1, 92:14). Furthermore, fruit is said to be the disaster that results from wickedness (Jeremiah 6:19). Hosea 10:13 uses the striking metaphor of fruit representing the results of wickedness and deceit. And in Amos 8:1–2, ripe luscious fruit is used as a metaphor for something that is getting ready to spoil, and will eventually incur the wrath of God. Paul speaks of the "fruit of the flesh" as representing all sorts of evil, including sexual sin (Galatians 5).

Yet another startling passage of Scripture might give us a hint for interpreting the Garden of Eden account. The verses come from Jeremiah 51:34. Jeremiah is lamenting King Nebuchadnezzar's plundering of Jerusalem. In that passage, he compares the king to a serpent:

> Like a serpent he has swallowed us and filled his stomach with our delicacies, and then has spewed us out.

The word translated as "delicacies" is a very interesting choice of terminology. In the original Hebrew text, the word is #5730 (*ednah*). The word most literally means "pleasures." The *NAS Exhaustive Concordance* identifies the word *ednah* as having derived directly from the word "Eden."[145]

Once again, we find imagery of evil (serpent), with connotations of a *stolen pleasure* that was subsequently tossed aside, having been used for a solely selfish purpose. Jeremiah chose a specific Hebrew word to describe the despicable scene of stealing the *delicacies* of Yahweh's beloved (Jeremiah 11:15). It is a word that possesses a direct tie to the Garden of Eden.

Regardless of one's final analysis of the matter, the question is legitimate. As repulsive or out of context as some might claim the suggestion of some sort of profane sensuality to be, there does exist a body of thought among certain classic commentators suggesting this possibility. There also appears to be a hefty amount of linguistic contextual consideration as well.

ARGUMENTS FROM THE HEBREW TEXT

There are sometimes several ways in which specific Hebrew words can be correctly translated into English phraseology. The real problem comes in attempting to determine which English translation is most appropriate to the overall context of the passage at hand. Our study of the word *elohim* is a prime example of this phenomenon.

As an example of an interpretation choice for the Garden narrative, have a look at Genesis 3:3 as represented in several common English translations: "But God did say, 'You must not eat fruit from the tree that is in the middle of the garden, and you must not *touch* it, or you will die.'"

The word "touch" (Strong's #5060, *naga*), is the pivotal translation word of this verse. Its Hebrew definition is as follows: "A primitive root; properly, to touch, i.e. Lay the hand upon (for any purpose; *euphemism—to lie with a woman*)." (emphasis added).[146]

The English word "touch" is certainly an appropriate translation for this text, especially in keeping with the obvious metaphorical narrative involving trees and fruit. However, it is quite amazing, in light of everything else we have discovered, that such an important word in this critical verse also possesses an undeniable euphemistic undertone of sexual impropriety.

BEGUILED

There is also this important tidbit coming straight from the Genesis 3 text:

> And the LORD God said unto the woman, What is this that thou hast done? And the woman said, The serpent beguiled me, and I did eat. (Genesis 3:13, KJV)

Eight of the top several dozen scholarly translations use the word "beguiled" in this passage. Other Bible versions use words like: "deceived," "tricked," "misled," or *caused me to forget.*"[147]

Why so many nuances in translations? Why do a third of them choose the specific word "beguiled"? Once again, we are faced with a Hebrew word that carries with it several legitimate translation choices, including the potential connotation of sexual seduction. The Hebrew word for "beguiled"/"deceived" is *nasha*, Strong's OT # 5277. Observe the *Strong's Exhaustive Concordance* definition possibilities for this word:

> Beguile, deceive, greatly, utterly. A primitive root; to lead astray, i.e. (mentally) to delude, *or (morally) to seduce—beguile*, deceive, X greatly, X utterly. (emphasis added)[148]

Interestingly, the *Merriam-Webster Dictionary* lists its very first definition of "seduction" as: "The enticement of a person to sexual intercourse."[149]

BACK TO EZEKIEL 28

One additional point. Since we have already determined that Ezekiel 28 speaks of Satan and his ultimate demise, it could be that this passage also holds an important clue to Satan's involvement in Eve's seduction. After we are informed that the fallen guardian cherub of Ezekiel 28 is actually in the Garden of Eden, we find that God pronounces judgment upon his actions in that garden—God calls Satan's conduct *profane*:

> And thou hast sinned: therefore I will cast thee as profane out of the mountain of God. (Ezekiel 28:16, KJV)

The Hebrew word in question, translated as "profane," is *chalal* (Strong's #2490). Believe it or not, one of the implications of this word's definition is "to defile" or "*to prostitute oneself.*"[150]

Consider the implications. The word "prostitution" is most typically defined as "the offering of one's sexuality in exchange for a payment or a bargain." In what process does the Bible say Satan and Eve were engaged? Was it not an offering of some sort, a bargaining process in exchange for the promise of a divine pay off? Of course it was. The only points that are real matters of debate are: Exactly what was the deal, and exactly what act was committed that might be represented by the "eating of fruit"?

Are those who hold to the potentiality of a profane act of seduction committed in the Garden-Fall merely seeing elephants and bunny rabbits in cloud formations, or is there really something here that the text intends to reveal? Why do so many Hebrew words used in the Garden text hold images of sensuality? Why does the overall image of trees, fruit, and eating hold corresponding biblical images of sexual involvement? Is all of this mere coincidence, or is something deeply sinister meant to be conveyed—in veiled format? These are the questions that stump biblical scholars to this day.

But we're not finished yet. There's still more to consider…a lot more.

24

THE CORRUPTION OF GOD'S GIFT

They slipped briskly into an intimacy from which they never recovered.
—F. SCOTT FITZGERALD, *THIS SIDE OF PARADISE*[151]

WHAT WE EXAMINE next might be a bit uncomfortable to consider. I am not proposing the following assertions as a dogmatic stance as to what actually transpired in the Garden rebellion. However, they reflect a quantity of historical evidence that we must at least investigate.

The twelve-volume *Jewish Encyclopedia,* published in 1901, presents a stunning entry under the section titled "Views of the Rabbis":

> Through the illicit intercourse of Eve with the serpent, however, the nature of her descendants was corrupted, Israel alone overcoming this fatal defect by accepting the Torah at Sinai.[152]

The online encyclopedic source *New World Encyclopedia* reiterates the theme we just observed in the *Jewish Encyclopedia.* The entry titled "Human Fall" similarly asserts:

Some early Christian sects and rabbinical sages, considered that the Fall was the result of sexual intercourse between Eve and the Serpent, usually understood to symbolize Satan....

Christianity traditionally teaches that the Original Sin is passed on through sexual intercourse, interpreting Psalm 51:5, "I was brought forth in iniquity, and in sin did my mother conceive me."

A condition that is the result of eating a literal fruit can hardly be passed down through the lineage. But the effects of illicit love can be.[153]

The same encyclopedia entry offers further explication upon the orthodox Jewish view of the Garden Fall through the eyes of ancient Hebrew Kabbalists:

The Bahir, a Kabbalistic text, states: "The serpent followed Eve, saying, 'Her soul comes from the north, and I will therefore quickly seduce her.' And how did he seduce her? He had intercourse with her." (Bahir 199)[154]

Additionally, an intricate scholarly work, published in 2010, offers a detailed examination of ancient Jewish thought relating to the Garden sin. Note the following assertion:

One finds in rabbinic writings a number of exegetical traditions evolving around the serpent's passion for Adam's wife. In general, these traditions can be divided into the two main groups: those where the serpent's plot in Gen 3 is directed against Adam in order to get to his wife, and those where he (or Satan) actually has sexual intercourse with Eve.

Although all these traditions are attested in the late Amoraic sources, both Palestinian and Babylonian, there is a high probability that the basic motif of Eve having intercourse with the serpent goes back well into the Second Temple Period. [Roughly four hundred years before Christ].[155]

I have not presented the preceding sources as an argument that insists *Satan had sex with Eve*. Plainly stated: Simply because a group of ancient rabbis state something to be "true" does not necessarily make it so, even if they insisted upon the belief for hundreds of years. However, it is important to be fully aware of this influential view that actually existed among early orthodox Jews and even certain components of the early New Testament church.

You will also discover in a few moments that even the apostolic assertions of John, Peter, and Paul appear to address the matter of original sin in a similar manner. Consequently, there *has* to be a legitimate reason a number of ancient Jewish scholars, as well as ~~some~~ several New Testament writers, seem to mirror this position.

ADDITIONAL CONTEXT

While *Adam Clarke's Commentary on the Bible* does not specifically say that the original sin was directly related to something sensual in nature, he does offer an extremely applicable observation:

> [The account of the Garden Fall] could never have been credited had not the indisputable proofs and evidences of it been continued by uninterrupted succession to the present time. All the descendants of this first guilty pair resemble their degenerate ancestors, and copy their conduct. The original mode of transgression is still continued, and the original sin in consequence.[156]

Having considered Clarke's astute observation, think with me for just a moment; what matter of sinful activity is an undeniably recurrent theme throughout the Scriptures, one in which Yahweh consistently warns His people never to participate? Is it not the problem of their involvement in all manner of sexual perversion? We cannot even get out of the book of Genesis before we run into the sin of Sodom and Gomorrah—a sexually perverse arena that is actually proclaimed from the lips of Jesus Christ as an example of a specific sign of end-time judgment (Luke 17: 28).

From Genesis to Revelation, we discover the corruption of God's gift of sexuality to be one of the most prevalent and destructive plagues upon humanity. Sexual perversion brings disease and death. It brings the ruin of marriage, home, family, and the spiritual/psychological demise of countless children, often passed down through the generations.

We also know from sad experience that acts of immersive sexual rebellion are often interrelated to substance abuse, suicide, self-destructive social behavior, and a complete separation from a saving relationship with Jesus Christ. Sexual perversion frequently leads to the specific exploitation of women and children (think *pornography*)—sometimes involving kidnapping, torture, or worse. As well, we are painfully aware that sexual corruption can lead to adultery, fornication, homosexuality, gender confusion, pedophilia, bestiality, and even the downfall of civilizations (Jude 1:7).

We see the possible origins of some sort of sexual perversion in the Garden, first in the covering of their sexual organs in shame, but we also might see it foreshadowed in the curse pronounced upon Satan, a curse that manifests itself through children—the seed of the woman—especially through a specific child (Genesis 3:15; Galatians 3:19, 4:4).

How can we deny that the New Testament echoes the manifold warnings and rebukes against sexual sin in particular, and the deeply spiritual connections thereof (Romans 12:1–3; 1 Corinthians 6: 9–20; 1 Thessalonians 4:3; Ephesians 5:5; Colossians 3:5; Galatians 5:19, etc.)

If there truly is any credibility to this line of exegetical approach, is there any wonder that, by the time we get all the way to the end of the Word of God, we run right into the theme of Satan attempting to destroy the *seed of the woman* (Revelation 12)? Apparently, the seed (and the womb) of the woman have always been a fixed target of Satan's most appalling schemes (Matthew 2:16).

THE SORROWFUL PRONOUNCEMENT

And the Lord God said, "The man has now become like one of us, knowing good and evil. He must not be allowed to reach out his hand and take also from the tree of life and eat, and live forever." (Genesis 3:22)

The *Cambridge Bible for Schools and Colleges* agrees that the Garden temptation's primary appeal was that Adam and Eve could somehow attain to the position of being on the divine council. *Cambridge* lays forth this understanding as the first choice of biblical possibilities:

[Yahweh here] speaks to the Heavenly Beings by whom the throne of God was believed to be surrounded. "As one of us" will then mean, not "like unto Jehovah personally," but "like to the dwellers in Heaven," who are in the possession of "the knowledge of the distinction between good and evil."[157]

Neither Adam nor Eve became a *god* by obtaining their new knowledge. However, a part of Satan's lie contained at least a kernel of truth—because Adam and Eve had, in fact, been made privy to something that apparently the divine council also knew. The first humans, possessing this new knowledge, were now *like* the members of that divine assembly. They held information pertaining to the evil in which they had participated—an evil so despicable that they, and their seed, would be forever cursed by Yahweh. And, God called Satan *profane* for having seduced them to do whatever it was that they did. Think logically upon this matter: Was the *Divine Knowledge* possessed by the *elohim* and offered by Satan to Adam and Eve trulyreally something along the lines of, "Oh! Don't eat that fruit! That stuff will kill you!" Or is the entire Garden account a divine metaphor for something utterly profane and devastating?

Whatever the precise thing was in which they participated, that "thing" became the germination point for every vile and wicked calamity that has since befallen humanity, as well as the earthly creation itself. Don't forget, it would not be too much later in humanity's chronicle before God would destroy everything with a global Flood, because by that time "all flesh had become corrupted" (Genesis 6:12, KJV). Now, there's an interesting choice of words: *corrupted flesh*. More on that later.

NEW TESTAMENT HINTS

The apostle John may have given a nod toward what might have happened in the Garden. In 1 John 2:16, he outlines what appears to be his assessment of the top three allurements to our sin nature:

> For all that is in the world, the lust of the flesh, and the lust of the eyes, and the pride of life, is not of the Father, but is of the world. (KJV)

Interestingly, almost every modern commentary identifies John's list in that passage with Eve's assessment of what lay before her in the Garden that day with *nachash*:

> And when the woman saw that the tree was good for food [lust of the flesh], and that it was pleasant to the eyes [lust of the eyes], and a tree to be desired to make one wise[(the pride of life], she took of the fruit thereof, and did eat, and gave also unto her husband with her; and he did eat. (Genesis 3:16, KJV)

It is difficult to ignore these biblical connections as potential hints to the Garden sin.[158]

Did Peter and Paul Spill the Beans?

Are you ready for another shocking revelation? Notice what Peter asserts in 2 Peter 1:4 as the ultimate reason, and point of origin, for the depravity of the entire planet:

> Whereby are given unto us exceeding great and precious promises: that by these ye might be partakers of the divine nature, having escaped **the corruption that is in the world through lust.** (KJV, emphasis added)

The word "corruption comes" from the Greek word *phthora* and literally means "destruction," "rot," "decay," and "decomposition." It carries with it the connotation of a continual process. And, as we know, every *process* has to first have a *beginning*.[159]

Peter then methodically moves from his striking declaration of 2 Peter 1:4 right into the judgment and fiery destruction that is to come upon the entirety of the first creation as a result of that pervasive corruption (2 Peter 3:7).

Of all words Peter could have used to describe the original sin, why did he choose the word "lust"? The Greek word in 2 Peter 1:4 translated as "lust" is Strong's #1939 (*epithumia*). It means, "A longing (especially for what is forbidden)—concupiscence (strong sexual desire), lust (after)."[160]

Admittedly, the word "lust" can be used in a variety of nuanced contexts in the Greek as well as in the English language. I often lust after a bowl of ice cream. But, that's not how I usually use the word. The prevailing implication of the word is that of longing for something that is deeply sensual in nature, and forbidden. Observe the following three scholarly attestations of this fact.

The *Jamieson-Fausset-Brown Bible Commentary* has this to say about Peter's declaration: "The corruption in the world" has its seat not so much in the surrounding elements, as in the "lust" or concupiscence [strong sexual desire] of men's hearts.[161]

Adam Clarke's Commentary on 2 Peter 1:4 states:

> We have *partaken* of an earthly, *sensual, and devilish nature*; the design of God by Christ is to remove this, and to make us partakers of the Divine nature; and save us from all the corruption in principle and fact which is in the world; *the source of which is lust.*... Lust, *or irregular, impure desire, is the source whence all the corruption which is in the world springs.* (emphasis added)[162]

John Gill's Exposition of the Bible references Peter's contextual use of the word "lust" in this manner:

> Not the corruption and depravity of nature, which is never escaped by any, nor got rid of so long as the saints are in the world; but the corrupt manners of the world, or those corruptions and vices which, are prevalent in the world, and under the power and dominion of which the world lies; *and particularly the sins of uncleanness, adultery, incest, sodomy, and such like filthy and unnatural lusts.* (emphasis added)[163]

To be "in this world *through* lust" is Peter's method of communicating that lust is the foundational vehicle through which the corruption was initiated, and whereby it continues to perpetrate itself. Again, we must ask the obvious: "If the foundation of that lustful corruption is hopelessly embedded in the heart of humanity, when did that particular corruption process actually begin? Where did the vehicle of *unnatural* lust first take off?" The only place in the Bible that speaks about the beginning of man's universally corrupt heart is the Garden account in Genesis. And that particular narrative, as we have demonstrated, is filled with nuanced words and images carrying with them the potential of unnatural sensuality.

PAUL'S LINK WITH PETER

In the book of Romans, the apostle Paul expresses much of the same idea laid out by Peter. Additionally, he used the same Greek word for "corruption" that Peter used. Paul's declaration also makes a direct connection back to the Garden sin concerning the "corruption that is in the world." Paul declared that this corruption not only infected all of humanity, but has also permeated the entire creation. Observe:

> I consider that our present sufferings are not worth comparing with the glory that will be revealed in us. For the creation waits in eager expectation for the children of God to be revealed. For the creation was subjected to frustration, not by its own choice, but by the will of the one who subjected it, in hope that the creation itself will be liberated from its bondage to decay [corruption] and brought into the freedom and glory of the children of God.
>
> We know that the whole creation has been groaning as in the pains of childbirth right up to the present time. Not only so, but we ourselves, who have the firstfruits of the Spirit, groan inwardly as we wait eagerly for our adoption to sonship, the redemption of our bodies. For in this hope we were saved. (Romans 8:18—24a, emphasis added)

Paul proclaims the same truth that Peter set forth in 2 Peter 1:4. He speaks of the corruption that is in this world and in our own bodies— and he emphasizes that it has its roots in the very beginning. Peter, of course, reveals corruption's vehicle: *lust.*

Once again, based upon Paul's declaration to the church at Rome, we are faced with asking the question, "When did creation actually fall into this *bondage to decay*?" Again, we are left with the only answer the Bible provides: I began in the Garden of Eden (Romans 5:12; 1 Corinthians 15:21).

Based upon all that we have examined on the topic thus far, many would say that John, Peter and Paul do not even come close to sanitizing the foundational problem of humanity—or where, and how, it began.

THE ELEPHANT IN THE ROOM

Let's ask a few obvious questions: "If sexual perversion of some sort truly *was* the sin perpetrated in the Garden, did Satan actually participate in that sexual perversion? Did Satan perhaps include other *elohim* in the act/acts? Or did *Nachash* merely instruct in the perversion, and/or instigate it? And, what, precisely could that specific perversion have been?"

Now, for my extremely deep theological answer to all those questions: I don't have a clue.

The truth is that the Genesis text does not directly address any of those questions. Of all the textual and historical evidence I have provided for the possibility, there is still no categorical proof that unnatural sexuality was involved in the Garden sin. It could very well be that the inability to answer those kinds of inquiries and many others like them is what leads so many commentaries to shy away from interpreting the Garden account as having anything to do with sexual sin. I feel their pain; this is a tough one, to be sure.

Accordingly, I am not willing to make an inflexible assertion in the matter. However, the possibility of the sexual perversion explanation has been explored by biblical scholars for thousands of years, and it is one that holds plenty of biblical and scholarly elements of consideration (Romans 12:1–3).

Regardless of the unknown details, the sin that took place in the Garden was no trivial matter. Something deeply profane occurred there. It was so degenerate that it caused God to ultimately pronounce the curse of death upon the whole of creationThat fact is no small consideration.

Now, we are finally prepared to examine that often-avoided passage in Genesis 6, perhaps ultimately related to Genesis 3…

25

The Corruption of All Flesh

The sons of God saw that the daughters of men were beautiful.

—Genesis 6:2

Would you like to read one of the most hotly contested passages in the entire Bible? Okay then, brace yourself. The following translation is from *The New International Version*. The passage is Genesis 6:1–8, and our understanding of it literally determines how we will interpret the rest of the biblical message—right up to some of the last words of the book of Revelation:

> [1] When men began to increase in number on the earth and daughters were born to them,
> [2] the sons of God saw that the daughters of men were beautiful, and they married any of them they chose.
> [3] Then the Lord said, "My Spirit will not contend with a man forever, for he is mortal; his days will be a hundred and twenty years."

197

⁴ The Nephilim were on the earth in those days—and also after-ward—**when the sons of God went to the daughters of men and had children by them.** They were the heroes of old, men of renown.

⁵ The Lord saw how great man's wickedness on the earth had become, and that every inclination of the thoughts of his heart was only evil all the time.

⁶ The Lord was grieved that he had made man on the earth, and his heart was filled with pain.

⁷ So the Lord said, "I will wipe mankind, whom I have created, from the face of the earth—men and animals, and creatures that move along the ground, and birds of the air—for I am grieved that I have made them."

⁸ But Noah found favor in the eyes of the Lord. (emphasis added)

First, let's deal with the facts of the plain reading as translated from the Hebrew text. Starting at the end of the passage, we discover that whatever happened in those days was so despicably evil that Yahweh determined to wipe every living thing from the face of the earth.

ALL FLESH

This same passage further tells us that God was specifically going to destroy *all flesh* on the earth, because every bit of it had become *corrupt* (Genesis 1:12, KJV). And the passage appears to suggest it was through a unique and particularly despicable union that the world-destroying corruption had come.

The Hebrew word for "flesh" is *basar* (Strong's #1320). The NIV translation interprets *basar* to mean "all people." The KJV translates the Hebrew phrase as "all flesh." This Hebrew word is used throughout the Old Testament to refer to humans and/or animals—*anything* created of flesh. Since we know the Flood was meant to destroy every living thing except for Noah, his family, and the animals set apart on the Ark, we can assume the word means what it says, all fleshliterally everything living had become corrupt.[164]

This is not a very pretty picture thus far, is it? Just wait.

NEPHILIM

Then we learn that something called the *Nephilim* were on the earth in those days. They were there because a very specific union had taken place. The word *Nephilim* is usually translated as "giants." The word often carries with it the connotation of something out of the ordinary.[165]

In Genesis 6:4, the word translated "heroes" comes from the Hebrew word #1368 (*gibbor*). The word means, "A powerful warrior, a tyrant, a mighty man—and *a giant* of a man." So, in both cases, *Nephilim* and *gibbor*, we find the connection to giants in the most literal sense of the word.[166]

The word translated as "renowned" simply means "well-known." So, what we truly have here are: notorious tyrant-warriors who were overwhelmingly powerful and huge—even gigantic in stature.

On top of that, the next verse (verse 5) tells us that these individuals were causing untold violence to flourish over the earth. To put it in modern vernacular, the *Nephilim* were brutal terrorists. These were terrifying beasts of men. And their existence was at least a part of the reason God destroyed every living thing on the earth.

SONS OF GOD

Now we come to that dreaded, ignored, denigrated, glossed-over, explained-away, and excoriated phrase found in Genesis 6:2: "the sons of God."

Whoever these fellows were, they "came unto the daughters of men," and evidently *produced* some evil offspring. There can be no doubt that this union, and the offspring issued forth, finally wore thin on God's patience and mercy. This had to have been a really bad seed of some sort.

The understanding of "daughters of men" is pretty straightforward: These were human women. But it's the biblical counterpart to this union that gives the commentators pure fits. Let's step off that ledge now.

BENE ELOHIM

Just who are these "sons of God?" As revealed in an earlier chapter of this book, we first see the sons of God in the book of Job. They are a part of the divine council—they are divine beings. The same Hebrew words *bene elohim* used in Job are also used here in the Genesis text. You would think every scholar could plainly see that fact, right? Think again.

A number of the modern commentaries completely skip Genesis 6:2 as far as giving an explanatory statement. That's how controversial this passage is. On the other hand, the various Bible translations have it a bit easier. Almost every one of them simply renders Genesis 6:2 as the Hebrew states it: "sons of God." They leave it to the readers, teachers, preachers, and scholars to debate the exact meaning of the phrase.

However, I did actually find one translation bold enough to render the verse into English within the plain Hebrew contextual implication. Observe the *International Standard Version's* translation of Genesis 6:2: "Some divine beings noticed how attractive human women were, so they took wives for themselves from a selection that pleased them."[167]

THREE POSSIBILITIES

The three most popular commentary choices for the interpretation of the "sons of God" in Genesis 6 are:

1. High-ranking noble men of the time
2. Divine beings—angels
3. The sons of Seth (from the line of Cain, the first murderer)

Ellicott's Commentary for English Readers offers a concise understanding of these three choices:

> Of the sons of the Elohim there are three principal interpretations: the first, that of the Targum and the chief Jewish expositors, that they were the nobles, and men of high rank;…
>
> …the second, that they were angels. Jude 1:6, and 2 Peter 2:4, **seem to favor this interpretation,** possibly as being the translation of the LXX [the Septuagint]. According to several MSS [manuscripts].
>
> The third, and **most generally accepted interpretation in modern times,** is that the sons of the Elohim were the Sethites, and that when they married for mere lust of beauty, universal corruption soon ensued. But **no modern commentator has shown how such marriages** could produce "mighty men…men of renown;" or how strong warriors could be the result of the intermarriage of pious men with women of an inferior race, such as the Cainites are assumed to have been. [168] (emphasis added)

Do you now understand the struggle numerous commentators have with this verse? First, to say that the "sons of God" are mere humans who were nobles among the people completely misses the point of the whole narrative. For goodness' sake, God destroyed the life of every living thing on the planet because of this union and their abnormal offspring! Whether it's high-ranking noblemen or the Sethites, how could mere human men, of any type or tribe, have produced a race of giant warrior-tyrants who were terrorizing the earth to the point God called *time out* on the whole creation? How could this have happened simply because they married beautiful women? That line of reasoning defies all logic.

Therein lies the rub, because now there is only one other logical choice for consideration, and it just happens to line up with every other time the Hebrew phrase *bene elohim* is used. It is choice number two in our list: *divine beings/angels.*

Notice also that the preceding *Ellicott's* commentary references two New Testament passages as contextual proof texts for rendering Genesis 6:4 as angels or divine beings (Jude 1:6; 2 Peter 2:4). Do you see why a number of commentators simply skip Genesis 6:4 without a single word of explanation? Few are prepared to call Jude and Peter wrong in their interpretation of what happened before the Flood of Noah. To call them incorrect comes very close to saying Peter and Jude did not write under the inspiration of the Holy Spirit. But to admit their Holy Spirit inspiration pretty much concedes the notion that divine beings somehow produced offspring with human women.

PRODUCED OFFSPRING?

Before the Flood we know very little about how life was lived between the upper family of the divine realm and the lower family of the earthly realm. In the beginning, the two obviously had contact with each other, even in the Garden. This seems to be one of the first purposes for the Garden's existence.

The Bible does not say anything about the sexual ability, knowledge, or technical mechanics of those matters as they might be applied to divine beings. We know divine beings can appear in the form of humans.

Although the Old Testament term "sons of God" refers to divine beings, that does not, in and of itself, prove all angels are male. The sexually generic terms "sons of God" (New Testament use), "sons of light," or "brethren" are also used to refer to both men and women throughout the Scriptures (Psalm 8:4; Luke 16:8; John 1:12, 12:36; 1 Thessalonians 5:1–5).

Consider the following illustration: If a deer lived its entire life deep within the forest and never saw a human, it would have to assume humans did not exist. But if that deer did one day see a human, it would probably see a hunter. That hunter would most likely be a male, and would probably be holding a high-powered rifle. At this point, the deer might finally *believe* in humans, but would mistakenly assume all humans were males with rifles, wearing camouflage and hunter's orange. That deer's assessment of humanity would be deeply flawed and incredibly limited, but that conclusion would be based on the only information the animal possessed.

Let's face it, there is much about the unseen realm we simply do not know (1 Corinthians 2:9). We would be foolish to presume otherwise, and then make categorical statements about what the beings of the divine realm can and cannot do apart from the clear declarations of God's Word to the contrary. We would be as foolish as a deer seeing its first and only man declaring it now understood everything about the entire realm of humankind.

However, we *do* know divine beings have the ability to choose, and they can sin and fall from grace. We also know they are capable of despicable evil deserving imprisonment and the ultimate sentence of eternal death. We have also seen that Jude and Peter connect the vivid possibility of sexual sin with a certain company of *angels* who are already in prison awaiting eternal judgment.

The text in Genesis 6 says the sons of God "produced" or "brought forth" children by the daughters of men. Remember, if these were truly fallen divine council members, they possessed divine knowledge. Abusing that knowledge, however they might have accomplished that feat, would certainly appear to be a logical reason for God to destroy everything in the Flood.

By now you might be asking, "Are there reliable and scholarly sources that venture within the realm of Genesis 6:2 as divine beings?"

Good question! Turn the page.

26

CHAINS OF DARKNESS

For if God did not spare angels when they sinned, but sent them to hell,
putting them in chains of darkness to be held for judgment.

— 2 PETER 2:4

HAVE YOU EVER given much attention to the biblical account concerning the conception of Jesus?

Think about it: An angel came to Mary and declared that she would soon find herself pregnant, even though she was a virgin and would remain so until after she delivered the child. She is also told that this miraculous feat would be accomplished by the Holy Spirit. We accept the account at face value, as we should, and we rejoice in the matter with songs, celebrations, and special services of worship and Christmas traditions, as we ought to do. The bottom line is that the impregnation of Mary was a supernatural occurrence that was initiated from the divine realm—in this case, decreed from the throne of God.

Please understand, I am not in any way proposing that an angel, or the Holy Spirit, had intimate physical relations with Mary—and neither does the Bible even come close to suggesting such a thing. However, through the immaculate conception account, we are explicitly introduced to the fact that a human woman can be *made* to conceive a child through a divine function of the heavenly realm. This fact is central to our understanding of the Christmas message, as well as the fulfillment of messianic prophecy; it is also the focal point of how Jesus could be both deity and human at the same time.

Why is it that we have no problem with the biblical truth of the divine incarnation, but at the same time many Bible scholars cannot bring themselves to deal with Genesis 6:4 for what it unambiguously states? Granted, the two accounts have important elements of variation; however, the result is the same: Human women were impregnated through an unknown (to us) function of the divine realm. One occasion was unquestionably holy and directed by Yahweh's decree; the other occurrences were perverse, and that perversion ultimately resulted in Yahweh destroying nearly every living thing on the planet through a worldwide Flood.

In the interest of academic integrity, I must admit that for much of my early preaching and teaching years, I avoided the Genesis 6 narrative as much as possible. When I did address the subject, I did so from the point of view represented by a couple of "conservative" commentaries that I had examined. Those entries completely rejected the notion of the sons of God as being divine beings. So, that was good enough for me. And it felt comfortable—for a while.

But, the more I compared Scripture to Scripture and conducted a number of in-depth word studies in the Hebrew language, the more I became increasingly uncomfortable with the position I had previously accepted. There was *something* more here—much more.

So what really happened when "the sons of God came unto the daughters of men"? This question may be one of the most important ones we can ask, because the truth of what happened here determines how we are to interpret practically every spiritual revelation that follows. Let's dig in and see what we can discover.

THE SCHOLARS SPEAK

The *Cambridge Bible for Schools and Colleges* says this about Genesis 6:

> This is one of the most disputed passages in the book [of Genesis]. But the difficulty, in a great measure, disappears, if it is frankly recognized, that the verse must be allowed to have its literal meaning.... Intermarriages took place between Heavenly Beings and mortal women.[169]

The *Jamieson, Fausset, and Brown Commentary*, while not ultimately taking the view that "sons of God" refer to divine beings (they prefer the Sethite view), admits:

> The term Nephilim...is commonly traced to [Hebrew] *naapal*, to fall, and considered to signify either fallen ones, apostates, or falling upon others. *In the first sense many of the fathers applied it to designate fallen angels.* (emphasis added)[170]

Keil and Delitzsch also present the following interesting piece of historical information about Genesis 6:

> The words of Jude agree so thoroughly with the tradition of the book of Enoch respecting the fall of the angels, that we must admit the allusion to the Enoch legend, and so indirectly to Genesis 6, since Jude could not have expressed himself more clearly to persons who possessed the book of Enoch, or were acquainted with the tradition it contained.[171, 172]

While the book of Enoch (Noah's great-grandson) is non-canonical, it is an influential ancient Jewish work, with parts of it dating to around 300 BC. Eleven fragments of the book were found among the Dead Sea Scrolls, proving its impact upon at least some within the earliest Jewish community. A particular passage in the book of Enoch is very similar to the reference in Jude 1:6–7.[173]

Enoch is mentioned by name in the New Testament in three different places (Luke 3:37; Hebrews 11:5; Jude 1:14). It is also alleged that there are a number of allusions (paraphrased quotes, etc.) to the book of Enoch throughout the New Testament as well. The identification of those particular passages as having Enochian influence is disputed, and hold varying degrees of interpretation among Bible students.

However, the greater point of *Keil and Delitzsch* in their Genesis 6 commentary entry is the affirmation that a good portion of early Jewish thought concerning the matter was that the sons of God were fallen *elohim*. This understanding apparently came from biblical, as well as non-biblical, sources, and was prevalent among early orthodox Jews as well as the early church.

There is yet another revealing *Keil and Delitzsch* attestation:

[That sons of God mean divine beings] *may be defended on* two plausible grounds: first, the fact that the "sons of God," in Job 1:6; Job 2:1, and Job 38:7, and in Daniel 3:25, are unquestionably angels (also בְּנֵי אֵלִים in Psalm 29:1 and Psalm 89:7); and secondly, the antithesis, "sons of God" and "daughters of men." … *these two points would lead us most naturally to regard the "sons of God" as angels, in distinction from men and the daughters of men.* But this explanation, though the first to suggest itself, can only lay claim to be received as the correct one, *provided the language itself admits of no other.* (emphasis added)[174]

The argument of *Keil and Delitzsch* is that if no other biblical example of *bene elohim* exists where they are not clearly represented as angels, then Genesis 6 must naturally be translated as angels, or divine beings. Then *Keil and Delitzsch* gives four examples wherein they claim that other texts do, in fact, use *bene elohim* as humans (Psalm 73:15, 80:17; Deuteronomy 32:5; Hosea 1:10).

There's only one problem: Those passages do not have the specific phrase *bene elohim* in the original Hebrew texts—not a single one. The word *bene* is there, which can also be translated as "children," but not the unique phrase *bene elohim* as found in Job and Genesis.[175]

Thus, according to their own admission, the most *natural* and contextual interpretation is that the sons of God in Genesis 6 are divine beings. This fact is borne out by the struggle so many commentators face in their attempt to make Genesis 6 into mere humans, rather than what *bene elohim* means every other time that phrase is used in the Old Testament.

The *Guzik Bible Commentary* puts Genesis 6 in this light:

The sons of God saw the daughters of men: It is more accurate to see the sons of God as either demons (angels in rebellion against God) or uniquely demon-possessed men, and the daughters of men as human women.... The phrase "sons of God" clearly refers to angelic creatures when it is used the three other times in the Old Testament (Job 1:6, 2:1, and 38:7). The translators of the Septuagint translated sons of God as "angels." They clearly thought it referred to angelic beings, not people descended from Seth.[176]

Dr. C. Fred Dickason, in his book titled *Names of Angels*, also comments upon the *bene elohim* of Genesis 6. He soundly disputes the use of the term in the sense of mere mortals:

Bene elohim is a technical term for angels and is probably the sense in which "the sons of God" in Gen 6 is used—Bene elohim—refers to angels as a class of mighty ones or powers. It is used of angels in Job 1:6; 2:1; 38:7. Some say that this term is also used of God's own people; *but close inspection of the passages usually listed (Deut. 14:1; Hos 1:10; 11:1) will show that the exact term is not bene elohim.* (emphasis added)[177]

Additionally, the doctrinally conservative *GotQuestions.org* has this to say about the Nephilim and the Genesis 6 account:

> The Bible calls Noah "blameless in his generation" (Genesis 6:9). This could be a reference to Noah's character, but it also could be that Noah was "blameless" in the sense that his bloodline had not been polluted by the fallen angels, so God saved him and his family to be the beginning of a new, genetically clean human race.
>
> However, the Bible mentions the Anakim and the Rephaim after the flood, so either the "giant" bloodline remained, or it is also possible that the fallen angels made a second attempt to pollute mankind after the flood. Whatever the case, there is the biblical evidence, plus written accounts outside of the Bible, that giants did exist.[178]

In a related article, *GotQuestions.org* offers the following commentary on the matter as it deals with the topic of demonic interaction with humanity:

> Another notable instance of [demonic] interaction with us is found in Genesis 6:4 with the arrival of the "sons of God." The Genesis account states that these powerful beings had sexual intercourse with women and produced a super race of beings known as the Nephilim. This sounds like the stuff of science fiction, yet it is right there in the Bible.[179]

There is also this affirmation from biblical language professor and renowned Bible scholar, Dr. Michael Heiser:

> It might seem unnecessary to mention this, given the enthusiasm many Bible readers have today for tapping into the Jewish mind to understand the words of Jesus and the apostles. When

it comes to Genesis 6:1-4, though, that enthusiasm often sours, since the result doesn't support the most comfortable modern Christian interpretation. The truth is that the writers of the New Testament know nothing of the Sethite view, nor of any view that makes the sons of God in Genesis 6:1–4 humans.[180]

Dr. Heiser's comprehensive conclusion is that the sons of God in Genesis 6 are divine beings.[181]

APPLICATION

The crux of the matter is this: It seems the most grammatically correct and contextually plausible translation of Genesis 6 is to render "sons of God" the same way it is rendered everywhere else in the Old Testament, as angels or fallen *elohim*. To not do so is to go down a path of forced sanitization that can become absolutely humorous at times.

As an example, I came upon more than one academic commentary where, when speaking of Genesis 6:2, the practical application lesson was stated as something along the lines of, "This passage is God's way of warning us to 'be careful who you marry.'"[182]

Be careful who you marry? That's a good piece of advice, to be sure—except this passage is not about instructions to young brides concerning marital bliss, nor is it about marrying someone who doesn't have the same faith as yours. Rather, it is an explanation of why the Lord devastatingly destroyed every living thing on the face of the earth. Something atrocious and unredeemable happened—*that* is the point of this particular biblical text. See what happens when we are bound and determined to not let the Bible simply say what it clearly intends to say? Why be afraid of what God's Word plainly says? Why try to sterilize the biblical text?

Which leads right into the next, and often misunderstood, declaration of Jesus...

27

LIKE THE ANGELS IN HEAVEN

At the resurrection people will neither marry nor be given in marriage.
—MATTHEW 22:30

AT THIS POINT one might ask, "If the sons of God really were some sort of divine being/fallen *elohim*, how can that be? I thought Jesus said angels don't marry, therefore they can't have sex either."

A number of the scholars will make this argument as their rock-solid proof that Genesis 6 simply cannot be referring to angelic beings. The dispute comes from Jesus' pointed statement in Matthew 22:30 (also Mark 12:25; Luke 20:35–36): "At the resurrection people will neither marry nor be given in marriage; they will be like the angels in heaven."

First, Jesus says absolutely nothing about angels being sexless. He speaks only of the human institution of marriage, which indeed appears to be of no concern in the divine realm.

Second, regarding marriage between angels, Jesus was referring to angels who were *in heaven*. These are the obedient angels living in divine bliss. Jesus was not referring to the fallen angels who apparently *came to earth* in lustful temptation and played house with the daughters of men in pre-Flood days, as the Genesis 6 narrative recounts. So the "Jesus said angels don't have sex" argument simply does not stand up to biblical scrutiny—despite arguments to the contrary.[183]

WHAT WAS THE DEBATE?

The passage, Matthew 22:23–31, begins with the Sadducees asking a hypothetical question concerning a doctrine to which they did not give credence in the first place—*the resurrection of the dead*. The question was designed as a trap against Jesus. While it is true the Sadducees presented children as a part of their hypothetical scenario, the context of their entire test is the question of, "How will we know who our *wife* will be in heaven, if we have been married multiple times?"

There was not a single question asked by the Sadducees about sexual relationships or the process of producing children. It might be argued that the Sadducees assumed these things; however, the Sadducees assumed there was no resurrection of the dead as well.

Since the Sadducees asked no direct question about sex and child-bearing, Jesus simply did not address what they did not ask. Despite arguments otherwise, there is no clear denial on Jesus' part about angels possessing the ability, or inability, to engage in sexual relations—especially divine beings of the pre-Flood era who made earth their habitation.

He did, however, directly address what the Sadducees actually asked. To that question, He responded that there was no human-like institution of marriage in heaven. Jesus told the Sadducees they were mistaken in their foundational question. Jesus, in effect, told them that life in Heaven was not a mere stepped-up reflection of earthly life; it is something much more glorious.

The truth is that we have no idea what was happening in the pre-

Flood world regarding the possibility of sexual relations among angelic beings and human women, other than what we learn from Jude and Peter. But, in the Hebrew grammar context of Genesis 6, there really is not much choice. We must therefore deal with the text as it stands without trying to force a refinement upon its interpretation.

The *Expositor's Greek New Testament* affirms what I have argued here, as it applies to Jesus' declaration about angels, marriage, and sex with this succinct statement: "[We will be] as angels, so far as marriage is concerned, not necessarily implying sexlessness."[184]

TIED TO THE GARDEN OF EDEN?

By now you have probably made the connection. How is it that even among the plethora of Bible scholars who clearly see the potentially sexual connotations of the Genesis 6 account (involving divine beings), many of them can't quite bring themselves to consider the possibility that the entire despicable situation probably originated in the Garden of Eden, at least to some degree? After all, is Satan not the prince of the fallen sons of God? (See Matthew 25:41; Luke 11:15.) These are tough matters to consider, to be sure. You can see why these topics have been so hotly debated across the ages, and why they are often so ardently avoided in many pulpits to this day.

NEW TESTAMENT ATTESTATIONS?

In a number of commentary entries dealing with Genesis 6, the New Testament books of Jude 1:6-7 and 2 Peter 2:4 are consistently referenced as having potential connections. This is especially true of those commentaries holding to the understanding that the *sons of God* of Noah's Flood are, in fact, fallen *elohim*.

Observe the words of Jude 1:6–7, as rendered in the NIV:

And the angels who did not keep their positions of authority but abandoned their own home—these he has kept in darkness, bound with everlasting chains for judgment on the great Day. In a similar way, Sodom and Gomorrah and the surrounding towns gave themselves up to sexual immorality and perversion. They serve as an example of those who suffer the punishment of eternal fire. (emphasis added)

Jude makes a straightforward case: Sometime in eons past, angels left the divine realm, obviously as an act of rebellion, and came to the earthly realm. Their sin is directly compared to that of the sexual perversion of Sodom and Gomorrah. Those particular angels are now in prison awaiting their ultimate destruction on the Day of Judgment.

Now, let's look at 2 Peter 2:4–6 and verses 9–10 as translated in the NIV:

[4] *For if God did not spare angels when they sinned,* but sent them to hell, putting them in chains of darkness to be held for judgment;
[5] if he did not spare the ancient world when he brought the flood on its ungodly people, but protected Noah, a preacher of righteousness, and seven others;
[6] *if he condemned the cities of Sodom and Gomorrah* by burning them to ashes, and made them an example of what is going to happen to the ungodly…
[9] if this is so, then the Lord knows how to rescue the godly from trials and to hold the unrighteous for punishment on the day of judgment.
[10] This is especially true of those who follow the corrupt desire of the flesh and despise authority. (emphasis added)

There it is again: We find angels in prison awaiting a judgment of eternal destruction, seemingly connected to a sexually perverted act they committed. Their deeds also appear to be directly linked to the days of

Noah as well as the sins of Sodom and Gomorrah.

While we are in the New Testament, we certainly cannot ignore the words of Jesus Hmself regarding the matter of our current study. Read Luke 17:26 and see what you think: "*Just as it was* in the days of Noah, so also will it be in the days of the Son of Man" (emphasis added).

The question is, "How *was it*, in the days of Noah?" It appears that Jesus was trying to warn us, "Something evil is on its way."

Which directs us to the next chapter.

28

SOMETHING WICKED

By the pricking of my thumbs, something wicked this way comes. Open, locks, whoever knocks.

—WILLIAM SHAKESPEARE, MACBETH

You're all set—your bags were packed long ago; there's a dozen solid gold coins stashed inside your belt and a pistol strapped round your waist. There's no need to say goodbye to the wife and children as they're already waiting for you 6,000 miles away in New Zealand, having slipped off quietly at the first whiff of global catastrophe.[185]

THOSE WORDS ARE from the opening paragraph in a 2017 story appearing in an international mainstream publication. The title of that particular article made a sensational statement and asked a startling question: "The Apocalypse island: Tech billionaires are building boltholes in New Zealand because they now fear social collapse or nuclear war. So what do they know that we don't?"

The last several years have seen a number of similar articles highlighting the global angst among the elite and wealthy. What exactly do the elite fear so much? The following two paragraphs were embedded about one-third into the "Apocalypse Island" news piece:

> What the catastrophe will precisely be remains unclear, but possibilities include a devastating asteroid impact, giant earthquake, nuclear war, civil war, pandemic, zombie invasion and *the Second Coming*.
>
> Tellingly, the geeks of Silicon Valley appear *to be most worried* that it will be a struggle between rich and poor in a *world economy turned upside down by new technology*—with them as the main targets. (emphasis added)

It seems the primary concern of the world's influential wealthy is that they sense something is about to snap. When reading the words of that article, how can a student of prophecy not think of the woeful warning of Revelation 6? That passage speaks of the time just before God's wrath is poured out upon the earth, in the very last days before the coming of the Lord. Notice the eerie similarity to the text of the "Apocalypse Island" article:

> Then the kings of the earth, the princes, the generals, the rich, the mighty, and everyone else, both slave and free, hid in caves and among the rocks of the mountains. They called to the mountains and the rocks, "Fall on us and hide us from the face of him who sits on the throne and from the wrath of the Lamb! For the great day of their wrath has come, and who can withstand it?" (Revelation 6:15–17)

I am not making a statement of eschatology and Rapture timing with this illustration. I am simply stating the obvious. The attitudes and fears of the last days, stated in Revelation 6, are beginning to play out in mainstream news articles of today.

The "Apocalypse Island" piece lamented the fact that the ones who are planning on running to the mountains are the same ones primarily responsible for creating the world's newest technologies. Ironically, these are the same technologies that even some industry leaders are beginning to fear.

At about the same time the "Apocalypse Island" article was featured, yet another prominent Internet news site touted this headline, "'Pandora's Box': Tech fueling urge to be 'gods on Earth.'"[186]

That piece stressed today's atmosphere of wanton technological expansion as well. It stressed the point-of-no-return feature, of which even some who are actually inventing the science-fiction-like technologies are currently speaking. The article sums up the situation as follows:

> For the first time in history, advances in technology are challenging the very meaning of what it is to be human. Human-animal hybrids. Relationships, emotional and sexual, with artificial intelligence. Even the promise to abolish death itself.
>
> In late 2016, U.S. astronaut Leroy Chiao, who spent a total of 230 days on board the International Space Station across four missions and conducted six space walks, said, "Indeed, there are strong arguments that after enabling life to thrive, technology is now hastening our collective demise.... Unlike many people, including several of my astronaut colleagues, I don't think that technology will save us."[187]

In March 2017, *Vanity Fair* ran an article featuring Elon Musk concerning his fears about the phenomenon of burgeoning technology. The multibillionaire entrepreneur, inventor, and CEO of SpaceX and Tesla, said that even with good intentions, we might "produce something evil by accident." The article headlined with these words:

Elon Musk is famous for his futuristic gambles, but Silicon Valley's latest rush to embrace artificial intelligence scares him. And he thinks you should be frightened too. [This article helps to understand] his efforts to influence the rapidly advancing field and its proponents, and to save humanity from machine-learning overlords.[188]

Even globally renowned physicist Stephen Hawking chimed in on the inherent dangers of burgeoning technologies—especially in the field of robotics, transhumanism, and artificial intelligence capabilities:

The real risk with AI isn't malice but competence.... You're probably not an evil ant-hater who steps on ants out of malice, but if you're in charge of a hydroelectric green energy project and there's an anthill in the region to be flooded, too bad for the ants. Let's not place humanity in the position of those ants.[189]

Human/animal hybrids and the latest developments in gene-splicing are of particular concern, not only to prophecy experts but also among secular scientists. Observe the following from an early 2017 report posted by *Natural News*:

Scientists say that the more human-like the animal is, the better suited it is for testing purposes—and for growing "spare parts."

The latest research from Salk Institute suggests that science is one step closer to reaching its goal, no matter how disturbing some people find it to be.

Some would argue that even creating and implanting chimeric embryos [human/animal hybrids] into non-consenting living animals is ethically concerning too.

The researchers say that one of the big concerns about chimera creation is the potential for the hybrid animal to become too human. As Science Daily reports, "For instance, researchers don't want human cells to contribute to the formation of the brain."[190]

Animal/human hybrids becoming *too human*? Animals potentially developing human brains? Growing human body parts for later harvesting? Artificial intelligence that might crush us like ants? Inventing something evil by accident? This is beginning to sound strangely like a *corruption-of-all-flesh* scenario. It's as if everything has been kicked into high gear, diving headlong into an abyss from which there will be no return. And it is largely today's intelligentsia who are the most outspoken about the impending dangers.

Consider this small sampling of mainstream media messages recently making their appearances through the headlines. See if you spot the common themes tied to what we have learned about Satan's very first deceptions:

- Scientists take a step closer to eternal life as they preserve and revive brain.[191]
- Can uploading our "minds" to computers be our key to eternal life?[192]
- Men could have babies without women, using skin cell cloning. "It could allow gay men to have babies with each other."[193]
- Part human, part pig embryos have been created by scientists. We can grow our own body parts![194]
- Now available! Artificially intelligent sex robots with programmable personalities and fully functioning "genitalia."[195]
- Sex in Virtual Reality Is Getting Even More Immersive in 2017. "It brings us one step closer to feeling the person on the other end without actually being in the same physical space."[196]
- "Sex robot theme parks 'better than Disney World" to offer raunchy getaways: Grab orgies on tap.[197]
- Virtual reality "sex suit" allows men to experience realistic intercourse.[198]

- The human universe: Could we actually become gods?[199]
- Through the singularity humans can very soon become "god-like."[200]
- Technology will turn us into super-humans sometime in the next 12 years.[201]

This short list barely scratches the surface of the weird-but-true technology that is now a part of our world's new paradigm. The disturbing thing is that a large portion of the world's population apparently does not seem to think there is anything prophetic or weird about any of this. We are extremely close to being biblically dumbed-down enough for Nachash to once again beguile humanity (Matthew 24:24;2 Thessalonians 2:11–17; Revelation 13)—in person.

Notice also, how so many of today's wonders are aimed at:

1. Unregenerate humanity's dreams of eternal life
2. Becoming as gods or super-humans
3. Free-flowing sexual perversion

All three of the potential elements of the rebellious Garden sin are now the headlines of today's media reporting. It is as if we are hearing the antediluvian lie of the serpent once again, "Just eat of this fruit. Not only will you not die, but you can truly be like the gods!" But this time, Satan doesn't have to merely whisper his lie in the ear of one couple; now he has the ear of the whole world—at one time.

Such is the nature of our day.

29

JUST LIKE THIS

The LORD saw how great the wickedness of the human race had become on the earth, and that every inclination of the thoughts of the human heart was only evil all the time.

—GENESIS 6:5

WHAT DID JESUS mean when He said the last days would be just like the days of Noah and the days of Lot? (Luke 17:28ff). To begin with, both of those periods involved unthinkable wickedness.

They were also marked by supernatural visitations from the angelic/demonic realm. With Noah's day, it was the sons of God, the Nephilim, and the continual growth of wanton evil. In Lot's day, it was unbridled sexual sin marked by rampant homosexuality, the angelic visitations to Abraham, and then finally their divinely tasked appearance in Sodom and Gomorrah. Even in Sodom, the wicked men of the city, of all things, desired to have sex with the angelic visitors (Genesis 19:5). Both of these periods of historically epic days had at least one painfully obvious common thread: perverted sexuality ruled the day. Gee, I wonder why that might be.

A number of prophecy scholars speculate that through those ominous words of Jesus, it could be that we are being warned of, at the very least, an outpouring of foreign visitations. Think about it: What has been one of the predominate fascinations of our own day? What is it to which the movie industry, media reporting, secular science, and a plethora of popular global websites are so often dedicated? The answer is that they are infatuated with visitations of all sorts.

Whether it's UFOs, alien beings, ghosts, demons, angels, roving spirits, witchcraft conjuring, satanic ritual summonsing, zombie infatuation, vampirism, or contacting entities from the realm of the dead, today's world is absolutely enraptured with thoughts of interaction with the darker supernatural realm and/or alien life forms.

Many in the biblical world of prophetic study believe Satan is getting ready to oblige those who are seeking to connect with the inner chambers of his dark domain. The fruit in the Garden once again appears ripe for the plucking.

OUTPOURING OF EVIL

The Bible tells us there will be "principalities and powers" in the end-time generations that will be instrumental in assisting humanity in achieving what they so desire. We are warned of an unprecedented demonic outpouring accompanied by a great perversion of the Word of God (1 Timothy 4:1). We are informed the outpouring will come upon the world rapidly, catching billions of people completely by surprise (Daniel 9:26; Matthew 24:22; 1 Thessalonians 5:2, 13; Revelation 16:15).

We are also warned of a massive delusion that will sweep the planet in the last-days generations (Matthew 24:24; Daniel 8:12; 2 Thessalonians 2:11). The Bible speaks of a time of unprecedented lawlessness and rebellion in those days (Daniel 8:12; 2 Thessalonians 2).

Jesus told us that those dreadful days will be worse than anything the earth has ever before seen (Mark 13:19; Mathew. 24:21). Corresponding Old Testament prophecies confirm this fact (Daniel 12:1).

We are also assured that in the very last days Satan will be enraged, and he and his host of fallen *elohim* will pour out their unmitigated fury upon the earth (Revelation 12). We are warned of demonic spirits that will lead the nations of the world astray (Revelation 12:9, 16:13, 20:8). We are also advised this demonic outpouring will ultimately culminate in a world ruler who will demand to be worshipped. He will command his subjects to be marked in obedience to his image *that lives* (Revelation 13–14).

According to the Word of God, those days are guaranteed to arrive upon a particular generation. Many believe we may be in the edges of that period even now. Look at a few examples of recent mainstream headline-grabbers:

- Exorcism Thriving in U.S., Say Experts (ABC News)[202]
- As a psychiatrist, I diagnose mental illness. Also, I help spot demonic possession. (*Washington Post*)[203]
- Exorcism expert warns, Global demonic possessions are reaching "emergency levels" (Express UK)[204]
- "Witchcraft" child abuse cases on the rise (BBC)[205]
- Witches of the world will cast a mass spell on President Trump (*NY Daily News*)[206]
- FBI: "Epidemic" levels of pedophilia, child sex trafficking (*Washington Examiner*)[207]
- STD rates reach record high in United States (CNN)[208]
- America May Be Heading into an STD Epidemic—Gay and Bi Men Are Going to Be the Hardest Hit (Slate.com)[209]
- UNAIDS report on the Global Aids Epidemic (World Health Organization)[210]
- Close to Half of American Adults Infected with HPV (*New York Times*)[211]

As end-times technologies burst forth, coupled with a consistent descent into a never-ending moral abyss, numerous prophecy observers are posing an important question: Will there once again be a demonically engineered hybridization effort—maybe something similar to the days of Noah?

Might it be that we will see some sort of return of the Nephilim? Could that be a hint of what we are witnessing concerning the early stages of our rapidly advancing technology? Could this debauched knowledge of good and evil be somehow demonically delivered—specifically to our generation, the first generation since the Garden and the Flood to possess anything like it? It's only a question, only a theory, but it has its basis in biblical roots. Many sincere scholars are asking the same questions.

God-Like?

In early 2017, ITechPost.com published this shocking headline: "Resurrecting Dead People Using Stem Cells Given the Green Light." To many prophecy watchers, it appeared as though rebellious humanity, under Satan's influence, was in a race to outsmart Yahweh.

The first two lines of the ITechPost story read:

Scientists are getting ethical permission from health watchdogs to resurrect dead people by using a combination of regeneration therapies. Starting this year, the groundbreaking Project Reanima will primarily use stem cells to stimulate the regrowth of neurons in clinically dead patients.[212]

As the year 2017 moved forward, those kinds of stories increasingly appeared in international technology headlines. There seemed to be a lustful expectation that becoming like god was tantalizingly within the literal reach of humanity—even the prospect of living forever.

By the last day of May 2017, NBC News ran a piece on their online site *Mach*. The article was titled, "Godlike 'Homo Deus' Could Replace Humans as Tech Evolves." The commentary touted the possibility of soon achieving unequalled—and, perhaps, divine—capacities. I have reproduced a few selected excerpts from the article that serve to illustrate its general *Nachash-like* message:

> Historian Yuval Noah Harari explores these questions in his runaway bestseller, "Homo Deus: A Brief History of Tomorrow," ...The title of his new book suggests a startling stage in our evolution: Homo sapiens ("wise man"), far from being the pinnacle of creation, is a temporary creature, one soon to be replaced by Homo deus ("god man").
>
> Churches, Harari suggested, may fade into history along with the very idea of religion. As he points out, the things that God does in Genesis—creating plants, animals, and people—may soon be things that humans can do. We'll see these new gods every time we look in the mirror.
>
> In the future, "techno-religions" may conquer the world, he said, not by promising salvation in the next world, but by radically changing our lives in this world.
>
> ..."until our descendants will look back and realize they are no longer the kind of animal that wrote the Bible.: (emphasis added)[213]

Did you ever think you would live to see such Garden of Eden-like haughtiness as the official tech-talk of the day—and in mainstream international media headlines?

From where is all this new knowledge flowing? From whence are the potential secrets of eternal life and superhuman, god-like powers springing forth? From where does the lust for such previously unimaginable things originate?

And why *now*?

By this point in our study, you probably have a good idea...

30

CONTACT

There's not much question that we're not alone in the universe. If we look hard enough we'll find it...it's just a question of when.
—JOHN REYNOLDS, PROGRAM DIRECTOR, CSIRO[214]

A GOOD NUMBER of biblical experts set forth the very real possibility that fallen *elohim* alien life forms might soon be making a public appearance, under the guise of being genuine visitors from other planets. Our culture so greatly desires to experience the phenomenon of an alien visitation; it seems Satan would surely grant it, if the ruse would help to pull off his final, grand delusion. Could something like this be a part of the demonic outpouring and delusion of the last days? Could the world be in the throes of a demonic "setup?"

GOING MAINSTREAM

To witness the world's fascination with the topic, simply browse through the popular program listings. The History Channel's acclaimed series,

*Ancient Ali*ens, feeds modern culture's fascination with the secularized questions: From where did our knowledge for modern technology come? And why did this boom in sci-fi-like technology only occur in the last several decades, given that man has been here for *millions of years*? Thus the theory of ancient astronauts was born. The concept is concisely stated in the following quote from *The Huffington Post*:

> The ancient astronaut theory posits that our ancestors experi-enced these huge leaps forward in advancement of scientific, astronomical, technological and medical knowledge that could simply not have happened on their own. We must have had some help from above, from entities far more intelligent and evolved than we.[215]

In 2006, the *BBC* ran a provocative story on the topic of alien tech-nology transference. The article revolved around the trial of a British man named Gary McKinnon, who was arrested by the UK's national high-tech crime unit in 2002. He was accused of hacking into NASA and US military computer networks at the Pentagon. Following is a sampling of the *BBC* interview with McKinnon:

> ***Spencer Kelly:*** Here's your list of charges: you hacked into the Army, the Navy, the Air Force, the Department of Defense, and NASA, amongst other things. Why?
> ***Gary McKinnon:*** I was in search of suppressed technology, laughingly referred to as UFO technology. I think it's the biggest kept secret in the world because of its comic value, but it's a very important thing.
> ***SK:*** Did you find what you were looking for?
> ***GM:*** Yes.
> ***SK:*** Tell us about it.
> ***GM:*** There was a group called the Disclosure Project. They published a book which had 400 expert witnesses ranging from

civilian air traffic controllers, through military radar operators, right up to the chaps who were responsible for whether or not to launch nuclear missiles.

They are some very credible, relied upon people, all saying yes, there is UFO technology, there's anti-gravity, there's free energy, and it's extra-terrestrial in origin, and we've captured spacecraft and reverse-engineered it.[216]

Even the *New York Times* got in on the act of examining possibilities of outside forces influencing our life through technological advancements seemingly far beyond our realm of knowledge. In an opinion piece titled "Can Evolution Have a Higher Purpose?" author Robert Wright penned:

You may scoff, but in 2003 the philosopher Nick Bostrom of Oxford University published a paper laying out reasons to think that we are pretty likely to be living in a simulation. And the simulation hypothesis has gained influential supporters. Neil deGrasse Tyson, director of the Hayden Planetarium and America's de facto astronomer laureate, finds it plausible. The visionary tech entrepreneur Elon Musk says there's almost no chance that we're living in "base reality." *The New Yorker* reported earlier this year that "two tech billionaires"—it didn't say whether Musk is one of them—"have gone so far as to secretly engage scientists to work on breaking us out of the simulation."[217]

Please understand where I am going with this. I do not believe in literal little green men from other planets, interplanetary humanoid time travelers, or space astronauts in the way secularists believe these things. Neither do I believe we are trapped in a giant supercomputer simulation being operated by a jokester alien genius. But, I do think it is highly plausible, from a biblical point of view, that the realm of fallen *elohim* could certainly present themselves in the fashion of an alien visitor. And

I also think it is at least a possibility that Satan may attempt to pull off a ploy staging an alien visitation of some sort as part of his last-days delusion, a grand deception allowing himself to be set up as "God" on earth (2 Thessalonians 2).

Regardless of the various theories on this subject, there can be no doubt about this one fact, the mainstream of the world population is absolutely fascinated with the idea of aliens potentially interacting with human affairs. Even presidents and presidential candidates are aware of the phenomenon. How could Satan resist the temptation to capitalize upon this human fascination?

IN PRESIDENTIAL POLITICS

During the 2016 U.S. presidential campaign, the *New York Times* reported that candidate Hillary Clinton vowed, if elected president, she would "open up the government files" on extraterrestrial beings and UFOs. "I think we may have been" visited already, she said in the interview. "We don't know for sure." Clinton's campaign chairman, John Podesta, was described in that same article as, "a crusader for the disclosure of government information on unexplained phenomena that could prove the existence of intelligent life outside Earth."[218]

The same *New York Times* article that reported on Hillary Clinton's and John Podesta's fascination with aliens and necromancy concluded with these words: "It shouldn't be a source of embarrassment to discuss [these matters]," said Christopher Mellon, a former intelligence official at the Defense Department and the Senate Intelligence Committee. "We should be humble in terms of recognizing the extreme limits of our own understanding of physics and the universe." I find it interesting that often these same people do not keep that same "humble" attitude when it comes to the things of God or His Word.

In the 2016 run-up to the ultimate election of Donald Trump as U.S. President, Hillary Clinton's campaign manager John Podesta gave these surprising comments to CNN's Jake Tapper: "The U.S. government could do a much better job in answering the quite legitimate questions that people have about what's going on with unidentified aerial phenomena.... The American people can handle the truth."[219]

These Podesta comments appeared to be an official hint that he possessed information about the matter—and that he now trusted that regular citizens could handle the information. Given the Clinton campaign's persistent mentioning of the possible release of government documents concerning UFOs, and Podesta's previous positioning of himself as a crusader for government UFO truth, the subject reached another fevered pitch of public discourse.

In October 2016, MSN.com ran a story that stated: "When Podesta stepped down in 2015 from his post in the Obama administration, he tweeted that his biggest regret about leaving the administration was some unfinished UFO business: 'My biggest failure of 2014: Once again not securing the disclosure of the UFO files.'"[220]

Here's a question for you: What do the Vatican, Hillary Clinton, President Barack Obama, John Podesta, WikiLeaks, a celebrated NASA astronaut, and UFO visitations have in common? In late 2016, MSN.com addressed the links:

> What does the Vatican know about alien life? And is there a threat of a war in space?
>
> These are among the issues that a former astronaut wanted to discuss with John Podesta, a former top adviser to President Barack Obama who is now Hillary Clinton's campaign chairman, according to new emails published Friday by WikiLeaks.
>
> The hacked emails have already drawn a great deal of attention.... But extraterrestrial enthusiasts are particularly interested in two documents that focus on UFOs, an alien presence around Earth and a belief that the Vatican has some knowledge about all of this.[221]

While making a speech to the 42nd United Nations General Assembly, on September 21, 1987, then President Ronald Reagan made a now-famous statement that was apparently intended as an example of mutual cooperation between nations. Regardless of how it was meant, it shocked many of those who heard it: "Perhaps we need some outside universal threat. I occasionally think how quickly our differences, worldwide, would vanish if we were facing an alien threat from outside this world."[222]

It's fairly clear that President Reagan was speaking metaphorically; however, others have seized upon his comments as possessing some sort of hint thereby applying much more serious overtones to his message. It probably does not help matters that President Reagan is famously known for making this same *alien threat* appeal in several public speeches.[223]

Then, in 2015, on a popular late-night talk show, former President Bill Clinton was trying to convince the audience that while he had been in office, he had personally investigated the possibility of the U.S. government having secret information about UFOs and alien visitations. After assuring the audience that he was never able to confirm such evidence, he then said: "I'm trying to tell you that 'I don't know,' but if we were visited someday, I wouldn't be surprised. I just hope that, uh, it's not like Independence Day—the movie…that it's not a conflict. But it may be the only way to unite this increasingly divided world of ours."[224]

Yet again, a world-renowned figure linked the possibility of an alien visitation to the need for global unification. Of course, the mainstream media is always too glad to promote the idea.

How convenient.

31

Mainstream Mind Control

Aliens have been observing us and have been here for some time
—Edgar Mitchell, NASA astronaut [225]

In March 2017, the headlines of *space.com* screamed, "Could Mysterious Cosmic Light Flashes Be Powering Alien Spacecraft?" The article centered on a new study from researchers at the Harvard-Smithsonian Center for Astrophysics, who were postulating that "bizarre flashes of cosmic light may actually be generated by advanced alien civilizations, as a way to accelerate interstellar spacecraft to tremendous speeds." The inference of the article appeared to be: *They're coming!* The new Harvard team study has been accepted for publication in *The Astrophysical Journal Letters.* [226]

In 2015, Fox News reported that Apollo 14 veteran Edgar Mitchell, the sixth person to walk on the moon, claimed his belief that peacekeeping aliens visited our planet to prevent a nuclear war between Russia and the United States:

The idea sounds far-fetched, but Mitchell claims that military insiders viewed strange flying crafts cruising over U.S. missile bases and the White Sands facility in New Mexico, the site of the first-ever nuclear bomb detonation in 1945.

> "They wanted to know about our military capabilities," he said. "My own experience talking to people has made it clear the ETs had been attempting to keep us from going to war and help create peace on Earth."
>
> "They told me UFOs were frequently seen overhead and often disabled their missiles," he added. "Other officers from bases on the Pacific coast told me their (test) missiles were frequently shot down by alien spacecraft."[227]

In 2016 *The Huffington Post* released an article titled "WikiLeaks Documents Reveal United Nations Interest in UFOs," which disclosed that WikiLeaks posted more than half a million U.S. State Department diplomatic documents from 1978 detailing America's interactions with countries all around the world concerning efforts to organize a United Nations-based committee to research and investigate global UFO reports.[228]

In April 2017, a major United Kingdom publication released these headlines to the globe: "Houston, We Have an Admission—Meet the NASA astronauts who believe aliens are visiting Earth and communicating with humanity." That astonishing piece listed several American astronauts who have made definitive statements regarding their beliefs that aliens have visited and/or are continuing to visit earth. Following is a sampling of some of their reported remarks:

> **Edgar Mitchell:** "Aliens have been observing us and have been here for some time.... The reason for the denial is they didn't know if they [the aliens] were hostile and they didn't want the Soviets to know so they devised to lie about it and cover it up."

Gordon Cooper: "I believe that these extraterrestrial vehicles and their crews are visiting this planet from other planets.... We may first have to show them that we have learned how to resolve our problems by peaceful means rather than warfare, before we are accepted as fully qualified universal team members."

Brian O'Leary: "There is abundant evidence that we are being contacted. Civilizations have been monitoring us for a very long time and their appearance is bizarre from any type of traditional materialistic western point of view."[229]

Then, on May 30, 2017, Robert Bigelow, a billionaire aerospace entrepreneur who has recently worked with NASA, proclaimed to the world in a *60-Minutes* interview that he is "absolutely convinced' that there are alien visitors living on Earth." Mr. Bigelow went on to say:

"I'm absolutely convinced. That's all there is to it.... There has been and is an existing presence, an ET presence [on Earth].

"I spent millions and millions and millions—I probably spent more as an individual than anybody else in the United States has ever spent on this subject [aliens]."

When asked whether he thought future human missions into space would result in alien encounters, he said: "You don't have to go anywhere. It's just like right under people's noses." (Bracketed words are in the original article)[230]

MAINSTREAMING THE MESSAGE

As you can see, this line of thinking is not merely the stuff of back-alley conspiracy theories; it's as mainstream as Harvard research papers, former presidents, important political candidates, renowned astrophysics journals, United Nations documents, billionaire tech gurus, and statements of former U.S. astronauts and moon-walkers. These are the declarations coming from today's world of science and international politics.

But as far back as the 1950s, renowned scientists have been publically speaking about their belief in visitations by intelligent life from other dimensions of space. One of the most famous and easily verifiable statements was made in an article written by the scientist himself, and published in a 1954 edition of *The American Weekly*. In that piece, titled "Flying Saucers Come from a Distant World," German rocket engineer and a founding father of the space age, Professor Hermann Oberth, wrote:

> It is my thesis that flying saucers are real and that they are space ships from another solar system. I think that they possibly are manned by intelligent observers who are members of a race that may have been investigating our earth for centuries.[231]

SECRETS OF LIFE

Could something of the magnitude of which Dr. Oberth penned actually be a part of the great demonic deception of the last days of which Jesus warned?

The doctrinally conservative evangelical biblical answer site *Got-Questions.org* describes themselves as, "We are Christian, Protestant, conservative, evangelical, fundamental, and non-denominational." They address the controversial subject of UFOs and a potential demonic connection like this:

> Recently, interest has been rising in the theory that this [last-days] deception will include alien beings from another planet. Odd as it may seem, this theory is entirely plausible from a Christian perspective. Although the Bible gives us no word about whether

or not aliens exist…the Bible does tell us about visitors from another world—the spiritual world.

We know from Eve's encounter with Satan that demons are interested in monitoring (and altering) the progress of humanity.… Another notable instance of their interaction with us is found in Genesis 6:4 with the arrival of the "sons of God." The Genesis account states that these powerful beings had sexual intercourse with women and produced a super race of beings known as the Nephilim. This sounds like the stuff of science fiction, yet it is right there in the Bible.[232]

MIND CONTROL

It is not just conservative evangelicals who are skeptical about little green men visiting us from other planets. The famed UFO and paranormal researcher John Keel who wrote the well-known book, *The Mothman Prophecies*, which was later made into the 2002 major Hollywood movie by the same title, wrote of a potential demonic connection:

The UFOs do not seem to exist as tangible, manufactured objects. They do not conform to the natural laws of our environment. They seem to be nothing more than transmogrifications tailoring themselves to our abilities to understand. The thousands of contacts with the entities indicate that they are liars and put-on artists. The UFO manifestations seem to be, by and large, merely minor variations of the age-old demonological phenomenon.[233]

Cited as one of the most famous UFO researchers of all time is Ph.D. scientist Jacques Vallée. Back in 1977, he insisted that he believes the UFO phenomenon is some sort of anciently existing "mind-control" technology:

I propose the hypothesis that there is a control system for human consciousness ... I am suggesting that what takes place through close encounters with UFOs is control of human beliefs, control of the relationship between our consciousness and physical reality, that this control has been in force throughout history and that it is of secondary importance that it should now assume the form of sightings of space visitors.[234]

Cited at creation.com is an interesting admission from ufologist Nick Redfern, who has written more than a dozen books, as well as numerous articles for various publications, and has appeared as a regular guest on The History Channel's *UFO Hunters*. Observe his progression of views over the years and where he has finally arrived:

...my views on the nature of the UFO phenomenon have radically changed over the years. Back when I was in my twenties, I was of the opinion that UFOs (the truly unknown ones) were extraterrestrial.... As I slid into my thirties, however, my thoughts slowly began to change (something which also happened for a few friends of mine in the field, too). And as many people will also know, my views—today—are far closer to those suggested by John Keel. Namely, that *we're dealing with something that co-exists with us and which masquerades as ET.* (emphasis added)[235]

PREPARING FOR THE ARRIVAL?

In February 2017, the mainstream international media reported that UFO sightings around the planet had reached an all-time high. The United States leads the way in the astronomical uptick as we reported sightings at a rate of almost three hundred times greater than the global median. The statistics assert that sightings have been rising dramatically since the 1980s. According to the report, there are now between thirty thousand to forty-five thousand worldwide sightings of UFOs each year.[236]

For numerous biblical prophecy prognosticators, and even the veiled admissions of secular ufologists, it appears highly possible that alien visitation occurrences could be tied to the coming days of the great delusion that Jesus warned would "deceive even the very elect, if that were possible" (Mark 13:22). Apparently, the last-days deception will be unlike anything the world has ever before witnessed—and practically everyone on the planet will fall for it. Its source could only be demonic, and from the realm of the fallen *elohim*.

> The coming of the lawless one is by the activity of Satan with all power and false signs and wonders, and with all wicked deception for those who are perishing, because they refused to love the truth and so be saved. Therefore God sends them a strong delusion, so that they may believe what is false, in order that all may be condemned who did not believe the truth but had pleasure in unrighteousness. (2 Thessalonians 2:9–12, KJV)

Is the world being prepared for the arrival? Are we closer than we could have previously imagined to the great deception the Bible assures will sweep the planet in the last days? What do we make of the fact that even some prominent secular UFO and alien contact experts are beginning to reach the conclusion that these alien encounters are something that *coexist with us* and which *masquerade* as ET? Sounds an awful lot like the fallen *elohim*, doesn't it?

I am not insisting that the *great deception* of the last days, culminating in the time of the Antichrist, will necessarily be some sort of UFO deception. It could well be that the deception that is to come will far outstrip even that possibility. Regardless, the ruse will be overwhelming, and it will be demonic in its origin. And, because the inhabitants of the earth refuse to believe the truth, God actually "sends" the delusion, or "gives them over" to the lie (2 Thessalonians 2:9–11; Romans 1:28).

However, considering the amount of global attention the subject of alien visitation is currently receiving, it would be wise of us to at least take into account the important biblical considerations that lend themselves to this demonic phenomenon, especially in light of the journey of study we have completed thus far.

Particularly in light of what comes next.

32

A New Age Dawning

Someone remarked that the best way to unite all the nations on this globe would be an attack from some other planet.

—John Dewey[237]

Without World Government, technological advances will destroy humans.

Those words marked a March 7, 2017, news headline on the Internet's top-ranked news site, the *Drudge Report*. The announcement corresponded to the following words spoken by, arguably, the world's most famous scientist, Dr. Stephen Hawking:

Technology has advanced at such a pace that [its potential future] aggression may destroy us all by nuclear or biological war. We need to control this inherited instinct by our logic and reason. We need to be quicker to identify such threats and act before they get out of control. This might mean some form of world government. But that might become a tyranny.[238]

A MERE RIGHT-WING CONSPIRACY THEORY?

So much for the insistence of naysayers who claim those that predict the eventual ascendency of a true global government are simply religious extremists and conspiracy theorists. As an example of the global-government-denial phenomenon, following is an excerpt from a lengthy repository-styled article on *Wikipedia*. The entry is titled "New World Order (Conspiracy Theory)":

> Observers note that the galvanizing of right-wing populist conspiracy theorists into militancy led to the rise of the militia movement, which spread its anti-government ideology through speeches at rallies and meetings, books and videotapes sold at gun shows, shortwave and satellite radio, fax networks and computer bulletin boards.
>
> However, it is overnight AM radio shows and viral propaganda on the Internet that have most effectively contributed to their extremist political ideas about the New World Order finding their way into the previously apolitical literature of numerous Kennedy assassinologists, ufologists, lost land theorists and, most recently, occultists.
>
> From the mid–1990s on, the worldwide appeal of those subcultures transmitted New World Order conspiracism like a "mind virus" to a large new audience of seekers of stigmatized knowledge.[239]

That article goes on to claim, "Many apocalyptic millennial Christian eschatologists…have predicted a globalist conspiracy to impose a tyrannical New World Order governing structure as the fulfillment of prophecies about the 'end time' in the Bible."

The context of the entire online entry appears to be dedicated to convincing its readers that the idea of a soon-coming one-world government is simply the stuff of conspiracy kooks and fringe Bible believing loons.

Regardless of the protestations of those who do not seem to be able to see the evidence before their eyes (2 Corinthians 4:3), a number of prominent international personalities openly call for a globalistic government as well.

PROPHETS OF GLOBAL GOVERNANCE

In 1999, Walter Cronkite, "The Most Trusted Man in America," appeared before the United Nations to accept the Norman Cousins Global Governance Award from the World Federalists Association. He told those assembled that the first step toward achieving the goal of global governance, which he claimed as a "personal dream," was to strengthen the United Nations.

At that event Cronkite opined:

> It seems to many of us that if we are to avoid the eventual catastrophic world conflict we must strengthen the United Nations as a first step toward a world government patterned after our own government with a legislature, executive and judiciary, and police to enforce its international laws and keep the peace. To do that, of course, we Americans will have to yield up some of our sovereignty. That would be a bitter pill. It would take a lot of courage, a lot of faith in the new order.

Cronkite mockingly added:

> Pat Robertson has written in a book a few years ago that we should have a world government, but only when the Messiah arrives. He wrote, literally, any attempt to achieve world order before that time must be the work of the devil. Well, join me. I'm glad to sit here at the right hand of Satan.[240]

Walter Cronkite is not the only one among the world's elite, past or present, to have brazenly called for or warned of, a one world government.

Carefully read through the following well-documented comments. If you were not previously aware of the pervasive magnitude of this globalist thinking, you are in for a surprise.

- **Paul Warburg** (financial adviser to Franklin D. Roosevelt and "father" of the Federal Reserve System, 1950): "We shall have world government, whether or not we like it. The question is only whether world government will be achieved by consent or by conquest."[241]
- **Senator Barry Goldwater** (1979): "What the Trilaterals truly intend is the creation of a worldwide economic power superior to the political governments of the nation-states involved…. As managers and creators of the system they will rule the future."[242]
- **David Rockefeller**, founder of the Trilateral Commission: "Some even believe we are part of a secret cabal working…to build a more integrated global political and economic structure—one world, if you will. If that is the charge, I stand guilty, and I am proud of it."[243]
- **David Rockefeller** (during a speech in which he "thanks" the mainstream media for withholding the secrets of the TLC's work): "It would have been impossible for us to develop our plan for the world if we had been subjected to the lights of publicity during those years. But, the world is more sophisticated and prepared to march towards a world government."[244]
- **Former National Security Advisor Zbigniew Brzezinski** (President Jimmy Carter): "More directly linked to the impact of technology, it involves the gradual appearance of a more controlled and directed society. Such a society would be dominated by an elite whose claim to political power would

rest on allegedly superior scientific knowhow. Unhindered by the restraints of traditional liberal values, this elite would not hesitate to achieve its political ends by using the latest modern techniques for influencing public behavior and keeping society under close surveillance and control."[245]

- **Zbigniew Brzezinski**: "The capacity to assert social and political control over the individual will vastly increase. As I have already noted, it will soon be possible to assert almost continuous surveillance over every citizen and to maintain up-to-date, complete files, containing even most personal information about the health or personal behaviour of the citizen, in addition to more customary data. These files will be subject to instantaneous retrieval by the authorities"[246]

- **Former Deputy Secretary of State Strobe Talbott** (1992): "In the next century, nations as we know it will be obsolete; *all states will* recognize a single, global authority.... Perhaps national sovereignty wasn't such a great idea after all."[247]

- **Former Soviet Union President Mikhail Gorbachev** (1996), "The threat of environmental crisis will be the international disaster key to unlock the New World Order."[248]

- **President Chirac of France** (2000): "For the first time, humanity is instituting a genuine instrument of global governance."[249]

- **Pope Francis** (2015): "To manage the global economy…to bring about integral and timely disarmament…to guarantee the protection of the environment and to regulate migration: for all this, there is urgent need of a true world political authority, as my predecessor Blessed John XXIII indicated."[250]

- **World Government Summit** (Dubai, 2016): "The World Government Summit has now transformed into the largest platform for the next generation of government leaders, and aims to prepare for the future and improve the lives of nearly seven billion people by gathering the world under one umbrella."[251]

- **Pope Francis** (2016): According to one report: "12 Times Pope Francis Has Openly Promoted a One World Religion or a New World Order."[252]
- **The Vatican** (2017): The Vatican called for the establishment of a "global public authority" and a "central world bank" to "rule" over financial institutions.[253]
- **Dr. Timothy J. Sinclair** (political scientist, author, professor, global finance expert): "Can we imagine a future without global governance?... But in the absence of an extra-planetary threat from marauding comets and malevolent aliens, this really does seem just a long-term possibility."[254]
- **Dr. Timothy J. Sinclair:** "By acting collectively as if global governance is a fact...we can make global governance a reality, that powerful agents cannot ignore. This sort of mobilization and transformation is what the Arab Spring was about, and this demonstrated the potential for change latent with global governance. That is something to get excited about!"[255]
- **Pierre Teilhard de Chardin** (considered by many as the Father of the New Age, and a heavy influence upon the UN): "The outcome of the world, the gates of the future, the entry into the super-human—They will open only to an advance of *all together*, in a direction in which all together can join and find completion in a spiritual renovation of the earth" (emphasis in original).[256]
- **Pierre Teilhard de Chardin:** "Although the form is not yet discernible, mankind tomorrow will awaken to a 'pan-organized' [global governance] world."[257]
- **Dr. Robert Muller**, former assistant secretary general of the United Nations (thirty-eight-year career with the UN): "Teilhard de Chardin...who inspired his colleagues, who started a rich process of global and long-term thinking in the UN, which affected many nations and people around the world. I have myself been deeply influenced by Teilhard."[258]

New Age Globalism in the United Nations

Knowing that Dr. Robert Muller was so heavily influenced by the one-world-governance doctrines of Teilhard, the following commentary from a prominent New Age website sheds even more light on how the United Nations might have been influenced during Dr. Muller's lengthy and prominent career. The publication, titled *Humanitad*, gives headline credit to Dr. Muller as a contributor. He is quoted and paraphrased throughout the article.

The *Humanitad* article's author claims:

> Of utmost importance in the creation of a "Planetary Declaration of Independence" would be the points so eloquently put forth by Dr. Robert Muller and Barbara Gaughen Muller in their "Agenda for the Future".... We must quickly learn to transcend personal egos, nationalistic, religious, and cultural differences and unite our efforts to stop the juggernaut of wanton destruction of our Natural Environment. Together we should work to make this Planet a Paradise.[259]

In the closing addendum comments, which the *Humanitad* article shows as signed by Dr. Muller in his own handwriting, we find this startling comment regarding the role of the Internet in developing a global consciousness:

> The Strategic Key to rapid and effective transformation of the Global Consciousness is through the Global Internet, which will remain relatively unrestricted as a medium of "free expression" for approximately the next 14 years. After this time the Internet will become so regulated and censored, that other means will need to be developed for the free expression and exchange of Ideas and Communications.[260]

AN US-AND-THEM WORLD

Then, on March 9, 2017, former president Bill Clinton gave an impassioned speech in Washington, D.C., at the Brookings Institute. The speech was given only weeks after the inauguration of President Donald Trump, who ran his campaign as a strong national-sovereignty and border-restoration candidate. Following is a portion of Clinton's speech:

> People who claim to want the nation-state are actually trying to have a pan-national movement to institutionalize separatism and division within borders all over the world. And it always comes down to two things—are we going to live in an us-and-them world, or a world that we live in together? If you got that, in every age and time, the challenges we face can be resolved in a way to keep us going forward instead of taking us to the edge of destruction. The whole history of humankind is basically the definition of who is us and who is them, and the question of whether we should all live under the same set of rules.[261]

Everyone from popes, former presidents, renowned scientists, media elites, United Nations statesmen, world financial magnates, celebrated educators, and authors to technology industry leaders continually sound the clarion call to install a globalist ruling authority. They desperately long to inaugurate a man-made dreamland of a new world order—a paradise on earth. In other words, they yearn for a world without the lordship of Yahweh. And, according to the Word of God, they will finally have it—if only for a short while.

The question of what will actually bring about the one-world Antichrist government system is a subject continually speculated upon within the world of prophecy examination. The globalist elites are discussing everything from a monumental environmental crisis, World War III, a looming financial meltdown, a technology nightmare scenario, and even an alien invasion as the possibilities that could be used to actuate their dream. The search is never ending for that one key factor that will finally flip the switch and cause the world to insist upon a one world leader and government.

THE END GAME

The globalist overlords will not just go away. They have been captivated by the demonic spirit of *Nachash*. Right before our eyes, every single day, we are watching the battle of the fallen *elohim* play out. The headlines are filled with the catalyst-agendas of the new world masters. Each of these potential catalysts is tied to clear biblical prophecies of the days just before the Antichrist system and the Second Coming of Jesus Christ.

Satan is furious. He will not relent, and neither must the people of God. We have been promised the gates of Hell will not prevail against God's ultimate plan (Matthew 16:18). We are in the midst of the sifting process. This was God's plan from the beginning.

Soon, Yahweh will bring His two families together under the headship of Jesus Christ, and we will rule and reign with Him. Let us then live within that foundational biblical promise in power, with love, and with sound minds (2 Timothy 1:7). We know the truth. We know what is really happening. We know *gods and thrones* are aligning themselves for the final showdown. We also know that the church has work to do.

Now, let's unfold yet another biblical bombshell and find out exactly *why* Satan is so furious…

33

REVERSING THE CURSE

Christ redeemed us from the curse of the law by becoming a curse for us.

—GALATIANS 3:13

HAVE YOU EVER wondered why Jesus was on the earth "showing him-self alive" for a specific period of forty days? Those forty days commenced on the day of His resurrection and lasted until the day of His ascension into Heaven. Observe the text of Acts 1:

> In my former book, Theophilus, I wrote about all that Jesus began to do and to teach until the day he was taken up to heaven, after giving instructions through the Holy Spirit to the apostles he had chosen. After his suffering, he presented himself to them and gave many convincing proofs that he was alive. He appeared to them over **a period of forty days** and spoke about the kingdom of God. (Acts 1:1–3, emphasis added)

While it might be easy to overlook this vital fact, the revelation of its significance should not be ignored, especially in light of what you have thus far discovered about the unfolding cosmic saga and the fallen *elo-him's* quest for earthly domination. The unveiling of the mystery at hand gives a shot of sheer adrenalin to the gospel message.

The number forty is found frequently throughout Scripture. In the vast majority of its uses, the number is interlaced with the idea of judgment and/or the calling of attention to something monumental that Yahweh is about to accomplish. This fact is true of the very first time the number forty is used (Genesis 7:4), as well as the very last time it is used (Hebrews 3:17).

THE CURSE AND THE JUDGMENT

Before God destroyed the earth in Noah's day, He explicitly stated that destruction was coming because of the "corruption of all flesh." We have discovered that the corruption of which God spoke actually started in the Garden and continued through the *sons of God* "coming unto the daughters of men" (Genesis 6:4).

When God finally brought His destructive verdict upon the world in those days, He did so through the worldwide Flood. God's judgment had come—embodied in the number forty. That flood commenced with the heavens being opened and a deluge falling upon the earth for forty straight days and nights (Genesis 7:11–12). This act of divine judgment is the first time the specific number "forty" is used in God's Word, and it is connected with the annihilation of the corrupted creation.

Also reflect upon the fact that when Yahweh delivered the nation of Israel out of Egypt, under the blood of the Passover lamb, He took them into a wilderness desert for their preparation.

What exactly was it that God was preparing Israel to do? As outlined in detail in a previous chapter, Yahweh was preparing them to be the conduit through which would eventually flow every vehicle of humanity's restoration—including Jesus Christ and the gospel of salvation. In other words, through a lengthy process, Israel would be uniquely used to reverse the curse brought upon the world through the Garden Fall and Satan's deception.

Those former slaves of Egypt could not have begun to fathom all that God had planned for them; nevertheless, it *was* His plan. But Israel rebelled. They refused to enter the Promised Land by faith. The spies brought back a bad report after *forty days* of spying out the land, and the people faltered. So God pronounced His judgment. They would remain in the desert wilderness *forty years*—one year for each day of faithless spying—until a faithful generation would rise up, take the Promised Land, and devotedly obey God's decree (Numbers 14:34).

THE REVERSAL BEGINS

Consider also, when Elohim covertly came unto His own creation through human flesh (Matthew 1:24), He went through a time of preparation before beginning His redemptive work. That time was precisely forty days. And it would be spent in a very specific locale: the wilderness desert area near Jericho. During that time, it is recorded that He ate no bread and drank no water (Luke 4).[262]

The setting of Jesus' desert wilderness preparation was no random piece of real estate. It was in the vicinity of the very place where the children of Israel had finally begun conquering the Promised Land. They would eventually enter that land of promise precisely forty years to the very day after the first Passover in Egypt (Joshua 5:10–12).

But there's more. Forty days and forty nights is the exact time period Moses spent on Sinai receiving the entirety of God's Law—also "without eating bread or drinking water" (Exodus 34:28).

Now consider these next truths. In Moses' case, the Law was given as judgment upon the sin nature of humanity (Romans 3:20). The giving of the Law at Sinai would also serve as the setting apart and the bringing forth of the nation of Israel, God's first messenger of His covenant of curse reversal.

In Jesus' case, He Himself would serve as the judgment of *humanity's* sin nature. And His death, resurrection, and ascension would affect the setting apart and birth of the Church. The number forty was central to the consecrating process of both Israel and the Church, as well as the ministry of both Moses and Jesus. It was also directly related to God's divine plan of wiping out the curse upon humanity, initiated in the Garden (Romans 5:17).

THE RETURN OF NACHASH

What happened during Jesus' opening forty days of ministry preparation? Satan launched a full-on frontal attack. Nachash was back. Once again, Nachash was whispering his deceptive challenges: "*If* you are the Son of God, command these stones to become bread, throw yourself down from this pinnacle…*if* you are the Son of God!" (Luke 4; Matthew 4; Mark 1).

Nachash, obviously, suspected that Elohim was in the process of thwarting his dastardly plan to usurp the Throne of Heaven. He just couldn't quite put his finger on the magnitude of it. Was this Jesus of Nazareth really Elohim in human form? If so, what could Nachash do to overturn the curse destined to fall upon him himself?

Nachash must have thought, "This *elohim*-in-the-flesh has to be stopped. He has to be shattered! This might be my chance to finally possess Heaven's Throne!" (Isaiah 14).

So Nachash went off to begin his counterattack of influencing the earthly thrones and principalities over which he had demonic sway—namely, the Roman Empire and the Jewish Sanhedrin council. Somehow, this Jesus of Nazareth had to be put to death. Little did Satan know what was really happening within the realm of Elohim's heavenly plan.

THE CROSS, THE RESURRECTION,
AND THE FORTY DAYS

Three days after what Satan thought was his victory, *Jesus was alive!* But, the humiliating blow didn't end there. The next weeks would be the absolute death blow to Satan's demonic pride, and an *in-your-face* assurance that his days were numbered. Not only did Jesus present Himself to many hundreds of His followers over the next forty days (1 Corinthians 15), but He also continued His work of miracles among the people (John 21; Acts 1), proving that *God in the flesh* was still very much alive. Satan's "best shot" had utterly failed, and Jesus was divinely flaunting the victory.

With each passing day, Jesus was declaring judgment on Satan's plan and disarming the powers of the demonic realm. Jesus was making a public spectacle of the ineptness of Satan's self-deluded brilliance. From this point forward, every born-again believer who entered through portals of glory through the veil of "death" would stand as God's "trophy" over Satan's domain of corruption. Want biblical affirmation of these truths? Read it for yourself:

> When you were dead in your sins and in the uncircumcision of your flesh, God made you alive with Christ. He forgave us all our sins, having canceled the charge of our legal indebtedness, which stood against us and condemned us; he has taken it away, nailing it to the cross. **And having disarmed the powers and authorities, he made a public spectacle of them, triumphing over them by the cross.** (Colossians 2:13–15, emphasis added)

> But thanks be to God, who always leads us in triumphal procession in Christ and through us spreads everywhere the fragrance of the knowledge of him. For we are to God the aroma of Christ among those who are being saved and those who are perishing. To the one we are the smell of death; to the other, the fragrance of life. (2 Corinthians 2:14–16)

THE SCHOLARS SPEAK

What do the biblical scholars say about our assertions in this matter? Observe the words of *Ellicott's Commentary for English Readers* regarding the Colossians 2 passage:

> The cross, as usual, is identified with the triumph over the powers of evil which it won. The very phrase "made a show," is cognate to the words "put Him to open shame" applied to the Crucifixion (Hebrews 6:6). The apparent triumph of the "power of darkness" over Him was His real and glorious triumph over them.[263]

And *Barnes' Notes on the Bible* address the passage like this:

> The "principalities and powers" here referred to, are the formidable enemies that had held man in subjection, and prevented his serving God. There can be no doubt, I think, that the apostle refers to the ranks of fallen, evil spirits which had usurped a dominion over the world.[264]

Deeper into *Barnes'* commentary on Colossians 2, he offers the following analysis of the matter, including the passage of 2 Corinthians 2:14:

> He made a show of them openly—As a conqueror, returning from a victory, displays in a triumphal procession the kings and princes whom he has taken, and the spoils of victory. This was commonly done when a "triumph" was decreed for a conqueror. On such occasions it sometimes happened that a considerable number of prisoners were led along amidst the scenes of triumph (see the notes at 2 Corinthians 2:14). *Paul says that this was now done "openly"—that is, it was in the face of the whole*

universe—a grand victory; a glorious triumph over all the powers of hell. (emphasis added)[265]

Vincent's Word Study also presents a vivid description of the metaphor Paul uses in his second letter to the Corinthian church:

[The specific Greek words found in this passage were] used to denote the Roman "triumph," celebrated by victorious generals on their return from their campaigns. The general entered the city in a chariot, preceded by the captives and spoils taken in war, and followed by his troops, and proceeded in state along the sacred way to the Capitol, where he offered sacrifices in the temple of Jupiter.

He was accompanied in his chariot by his young children, and sometimes by confidential friends, while behind him stood a slave, holding over his head a jewelled crown. The body of the infantry brought up the rear, their spears adorned with laurel. They shouted "triumph!" and sang hymns in praise of the gods or of their leader.

Paul describes himself and the other subjects of Christ's grace under the figure of this triumphal pomp, in which they are led as trophies of the Redeemer's conquest.[266]

THE ASCENSION CONNECTION

Nothing could have been more disheartening to Satan than Jesus' divinely powered ascension to the throne of Heaven. Seven passages in the New Testament mention the ascension of Jesus Christ: Mark 16:19; John 6:62; Acts 1:9ff; Acts 2:34ff; Ephesians 4:8–11; 1 Peter 3:22; and Revelation 12:5. In the passage at John 6:62, Jesus even used His imminent ascension as the "final" proof of His absolute deity and saving power:

Jesus asked them, "Does this offend you? Then what will happen if you see the Son of Man ascend to where He was before?" (John 6:61–62)

Furthermore, Jesus' ascension is biblically connected to the "taking of captives in victory" and the disarming of the demonic powers that are mentioned in 2 Corinthians and in Colossians. The connection is made through the passage of Ephesians 4:8–11. Observe:

> This is why it says: "When he ascended on high, He led captives in his train and gave gifts to men." (What does "he ascended" mean except that he also descended to the lower, earthly regions? He who descended is the very one who ascended higher than all the heavens, in order to fill the whole universe.). (Ephesians 4:8–11; parentheses in the quote are original to the NIV translation)

Ellicott's Commentary for English Readers makes the connection between Ephesians 4 and Colossians 2. As we have already seen from other commentaries, Colossians 2 and 2 Corinthians 2 are directly related as well:

> Paul's use of [captives] here is probably best interpreted by Colossians 2:15, where it is said of the "principalities and powers"—the powers of sin and death—that "He made a show of them openly, triumphing over them in the cross."[267]

The "captives" spoken of in the passages we just explored are the redeemed of God who have been saved through the work of Jesus' blood, Calvary's cross, an empty tomb, and an ascended and eternally triumphant Savior. And if you are a born-again child of God, these passages are about you! They are about how Jesus reversed the curse of the Garden Fall in your own life in order to prepare you for the coming restoration of your divine nature, which, by the way, is Satan's worst nightmare.

THE MOUNT OF OLIVES

In the book of Acts, Luke tells us in no uncertain terms that the ascension took place on the Mount of Olives, just outside the city of Jerusalem (Acts 1:12). He even describes the distance from where Jesus ascended from that mount as "a Sabbath day's journey from [Jerusalem]," about three-quarters of a mile.

It is not a mere coincidence that Jesus would begin His night of great agony *in a garden*—the Garden of Gethsemane. There, in that garden, is where He prepared to "reverse the curse" upon humanity, the curse that began in another garden thousands of years prior. Exactly where was this particular garden from which Jesus was now operating? It was at the foot of the Mount of Olives, the top of which would be from where He would ultimately ascend into Heaven. Jesus went from a garden-valley of dread and doom to a mountaintop of exaltation—both places, at the Mount of Olives, proclaiming to Satan, "You are finished!"[268]

The prophet Zechariah saw this place as well, four hundred years before Jesus went to Calvary's cross. Zechariah was prophetically shown the return of Yeshua: In the very last days, "On that day his feet will stand on the Mount of Olives." (Zechariah 14:4).

THE VICTORY

The following words from Revelation 12 should now burst forth with a clearer understanding:

> She gave birth to a son, a male child, who "will rule all the nations with an iron scepter." And her child was **snatched up to God and to his throne**....
>
> Therefore rejoice, you heavens and you who dwell in them! But woe to the earth and the sea, because the devil has gone

down to you! He is filled with fury, because **he knows that his time is short.**...

Then the dragon was enraged at the woman and went off to wage war against the rest of her offspring—**those who keep God's commands and hold fast their testimony about Jesus.** (Revelation 12:5, 12, 17, emphasis added)

Make no mistake: Jesus' forty days upon the earth after the resurrection and His subsequent ascension into Heaven were absolute death-nail signals to Satan's dreams of victory over the Throne of God. They were also declarations of Jesus' victory over your life. That's why Satan's attacks upon you are so vicious (Revelation 12:17). Every single day that you live for Jesus Christ stands as an embarrassing reminder of Nachash's utter defeat and his soon-coming judgment of death (Isaiah 14:15).

No—the specific number of Jesus' forty days upon the earth after the resurrection was no accident. It is the number of Yahweh's divine judgment, and it was the announcement that He had just accomplished something huge...and eternal. More than likely, the divine council of *elohim* rejoiced and celebrated the moment around the Throne of Heaven.

Perhaps they sang or shouted something like this:

No longer will there be any curse. The throne of God and of the Lamb will be in the city, and his servants will serve him. (Revelation 22:3)

⊰⊱

PART FOUR

THE PURPOSE

*I don't think life is absurd. I think we are all here
for a huge purpose. I think we shrink from the
immensity of the purpose we are here for.*
—NORMAN MAILER

34

Our Eternal Destiny

We are unceasing spiritual beings with an eternal destiny in God's great universe.

—Dr. Dallas Willard[269]

The pieces of the puzzle that were originally scattered all over our figurative table of biblical study are finally coming together into a discernable picture.

Our journey started with the scriptural declaration that Yahweh's two families (Ephesians 3: 15) will eventually be brought together into one enormous, redeemed family under the headship of Jesus Christ (Ephesians 1:9–10). All of creation will be restored to perfection. This was Yahweh's strategy from the beginning. Everything in the middle has been God's divinely ordained, cosmic separating process.

WE WILL BE LIKE THE ELOHIM

The fact that redeemed humanity, the lower family, will be *like* the *elohim*, in the upper family, is a clear New Testament truth, assuring us that when the times have reached their fulfillment, we will finally participate in that promised divine nature. In context, this means our originally intended condition of living as eternal beings in perfect concert with our Creator, will ultimately be restored. It promises that our original divine purpose of representing the majesty, glory, image, and love of Yahweh will be realized to its fullest potential.

Peter states the truth like this:

> Whereby are given unto us exceeding great and precious promises: that by these ye might be **partakers of the divine nature.** (2 Peter 1:4, KJV, emphasis added)

Obviously, the message of Peter's declaration is not that we become divine in the sense of obtaining literal "godhood," but that the seed of the redeemed nature has been divinely embedded within us. We are now made one with Jesus Christ, who is the ultimate divinity (John 15:1–6). In other words, born-again believers will partake in the divine nature, but we will not become gods.

This promise means that in Jesus Christ, even while we are in this earthly body, we can at least participate, through the Holy Spirit, in the eternally existent nature that God intended for us to possess in the beginning. But, it also means there is an even richer fulfillment of that promise yet to come.

THE DIVINE NATURE

MacLaren's Exposition of the Scriptures offers the following commentary concerning the partaking of the divine nature. The fullest meaning of the phrase largely escapes our earthbound ability to understand it, even though, as *MacLaren* states, the New Testament is "full" of the promise:

> "Partakers of the Divine nature." These are bold words, and may be so understood as to excite the wildest and most presumptuous dreams. But bold as they are, and startling as they may sound to some of us, they are only putting into other language the **teaching of which the whole New Testament is full**, that men may, and do, by their faith, receive into their spirits a real communication of the life of God. **What else does the language about being "the sons and daughters of the Lord Almighty" mean?**
>
> What else does the teaching of regeneration mean? What else mean Christ's frequent declarations that He dwells in us and we in Him, as the branch in the vine, as the members in the body? What else does "he that is joined to the Lord in one spirit" mean? Do not all teach that in some most real sense the very purpose of Christianity, for which God has sent His Son, and His Son has come, is that we, poor, sinful, weak, limited, ignorant creatures as we are, **may be lifted up into that solemn and awful elevation**, and receive in our trembling and yet strengthened souls a spark of God?
>
> "That ye may be partakers of the Divine nature" means more than "that you may share in the blessings which that nature bestows." **It means that into us** may come the very God Himself.[270] (emphasis added)

Matthew Poole's Commentary reiterates the fact that the divine nature has its greatest and ultimate fulfillment in the culmination of the ages, when we are with the Lord in glory: "The Divine nature may be understood of the glory and immortality of the other life, wherein we shall be conformed to God, and whereof by the promises we are made partakers."[271]

THE TRUTH PROTECTS US

Having discovered these truths affords us another great benefit: We are now protected from false teachings and cultic movements that portray an unbiblical picture of what lies on the other side of this earthly existence. Because now we know that to partake of the divine nature does not mean we are somehow swallowed up into an eternal oneness as New Age teachings attest. Nor does sharing in the divine nature mean that we become as unto God Himself, or anything nearly equal to Him, as other cult groups insist.

The term "divine nature" does not mean we will be absorbed into "Mother Earth," will go through cycles of reincarnation, or that aliens from other planets are our creators. Nor does it mean that we will become our own Gods, managing our own planets, and becoming exactly "as God is," as still other false religious sects teach.[272]

And having our divine purpose ultimately restored to us certainly does not mean that we are "absorbed into the *divine essence*," as the Buddhists explain it.[273]

Rather, the promise of possessing our divine nature means that we will ultimately take our place in God's heavenly council and among the reunited eternal family where we will rule and reign with Yahweh forever (2 Timothy 2:12; Revelation 20:6). This is how it was meant to be from the beginning. And this is how it will be realized at the last. Our heritage of a divine nature has been restored *only* in Jesus Christ (John 3:16, 14:6; Romans 10:9; Acts 4:12; 1 John 5:11–12).

> To the one who is victorious, I will give the right to sit with me on my throne, just as I was victorious and sat down with my Father on his throne. (Revelation 3:21)

THE PROMISE OF GOD'S WORD

Have a look at the following New Testament promises. You will probably recognize every one of them. However, I would venture to say that you will not look at them in exactly the same way as you did before.

Significant words are highlighted in each verse:

- Behold, what manner of love the Father hath bestowed upon us, that *we should be called the sons of God*: therefore the world knoweth us not, because it knew him not. (1 John 3:1, KJV)
- And we, who with unveiled faces all reflect the Lord's glory, *are being transformed into his likeness* with ever-increasing glory, which comes from the Lord, who is the Spirit. (2 Corinthians 3:18)
- Beloved, *now are we the sons of God*, and it doth not yet appear *what we shall be*: but we know that, *when he shall appear, we shall be like him;* for we shall see him as he is. (1 John 3:2, KJV)
- Now if we are children, *then we are heirs*—heirs of God and *co-heirs with Christ*, if indeed we share in his sufferings in order that *we may also share in his glory.* (Romans 8:17)
- I consider that our present sufferings are not worth comparing with *the glory that will be revealed* in us. The creation waits in eager expectation for *the sons of God to be revealed.* (Romans 8:18–19)
- But as many as received him, to them *gave He power to become the sons of God*, even to them that believe on his name: Which were born, not of blood, nor of the will of the flesh, nor of the will of man, but of God. (John 1:12–13, KJV)
- For the creation was subjected to frustration, not by its own choice, but by the will of the one who subjected it, in hope that the creation itself will be liberated from its bondage to decay and brought into the glorious freedom *of the children of God.* We

know that the whole creation has been groaning as in the pains of childbirth right up to the present time. Not only so, but we ourselves, who have the first fruits of the Spirit, groan inwardly *as we wait eagerly for our adoption as sons, the redemption of our bodies.* (Romans 8:20–23)

- At the resurrection people will neither marry nor be given in marriage; *they will be like the angels* in heaven. (Matthew 22:30)
- And [those who belong to Jesus] can no longer die; *for they are like the angels.* They *are God's children*, since they are children of the resurrection. (Luke 20:36)

Now that we know what we're looking for, the truth of the promise is almost impossible to miss. The New Testament is bursting with the assurance of the restoration of the divine nature that was rightfully ours from the beginning. When the Church was born in downtown Jerusalem over two thousand years ago, Peter proclaimed this certainty in his first sermon. Not only did Peter insist that "the restitution of all things" (the uniting of both of Yahweh's families) would be our ultimate reward and destiny, but he also preached that this fact had been clearly proclaimed by "all the prophets" in the past.

Read that portion of Peter's Pentecost sermon:

But those things, which God before had showed by the mouth of all his prophets, that Christ should suffer, he has so fulfilled. Repent you therefore, and be converted, that your sins may be blotted out, when the times of refreshing shall come from the presence of the Lord. And he shall send Jesus Christ, which before was preached to you: Whom the heaven must receive until the times of restitution of all things, which God has spoken by the mouth of all his holy prophets since the world began. (Acts 3:18–21, AKJV)

Before we close this chapter, have a look at 1 Corinthians 15 again:

As was the earthly man, so are those who are of the earth; and
as is the man from heaven, so also are those who are of heaven.
And just as we have borne the likeness of the earthly man, so
shall we bear the likeness of the man from heaven. (1 Corinthians 15:48–49, emphasis added)

There can be no mistaking the plain truth of this passage: As is Jesus,
so also are "those who are of heaven." And who are *those* of heaven?
They are the *elohim*, the upper family; our ambassador counterparts—
the angels, the sons of God, the divine court, or...*the heavenly host.*

Of course, we know that Jesus is greater than the angels (Hebrews
1:4), and He is *God with us*—Creator of all things, including the *elohim*.
Jesus is not *like* the *elohim*; rather, they are *like Him*. They were created
by His word and at His command (Colossians 1:16–20). Therefore,
they were created in His image. However, we also have been designed to
bear that same likeness. And, at the end of the ages, we will indeed reflect
His glory and image.

But our citizenship is in heaven. And we eagerly await a Savior from there, the Lord Jesus Christ, who, by the power that
enables him to bring everything under his control, will trans-
form our lowly bodies so that they will be like his glorious body.
(Philippians 3:20–21)

THE PROMISES

We shall be like Jesus. We shall be like the angels. We shall be called *the
sons of God*, co-heirs with Christ, and partakers of the divine nature.
There should be no mistaking these promises of the glory to which we
are headed. It is our divine destiny.

It is staggering to consider the depths of it all.

But wait...there's still more!

35

OUR HIGHER CALLING

This is the glory of all his faithful people. Praise the LORD.

—PSALM 149:9

HERE IS A shocking revelation for a number of modern Christians: The Bible is clear that we will ultimately have a literal part in judging the world; we will participate in that divine assignment because we will have been made a part of the divine council.

That heavenly appointment includes the judgment of all nations and their rulers. It also entails the judgment of angels who are now held in prison until the very last days. If you are in Christ Jesus, in a biblical, born-again relationship, this is yet another important part of your eternal and Heaven-fashioned purpose.

Read this reminder that Paul penned to the church at Corinth:

Or do you not know that the Lord's people will judge the world? And if you are to judge the world, are you not competent to judge trivial cases? Do you not know that **we will judge angels**? How much more the things of this life! (1 Corinthians 6:2–3, emphasis added)

John saw the future court of Heaven as well:

> I saw thrones on which were seated those who had been given authority to judge. And I saw the souls of those who had been beheaded because of their testimony about Jesus and because of the word of God. (Revelation 20:4)

Barnes' Notes on the Bible offers this commentary on Revelation 20:4:

> Paul asks the question [1 Corin. 6], "Do ye not know that the saints shall judge the world?" The meaning as thus explained is, that Christians will, in some way, be employed in judging the world; that is, that they will be exalted to the right hand of the Judge, and be elevated to a station of honor, as if they were associated with the Son of God in the judgment. Something of that kind is, doubtless, referred to here [Rev. 20:4]; and John probably means to say that he saw the thrones placed on which those will sit who will be employed in judging the world.[274]

The apostle Paul also endeavored to keep Timothy, the sometimes-fearful pastor, focused on the higher calling of his life and eternity. He reminded the young leader of the early Church that it was our divine and ultimate purpose to reign over God's kingdom with Jesus Christ:

> This is a trustworthy saying: If we died with Him, we will also live with Him; if we endure, **we will also reign with Him**; if we deny Him, He will also deny us. (2 Timothy 2:12, emphasis added)

Even the Old Testament speaks of the saints taking a place in the divine assembly of the last days, for the purpose of judging the nations:

> May the praise of God be in their mouths and a double-edged sword in their hands, to inflict vengeance on the nations and

punishment on the peoples, to bind their kings with fetters, their nobles with shackles of iron, to carry out the sentence written against them—this is the glory of all his faithful people. Praise the LORD. (Psalm149:6–9)

Matthew Henry's Concise Commentary says of Psalm 149:

The completing of this will be in the judgement of the great day. Then shall the judgement be executed. Behold Jesus, and his gospel church, chiefly in her millennial state.[275]

And we hear the same theme echoed in the book of Jude as well:

See, the Lord is coming with thousands upon thousands of his holy ones to judge everyone, and to convict all the ungodly of all the ungodly acts they have done in the ungodly way, and of all the harsh words ungodly sinners have spoken against him. (Jude 1:14–15)

The phrase "holy ones" comes from the Greek word *hagios*. The word simply means "separated unto God." Usually it is translated as "saints." In this case, it probably means the *elohim* as well as the redeemed earthly believers who are returning with Jesus.

Barnes' Notes on the Bible affirms this understanding:

With ten thousand of his saints—Or, "of his holy ones." The word "saints" we now apply commonly to "redeemed" saints, or to Christians. The original word is, however, applicable to all who are "holy," angels as well as men.[276]

The Bible is clear: We will judge the nations, we will judge the earth, we will judge the fallen angels, and we will reign over God's creation with Jesus Christ. Furthermore, we will do these things in conjunction with the faithful *elohim* who are also a part of the divine assembly of Yahweh.

All of this sounds much different than merely floating around on a cloud playing a harp, doesn't it? It does not sound anything like "getting saved" and securing a ticket to Heaven so that we might exist in some state of a perpetual dinner on the grounds rather than going to Hell. No, this sounds much more like we are going to be part of an eternal continuation of Yahweh's divine plan—beginning, at least, with being a part of His divine court. Who knows what Yahweh will do with His creation after that? The fact, though, is that whatever He does, *we will rule and reign with Him*—and will have an assignment in the entire affair with, and under the authority of, Jesus Christ!

ETERNAL PERSPECTIVE

The bottom line is this: Whatever we must sacrifice in this life will be well worth the trouble, pain, and heartache at the end of all things (Mark 8:36). We are going to be a part of Yahweh's divine realm. All things will be made new, and all things will be set right. There will be no more crying, death, or pain; we will be a part of restoring the order of God's divine kingdom throughout the universe (Revelation 21).

As mentioned in a prior chapter, Paul was caught up to paradise (2 Corinthians 12:4), and he saw what was in store for those who believe and are faithful. Once he saw and experienced that divine realm, he always longed to go back, but he knew he would stay on earth until his appointed task was complete. However, that little glimpse of glory Yahweh allowed him to see forever changed his life and ministry:

Eye has not seen, nor ear heard, nor have entered into the heart of man the things which God has prepared for those who love Him. (1 Corinthians 2:9, NKJV)

After that dramatic event in his life, the apostle Paul continually encouraged the early church to have their minds ever set on the eternal perspective:

Set your affection on things above, not on things on the earth. For ye are dead, and your life is hid with Christ in God. When Christ, who is our life, shall appear, then shall ye also appear with him in glory. (Colossians 3:2–4).

Having tasted of the glorious eternal calling that awaited him in in the divine realm, Paul wrote to the church at Corinth:

Therefore we are always confident and know that as long as we are at home in the body we are away from the Lord. For we live by faith, not by sight. We are confident, I say, and would prefer to be away from the body and at home with the Lord. So we make it our goal to please him, whether we are at home in the body or away from it. (2 Corinthians 5:6–9)

He wrote the same truth to the church at Philippi:

For to me, to live is Christ and to die is gain. If I am to go on living in the body, this will mean fruitful labor for me. Yet what shall I choose? I do not know! I am torn between the two: I desire to depart and be with Christ, which is better by far; but it is more necessary for you that I remain in the body. (Philippians 1:21–24)

KEPT FOR YOU

I suppose one of the most profound truths of all is the fact that our divine inheritance, secured in Jesus Christ, is awaiting us in Heaven even now. It is being kept there for us. Our divine destiny is secure. But for now, we must faithfully endure until He comes for us. Here is the biblical evidence of those truths found in 1 Peter 1:3–9:

[3] Praise be to the God and Father of our Lord Jesus Christ! In his great mercy he has given us new birth into a living hope through the resurrection of Jesus Christ from the dead,
[4] and into an inheritance that can never perish, spoil or fade. This inheritance is kept in heaven for you,
[5] who through faith are shielded by God's power until the coming of the salvation that is ready to be revealed in the last time.
[6] In all this you greatly rejoice, though now for a little while you may have had to suffer grief in all kinds of trials.
[7] These have come so that the proven genuineness of your faith—of greater worth than gold, which perishes even though refined by fire—may result in praise, glory and honor when Jesus Christ is revealed.
[8] Though you have not seen him, you love him; and even though you do not see him now, you believe in him and are filled with an inexpressible and glorious joy,
[9] for you are receiving the end result of your faith, the salvation of your souls.

LONGING FOR HIS APPEARING

Near the very end of Paul's life, when God had revealed to him that it was time for him to come home and take his place among the divine assembly, he wrote to Timothy again. One last time, Paul would use his life as a means to encourage a fellow ambassador and to remind that brother of his own eternally divine purpose:

For I am already being poured out like a drink offering, and the time for my departure is near. I have fought the good fight,

I have finished the race, I have kept the faith. Now there is in store for me the crown of righteousness, which the Lord, the righteous Judge, will award to me on that day—and not only to me, but also to all who have longed for his appearing. (2 Timothy 4:6–8)

May we all be so faithful. May we also possess and hold dear that same divine perspective. For it truly is our higher calling that keeps us moving forth, faithfully, while we are in these earthly tents.

I often find myself longing for His appearing. Do you?

36

How Then Shall We Live?

If you belonged to the world, it would love you as its own. As it is, you do not belong to the world, but I have chosen you out of the world.

—John 15:19

OUR DIVINE HERITAGE of salvation's promise is not a *back-pocket passport* merely guaranteeing our entry through the pearly gates of heaven. Salvation in Jesus Christ is also a *divine assignment*, and we only have a short lifetime upon this earth in which to accomplish our task. How then should we live (2 Peter 3:11–18)?

Jesus said we are to *occupy* until He returns (Luke 19:13). We have been given the designation of being Yahweh's ambassadors, holy representatives of His coming kingdom. *Elohim*/angels are continually dispatched to assist us in our work (Hebrews 1:14; Revelation 22:9). The powers of Heaven are counting on us. Those who have faithfully gone before us have shown the way (Hebrews 11). They are awaiting our arrival at their side (Hebrews 12). The restoration of all things is at hand, when we will finally judge the earth and the fallen angels. In the meantime, we are engaged in a great spiritual civil war (Ephesians 6:10ff).

For God's people to be actively operating as ambassadors for His kingdom is evidence that the Garden of Eden rebellion is in the process of being recovered. For that is truly what we were created to be in the first place—we were created in God's divine image to be His emissaries throughout the earthly realm. We are charging the gates of Hell, and those gates will not prevail against our daily assault upon them (Matthew 16:18).

Observe several biblical attestations of the foregoing truths:

- And he called his ten servants, and delivered them ten pounds, and said unto them, "Occupy till I come." (Luke 19:13, KJV)
- We are therefore Christ's ambassadors, as though God were making his appeal through us. (2 Corinthians 5:20)
- Are not all angels ministering spirits sent to serve those who will inherit salvation? (Hebrews 1:14)
- But [the angel] said to me. "I am a fellow servant with you and with your fellow prophets and with all who keep the words of this scroll. Worship God!" (Revelation 22:9)
- Therefore, since we are surrounded by such a great cloud of witnesses, let us throw off everything that hinders and the sin that so easily entangles. And let us run with perseverance the race marked out for us. (Hebrews 12:1)
- For our struggle is not against flesh and blood, but against the rulers, against the authorities, against the powers of this dark world and against the spiritual forces of evil in the heavenly realms. (Ephesians 6:12)

REMEMBER...

Of all that could be said in this chapter, the most important take-away would be: *At all times, remember who you are.* We are eternally existing beings created in the image of Yahweh, with a divine nature and purpose. We were fashioned for the direct objective of displaying the glory and the love of the Creator throughout the universe.

And, remember *whose* you are. You belong to Yahweh—through Jesus Christ. You do not belong to this world, nor do you belong to the spirit of *Nachash* that now rules within it (John 15:19). You are under the seal of the Holy Spirit of God (Ephesians 1:13).

> For this world is not our permanent home; we look forward to a home yet to come. (Hebrews 13:14, NLT)

Furthermore, remember *why* you are really here. You are on this earth, at this particular time, to be Yahweh's representative—and as a reminder to Nachash that his time is almost over. Your life is meant to be a monument to the truthfulness of God's promises and a demonstration of His sovereign and eternal power (1 Corinthians 1:18–31, 2:3–5; Revelation 12:11).

With this perspective in view, and the totality of what we have learned on our biblical journey thus far, do you now understand more fully the importance of guarding your heart, body, and mind in Jesus Christ? This is why there are so many New Testament commands directing us to keep this pledge.

Remember, all the way back to the Garden, the corruption of humanity involved the perversion of our loyalty to Yahweh, in whose image we have been created. In his diabolical outrage Satan desperately desires to continue the corruption of God's image within us.

Now we know that *the corruption that is in this world* originated in the Garden of Eden and continued through the perverted intervention of the fallen realm of the *elohim*. We have also discovered that the corruption that brought death to humankind, and even to the creation itself, most likely involved the perverted exploitation of human sexuality—and the deeply spiritual connection that is involved in that divinely designed gift. That explicitly corrupt distortion is the spirit of Baal. It is the spirit of Antichrist. And that spirit is spreading with a suffocating heaviness throughout the planet like never before.

Thus, the Word of God persistently reminds us to keep our bodies and our minds pure. When we step into areas of sexual sin, we open abysmally dark and demonic doors of harassment, infestation, and perhaps even habitation (Romans 12:1–3; 1 Corinthians 6:18–20). To immerse ourselves in that Antichrist spirit spoils our "image" of God, and it blemishes our witness before the world. Sexual sin is a deeply spiritual matter; it is one of the preeminent domains of the fallen *elohim*.

> Or do you not know that wrongdoers will not inherit the kingdom of God? Do not be deceived: Neither the sexually immoral nor idolaters nor adulterers nor men who have sex with men nor thieves nor the greedy nor drunkards nor slanderers nor swindlers will inherit the kingdom of God. And that is what some of you were. But you were washed, you were sanctified, you were justified in the name of the Lord Jesus Christ and by the Spirit of our God. (1 Corinthians 6:9–11)

> Flee from sexual immorality. All other sins a person commits are outside the body, but whoever sins sexually, sins against their own body. Do you not know that your bodies are temples of the Holy Spirit, who is in you, whom you have received from God? You are not your own; you were bought at a price. Therefore honor God with your bodies. (1 Corinthians 6:18–20)

Of course, sexual purity is not the only area in which the born-again Christian should be vigilant. Any arena of overtly rebellious activity and/or attitude can severely restrict the flow of the anointing that the Holy Spirit desires to impart to us. So, our struggle to be a faithful witness is not a one-time thing; it is a daily commitment and recommitment (Galatians 5:19–21). All the demonic forces of the rebellious *elohim* will be against us, using and manipulating our sin nature every step of the way.

You, dear children, are from God and have overcome them [the demonic powers], because the one who is in you is greater than the one who is in the world. (1 John 4:4)

The apostle Peter wrote some words to the early Church that have served to remind us down through the ages of the higher goal of daily living. The word of God still stands, and so do these words from 1 Peter 1:10–16—especially in our prophetic epoch of time:

[10] Concerning this salvation, the prophets, who spoke of the grace that was to come to you, searched intently and with the greatest care,
[11] trying to find out the time and circumstances to which the Spirit of Christ in them was pointing when he predicted the sufferings of the Messiah and the glories that would follow.
[12] It was revealed to them that they were not serving themselves but you, when they spoke of the things that have now been told you by those who have preached the gospel to you by the Holy Spirit sent from heaven. Even angels long to look into these things.
[13] Therefore, with minds that are alert and fully sober, set your hope on the grace to be brought to you when Jesus Christ is revealed at his coming.
[14] As obedient children, do not conform to the evil desires you had when you lived in ignorance.
[15] But just as he who called you is holy, so be holy in all you do;
[16] for it is written: "Be holy, because I am holy."

Yes, even angels have longed to pull back the veil of God's plan of the ages as it has slowly unfolded through the years of human existence. But, in these last days, the mystery is being revealed—to the Church—to those who have eyes to see. And because you are reading this book, and intently studying the Word of God as we move along, now *you* know!

The angels are cheering you on. They know the time of judgment and the restitution of all things is quickly approaching.

It is just down the road.

37

Just Down the Road

And they shall reign for ever and ever.

—Revelation 22:5

PROBABLY ONE OF the least understood truths about our new life in Christ is that once a person is born again, we are then held accountable for what we do with salvation's gift. This truth is an important part of the message of several of Jesus' parables. Do you remember the Parable of the Talents, the Parable of the Good Steward, or the Parable of the Vineyard Workers? (Matthew 25:14–30; Luke 16:1–13; Matthew 20:1–16).

God's servants must answer for what we do with the gifts and resources the Lord has given us through our relationship to Him. Paul reiterates this truth in both of his letters to the church at Corinth:

> [Your] work will be shown for what it is, because the Day will bring it to light. It will be revealed with fire, and the fire will test the quality of each person's work. If what has been built survives, the builder will receive a reward. If it is burned up, the builder

will suffer loss but yet will be saved—even though only as one escaping through the flames. (1 Corinthians 3:13–15)

For we must all appear before the judgment seat of Christ, that each one may receive what is due him for the things done while in the body, whether good or bad. (2 Corinthians 5:10)

Peter reminds us of this same truth along with the overarching reason for living it:

Since you call on a Father who judges each person's work impartially, live out your time as foreigners here in reverent fear. For you know that it was not with perishable things such as silver or gold that you were redeemed from the empty way of life handed down to you from your ancestors.... Now that you have purified yourselves by obeying the truth so that you have sincere love for each other, love one another deeply, from the heart. For you have been born again, not of perishable seed, but of imperishable, through the living and enduring word of God. (1 Peter 1:17–18, 22–23)

MAKE CERTAIN

Consider the words of Jesus as recorded in Luke 12:8–9:

I tell you, whoever publicly acknowledges me before others, the Son of Man will also acknowledge before the angels of God. But whoever **disowns me before others will be disowned before the angels of God**. (emphasis added)

Of course, now we understand that to be "denied before the angels in heaven" is a much more serious matter than many of today's Christians even begin to fathom, because that specific designation refers to our eventual appearance before the divine council of Heaven.

In this passage, Jesus affirms the measure of accountability we possess when we claim to be His disciple. We are answerable to the divine court of Heaven; they are witnesses to the reality of our kingdom loyalty. Observe the ominous declaration of this fact through the words of the *Pulpit Commentary* concerning Luke 12:8–9:

> Before that glorious throng of heavenly beings, whose existence was a part of the creed of every true Jew; before the mighty angels, the awful seraphim; before that countless crowd of winged and burning ones who assisted at the awful mysteries of Sinai, would they who witnessed for him, and suffered because of him, be acknowledged by him.
>
> Their sufferings in the service of the King of heaven, whom they knew on earth as the poor Galilee Teacher, would be recounted before the angels by the same King of heaven, when he returned to his home of grandeur and of peace in heaven.[277]

If we are to rule and reign with Jesus in the coming ages, how can we expect that great assignment to be fulfilled if our earthly ambassadorship is largely squandered on the trappings of this ever-decaying world, or if we are consistently timid in declaring before the world around us that *Jesus is Lord*?

In the meantime, what we do with our bodies as well as how we use our minds, time, gifts, anointing, ministry endeavors, and how we presently conduct ourselves in the family of God—every bit of it makes a difference as to how and where we will serve in eternity.

Therefore, it is vitally important that we are absolutely certain of our biblical born-again salvation (Romans 10:9). This matter is not something to be taken lightly. The matter of "salvation" is not a mere game of religiosity and cultural or denominational acceptance. What is at stake is our eternal destiny, our eternal home, and the restoration of our divine purpose.

Also at stake, even if we are confident of our biblically born-again status, is our ultimate assignment in the restored paradise and the kingdom work that is to come. Once again, we are confronted with the fact that true biblical salvation is not even close to the often-portrayed *ticket-to-heaven* scenario currently proclaimed from many of America's pulpits.

IT WILL BE WORTH IT

The apostle Paul reminded the church at Rome, during the days of rising persecution against the Church:

> Now if we are children, then we are heirs—heirs of God and co-heirs with Christ, if indeed we share in his sufferings in order that we may also share in his glory. I consider that our present sufferings are not worth comparing with the glory that will be revealed in us. For the creation waits in eager expectation for the children of God to be revealed. (Romans 8:17–19)

Think of it like this: When a baby is in the mother's womb, he or she is in a state of total bliss. The umbilical cord is a continual source of provision, coming straight from the baby's creator. The baby does not want for nourishment, comfort, protection, or any greater love than what he or she is currently experiencing—*or so the baby believes*. And then, finally, it is time to be born.

When that time comes, so do the contractions, forcing the child out of the cozy environment. "Wait! I don't want to leave! I like it where I am now!" But there's no stopping the process. The birth takes place in spite of the resistance.

Then… *The light is so bright!* The noises, sights, smells, and faces are wonderfully unexpected. Soon, an indescribable love is felt. A *touch*— something never before experienced! Snuggling. Warmth. Whispers of *love-words*. A mother's breath. A sweet lullaby. A kiss on the cheek.

Surrounded by an adoring family. Blissful, cuddled, love-bathed sleep. *Okay, I was wrong…*I've changed my mind…*this* is where I want to live!

If the child were able to remember the event of his/her birth over the months and years ahead, he or she might wonder, "What was I thinking? Why did I even dream of holding back? Life outside is awesome! I could never have imagined it!" As wonderful as life in the womb was, back in the good old days, you would not dream of going back into the womb after tasting of real life, would you? *Gross!*

But wait, it wasn't gross when that was *all* you knew. In fact, you didn't think you would ever want to leave the womb. But here you are, in a completely different world. Even though you are the *same you*, you are, at the same time, a very *different you*. You are a unique person living a glorified life, and the idea of going back would be completely unthinkable—even repulsive. Why would you want to go back to your fetus nature? So it will be when we are birthed one more time—into His presence, and into your divine nature. You will be *you*, but your life will be eternally different and more gloriously wonderful than you could ever have imagined…or heard…or seen!

IN THE MEANTIME…

Our journey began in Ephesians as we examined the eternal truths of Yahweh's two families. It is only appropriate that we bring our study to a close by returning to that same New Testament book. This is what is happening behind the veil of the unseen realm:

> Finally, be strong in the Lord and in his mighty power. Put on the full armor of God, so that you can take your stand against the devil's schemes. For our struggle is not against flesh and blood, but against the rulers, against the authorities, against the powers of this dark world and against the spiritual forces of evil in the heavenly realms. Therefore put on the full armor of God, so

that when the day of evil comes, you may be able to stand your ground, and after you have done everything, to stand. (Ephesians 6:10–13)

This is what we are up against. This earthly life is a battle between *Gods and Thrones*—and you, my friend, are an ambassador of the Kingdom of Yahweh—the *Elohim of elohim*. You are right in the middle of that raging war.

A TALE OF TWO TREES

Humanity's journey began with a choice placed before Adam and Eve in the Garden of Eden. The choice involved two trees. Their ungodly choice initiated the devastating fall of creation and humanity.

Yet, at the restoration of all things, as presented in the book of Revelation, we are once again confronted with a scene involving trees. This time, they line the side of a river. That river is called *the water of life*, and it flows from the Throne of God. On each side of that river stands the tree of life, and all the trees along that river bear fruit—the leaves are for the healing of the nations.

In Psalm 82, we discovered it was the nations and the gods behind the thrones of those principalities that had come under the direct judgment of GodThe nations had been thrown into demonic disarray, plunging humanity into corruption, vileness, misery, and destruction. Because of that celestial rebellion, God's eternal judgment had been pronounced upon the wicked *elohim* and the nations that allowed their influence upon them. However, at the culmination of the ages, nations will be healed, paradise will be restored, and once again humanity will walk with their Creator, as it was intended from the beginning.

Revelation 22:1–5 reminds us of the paradise-bliss for which our soul longs. Have another look. Be reminded. Come to this promise often. It is a little glimpse of the glory that is to come. It is down the road, just ahead. You will eventually be born again into this, and everything you left behind will be as utter corruption. You'll never imagine wanting to go back. This is your divine destiny, it is your eternal inheritance. It is why you were created, saved, separated, and sealed:

> Then the angel showed me the river of the water of life, as clear as crystal, flowing from the throne of God and of the Lamb down the middle of the great street of the city. On each side of the river stood the tree of life, bearing twelve crops of fruit, yielding its fruit every month. And the leaves of the tree are for the healing of the nations. No longer will there be any curse. The throne of God and of the Lamb will be in the city, and his servants will serve him. They will see his face, and his name will be on their foreheads. There will be no more night. They will not need the light of a lamp or the light of the sun, for the Lord God will give them light.
>
> And they will reign for ever and ever.

AT THE BEGINNING—AGAIN...

At the end of Yahweh's eternal plan, and at the restitution of all things, when our divine nature will have been graciously and mercifully restored to us through the sacrifice and blood of Jesus Christ, Nachash and his fallen *elohim* will finally be "gods" of nothing—they will be utterly destroyed.

Now that we have discovered these eternal truths together, in depths that are seldom plumbed by the average Bible reader, perhaps the words of the apostle Paul found in 1 Corinthians chapter 2 will burst into yet another exhilarating revelation for you. Pore over the words slowly, and prayerfully:

[6] We do, however, speak a message of wisdom among the mature, but not the wisdom of this age or of the rulers of this age, who are coming to nothing.

[7] No, we declare God's wisdom, a mystery that has been hidden and that God destined for our glory before time began.

[8] None of the rulers of this age understood it, for if they had, they would not have crucified the Lord of glory.

[9] However, as it is written: "What no eye has seen, what no ear has heard, and what no human mind has conceived"—the things God has prepared for those who love him —

[10] these are the things God has revealed to us by his Spirit. (1 Corinthians 2:6–10)

Thank you for taking this journey with me. I pray that the Holy Spirit of Yahweh has revealed marvelous and eternal truths to you. May the Lord Jesus Christ bless you and keep you until we finally arrive on the other side.

I will look for you there—somewhere around *The Throne*.

About the Author

CARL GALLUPS HAS been the senior pastor of Hickory Hammock Baptist Church in Milton, Florida, since 1987. He is the founder of the online PNN News and Ministry Network and is a longtime member of the Board of Regents at the University of Mobile in Mobile, Alabama. Pastor Gallups is also an Amazon Top-60 bestselling author, a talk-radio host since 2002, and a regular guest pundit on numerous international TV and radio programs as well as various print media sources. He has been featured on Fox News Business Report as an "influential evangelical leader." Carl was asked by the Trump campaign to open the internationally broadcast *Trump for President Rally* in Pensacola, Florida, in January 2016. Pastor Gallups lives in Milton, Florida, with his wife, Pam.

You can find more information about Carl at www.carlgallups.com.

Notes

Introduction—Unveiling the Mysterious

1. NPR (Commentary), "An Ideal of Service to Our Fellow Man," 5-28-05, http://www.npr.org/templates/story/story.php?storyId=4670423.

Chapter 2—The Seen and the Unseen

2. Dr. Graham, Billy. "Answers" (Topic: Heaven), 6-1-04, https://billygraham.org/answer/where-is-heaven/.

3. It has only been very recently that quantum science has claimed it can "see" the invisible particles and forces that they have "measured" and proven to exist. But this "seeing" is not the same sense in which we would normally call something "visible," as admitted by this late 2016 scientific article: "Invisible particles 'seen' for the first time," July 13, 2016, https://phys.org/news/2016-07-invisible-particles.html.

4. Davis, John, "Strange behavior of quantum particles may indicate the existence of other parallel universes." PHYS.org, June 3, 2015, https://phys.org/news/2015-06-strange-behavior-quantum-particles-parallel.html#jCp.

5. "Many Interacting Worlds theory: Scientists propose existence and interaction of parallel worlds," PHYS.org, 10-30-14, https://phys.org/news/2014-10-interacting-worlds-theory-scientists-interaction.html.

6. Clark, Stuart. "Multiverse: have astronomers found evidence of parallel universes?" The Guardian, May 17, 2017, https://www.theguardian.com/science/across-the-universe/2017/may/17/multiverse-have-astronomers-found-evidence-of-parallel-universes.

7. Chemistry of seabed's hot vents could explain emergence of life. Astrobiology Magazine, 27 April 2015, http://www.astrobio.net/topic/origins/origin-and-evolution-of-life/chemistry-of-seabeds-hot-vents-could-explain-emergence-of-life/.

8. Osborne, Hannah. "Time Travel Is Mathematically Possible with New Mind-Boggling Model," Newsweek, 4-2-17, http://www.newsweek.com/time-travel-physics-einstein-spacetime-tardis-592908.

9. Dr. Graham, Billy. "Answers" (Topic: Heaven), 6-1-04, https://billygraham.org/answer/where-is-heaven/.

Chapter 3—Meet the Relatives

10. *Patria*, Strong's Greek #3965, Biblehub.com, http://biblehub.com/greek/3965.htm.

11. Ephesians 3:15, Parallel Versions, Biblehub.com, http://biblehub.com/ephesians/3-15.htm.

12. Ephesians 3:15, Commentary, "Cambridge Bible for Schools and Colleges," Biblehub.com, http://biblehub.com/ephesians/3-15.htm.4.

13. Ephesians 3:15, Jamieson, Fausset, and Brown Commentary, Electronic Database. Copyright © 1997, 2003, 2005, 2006 by Biblesoft, Inc. All rights reserved.

14. Ephesians 3:15, Commentary, "Ellicott's Commentary for English Readers," Biblehub.com, http://biblehub.com/ephesians/3-15.htm.

Chapter 4—Restoring Paradise

15. Ephesians 1:10, Jamieson, Fausset, and Brown Commentary, (Electronic Database. Copyright © 1997, 2003, 2005, 2006 by Biblesoft, Inc. All rights reserved.).

16. Ephesians 1:10, Commentaries, "Barnes' Notes on the Bible," Biblehub.com, http://biblehub.com/commentaries/ephesians/1-10.htm.

17. Smith III, James D., "Where Did We Get the Doxology?" Accessed on April 19, 2017, http://www.christianitytoday.com/history/issues/issue-31/where-did-we-get-doxology.html.

Chapter 5—Elohim

18. Sumner, Paul, "'Elohim' in Biblical Context," Hebrew Streams, accessed on April 19, 2017, http://www.hebrew-streams.org/works/monotheism/context-elohim.html.

19. For an example of where *elohim* is translated as "angels" in at least eleven different scholarly translations, and as "divine or heavenly beings" in several other translations, see http://biblehub.com/psalms/8-5.htm.
For an example of where *elohim* is translated as "demons" seventeen times and as "devils" five different times, see: http://biblehub.com/deuteronomy/32-17.htm.

20. *Elohim*, Strong's # 430, Biblehub.com, http://biblehub.com/hebrew/430.htm.

Chapter 6—The Heavenly Council

21. Sumner, Paul B., "The Heavenly Council in the Hebrew Bible and New Testament," Hebrew Streams, accessed on April 19, 2017, http://www.hebrew-streams.org/works/hebrew/council.pdf.

22. Psalms 82:1, Parallel Versions, Biblehub.com, http://biblehub.com/psalms/82-1.htm.

23. For in-depth graduate thesis studies on the topic of the divine council in the Hebrew Scriptures, see:

a). Sumner, Paul B., "The Divine Council in the Hebrew Bible—Chapter 2 of: Visions of the Divine Council in the Hebrew Bible," April 1991, http://www.hebrew-streams.org/works/hebrew/divinecouncil-ch2.pdfcil-ch2.pdf.

b). Sumner, Paul B., "The Heavenly Council in the Hebrew Bible and New Testament," Hebrew Streams, accessed April 19, 2017, http://www.hebrew-streams.org/works/hebrew/council.pdf.

c). Heiser, Michael S. Ph.D., "What Is the Divine Council?" accessed April 19, 2017, http://www.thedivinecouncil.com.

24. For an authoritative study on the sons of God in every Old Testament location of the phrase, see: http://www.biblestudytools.com/encyclopedias/isbe/sons-of-god.html.
Ps. 29:1 For "Sons of God" translated as "heavenly beings," see: http://biblehub.com/psalms/29-1.htm.
Ps. 89:6 For "Sons of God'" translated as "heavenly beings," "angels,"

"divine beings," "Sons of the mighty," and "sons of God," see: http://biblehub.com/psalms/89-6.htm.

Job 1:6 For "Sons of God" translated as "angels," "members of the heavenly court," "divine beings," and "sons of God," see: http://biblehub.com/job/1-6.htm.

25. Ibid. (All references).

26. Job 1:6, Commentaries, Biblehub.com, http://biblehub.com/commentaries/job/1-6.htm.

27. Psalm 89:7, Matthew Poole's Commentary, Biblehub.com, http://biblehub.com/commentaries/job/1-6.htm.

28. `Iyr (Aramaic); from a root corresponding to OT:5782; a watcher, i.e. an angel (as guardian): (Biblesoft's New Exhaustive Strong's Numbers and Concordance with Expanded Greek-Hebrew Dictionary. Copyright © 1994, 2003, 2006 Biblesoft, Inc. and International Bible Translators, Inc.).

29. Daniel 4:17, Cambridge Bible for Schools and Colleges, Biblehub.com, http://biblehub.com/commentaries/daniel/4-17.htm

Chapter 7—The Throne, the Law, and the Scroll

30. Daniel 7:9, "Pulpit Commentary," Biblehub.com, http://biblehub.com/commentaries/daniel/7-9.htm.

31. Daniel 7:9, "Barnes' Notes on the Bible," Biblehub.com, http://biblehub.com/commentaries/daniel/7-9.htm.

32. Daniel 7:9, "Cambridge Bible for Schools and Colleges," Biblehub.com, http://biblehub.com/commentaries/daniel/7-9.htm.

33. Galatians 3:19, From Jamieson, Fausset, and Brown Commentary, Electronic Database. Copyright © 1997, 2003, 2005, 2006 by Biblesoft, Inc. All rights reserved.

34. Acts 7:53, From Jamieson, Fausset, and Brown Commentary, Electronic Database. Copyright © 1997, 2003, 2005, 2006 by Biblesoft, Inc. All rights reserved.

35. Acts 7:53, "Ellicott's Commentary for English Readers," Biblehub.com, http://biblehub.com/commentaries/acts/7-53.htm.

36. Acts 7:53, "Meyers New Testament Commentary," Biblehub.com, http://biblehub.com/commentaries/acts/7-53.htm.

37. Deuteronomy 33, "Ellicott's Commentary for English Readers," Biblehub.com, http://biblehub.com/commentaries/ellicott/deuteronomy/33.htm.

Chapter 8—I Said, "You Are 'gods'"

38. Following are two scholarly resources that affirm the contextual understanding of John 10 and Jesus' quoting of Psalm 82 as a defense of His deity, and not as somehow trying to show the Jews that they also were "gods"—as some commentaries and authors wish to present.

   a) Dr. Jerome H. Neyrey is professor of New Testament at the University of Notre Dame and the author of over dozen scholarly books and commentaries on biblical understanding says:

   Biblical texts that called mortals "gods" attracted attention from commentators and became the focus of ingenious interpretations and exegetical principles. This is certainly true of Ps 82:6, "I said: 'You are Gods.'"…

   Ps 82:6b ("sons of the Most High") is cited by Jesus when he calls himself "Son of God" (10:36), and it refers to his godlikeness in terms of holiness…Ps 82:6…functions as an adequate refutation of the erroneous judgment of Jesus' judges, who charged that he, "a man, makes himself equal to God," This judgment is false because God makes him "Son of God." …

   According to the apology in [John] 10:34–36 … [Jesus is] No mere human being, Jesus is a heavenly figure who is "equal to God." His equality rests not on holiness but on divine powers intrinsic to him, that is, full eschatological power. *

   *Neyrey, Jerome, SJ, "I Said: You Are Gods": Psalm 82:6 and John 10," accessed April 19, 2017, (Excerpted, in context, from the first paragraph of the paper and the concluding statements), https://www3.nd.edu/~jneyrey1/Gods.html#_ftn1.

   b) Dr. Michael S. Heiser, in a publically delivered and peer reviewed academic paper titled "Jesus' Quotation of Psalm 82:6 in John 10:34: A Different View of John's Theological Strategy," delivers the following conclusion:

   …John uses Psalm 82 as part of his portrayal of Jesus as divine—and even more than merely divine, as he has Jesus equal to the Father. When Jesus references the (plural) sons of God of Psalm 82 he does not have corporate Israel in mind, for corporate Israel does not rule in a council in the heavens (Psa

89:5–8; the council of the sons of God is in the heavens), nor were Israelites ever set over the nations, as the elohim of Psalm 82 were (cp. Deut 32:8–9, with LXX and DSS).

[Jesus claims to be divine] (John 10:30, 35-36). John wants his readers to know that Jesus was divine—a claim consistent with, "sons of God" being used of divine beings. Further, Jesus was not only more than man, he was equal to the Father (John 10:30) and had the Father living in him (John 10:35–36).

The "mortal" view of Psalm 82 therefore does nothing to assist the claim of Jesus' deity … *

*Heiser, Dr. Michael S., "Jesus' Quotation of Psalm 82:6 in John 10:34: A Different View of John's Theological Strategy" (presented at the Pacific Northwest Regional Meeting of the Society of Biblical Literature, Gonzaga University, Spokane, WA, May 13–15, 2011, https://booksmovie.org/similar-pdf-what-does-psalm-82-mean.html.

39. Buster, Aubrey, "Asaph and the Psalms," accessed April 19, 2017, https://www.bibleodyssey.org/en/tools/ask-a-scholar/asaph-and-the-psalms.aspx.

40. Psalm 82: 1, Parallel Translations, Biblehub.com, http://biblehub.com/psalms/82-1.htm.

41. Heiser, Dr. Michael S., *The Unseen Realm: Recovering the Supernatural Worldview of the Bible*, Lexham Press (September 1, 2015): 322.Michael Heiser is a scholar in the fields of biblical studies and the ancient Near East, and he is a Scholar-in-Residence at Faithlife, the makers of Logos Bible Software. Michael has an MA in ancient history from the University of Pennsylvania, and he has an MA in Hebrew studies and a PhD in Hebrew Bible and Semitic languages from the University of Wisconsin-Madison. He has published widely in scholarly journals and popular periodicals such as Bible Study Magazine, and he teaches ancient languages online at MEMRA.

42. Luke 1:52, Commentaries, "Gill's Exposition of the Entire Bible," Biblehub.com, http://biblehub.com/commentaries/luke/1-52.htm.

Chapter 9—Malevolent Thrones

43. Psalms 82:1, The Pulpit Commentary, Biblehub.com, http://biblehub.com/commentaries/psalms/82-1.htm.

44. Psalms 82:1, Gill's Expository of the Entire Bible, Biblehub.com, http://biblehub.com/commentaries/psalms/82-1.htm.

45. Psalms 82:1, Cambridge Bible for Schools and Colleges, Biblehub.com, http://biblehub.com/commentaries/psalms/82-1.htm.

46. Dr. Metzger, Bruce M., "The Early Versions of the New Testament," Accessed on April 19, 2017, Oxford: Clarendon Press (1977): 4–5.

47. Dr. Heiser, Michael S., "The Unseen Realm: Recovering the Supernatural Worldview of the Bible," Lexham Press (September 1, 2015): 27 and 29.

48. Isaiah 14, "The Bible Exposition Commentary: Old Testament," (from The Bible Exposition Commentary: Old Testament © 2001–2004 by Warren W. Wiersbe. All rights reserved.), accessed April 19, 2017, https://books.google.com/books?id=Hg444gp41loC&pg=PA24&lpg=PA24&dq=The+Bible+Exposition+Commentary+This+highest+of+God%27s+angels+tried+to+usurp&source=bl&ots=Rvy9Q4Zhpx&sig=q4TRkgV4yB-bKac0gB0aZFR4EOg&hl=en&sa=X&ved=0ahUKEwjU4cii9vHSAhVBC2MKHYglAgoQ6AEIGjAA#v=onepage&q=The%20Bible%20Exposition%20Commentary%20This%20highest%20of%20God's%20angels%20tried%20to%20usurp&f=false.

Chapter 10—No Other Gods

49. Was the Law Given at Mount Sinai on Shavuot? Accessed April 19, 2017, http://talmidimyeshua.org/lawgiven.htm.

50. Revelation 4:7, Parallel Translations, Biblehub.com, http://biblehub.com/revelation/4-7.htm.

51. .Moschos, Strong's #3448, Biblehub.com, http://biblehub.com/greek/3448.htm.

52. Exodus 32:8, Commentaries, Biblehub.com, http://biblehub.com/commentaries/exodus/32-8.htm.

53. Mizrachi, Murray J., "The Symbolism of the Bull as Understood in the Holy Books," May 2014, http://www.jewishmag.com/184mag/bull_imagery/bull_imagery.htm.

54. [Lesson] 8. The Tabernacle: A Picture of Jesus (Exodus 25-30), accessed April 19, 2017, bible.org, https://bible.org/seriespage/8-tabernacle-picture-jesus-exodus-25-30.

55. Gurkow, Lazer, "Why the Israelites Made a Calf," Chabad.org, accessed

April 19, 2017, http://www.chabad.org/parshah/article_cdo/aid/259461/
jewish/Why-the-Israelites-Made-a-Calf.htm

Chapter 11—Worthless Idols

56. Deuteronomy 32:17, Matthew Poole's Commentary, Biblehub.com, http://
biblehub.com/commentaries/deuteronomy/32-17.htm.

57. Leviticus 17:7, Elliot's Commentary for English Readers, Biblehub.com,
http://biblehub.com/commentaries/leviticus/17-7.htm.

58. Leviticus 17:7, Benson Commentary, Biblehub.com, http://biblehub.com/
commentaries/leviticus/17-7.htm.

59. Leviticus 17:7, Jamieson-Fausset-Brown Bible Commentary, Biblehub.
com, http://biblehub.com/commentaries/leviticus/17-7.htm.

60. Hohmann, Leo. "New Tunnel Unveiled in Bizarre 'Demonic'
Ceremony: Has women simulating sex with each other, resurrected
goat-man," WND.com, 6-6-16, http://www.wnd.com/2016/06/
new-tunnel-christened-by-bizarre-demonic-ceremony.

61. Swann, Jenifer, "Is a Trump Presidency the Satanic Temple's Chance to Go
Mainstream?" 2-27-17, LA Weekly, http://www.laweekly.com/arts/is-a-
trump-presidency-the-satanic-temples-chance-to-go-mainstream-7975996.

62. Jagannathan, Meera. "Witches of the world will cast a mass
spell on President Trump on Friday night," New York Daily
News, 2-24-17, http://www.nydailynews.com/news/politics/
witches-world-cast-mass-spell-president-trump-article-1.2981290.

63. Psalm 106: 36-38, Gill's Exposition of the Entire Bible, Biblehub.com,
http://biblehub.com/psalms/106-37.htm.

Chapter 12—Lord of the Flies

64. Ingersoll, Robert G., "Some Mistakes of Moses," accessed April 19, 2017,
http://www.goodreads.com/quotes/tag/baal.

65. Institute for Creation Research, "Baal and Ashtaroth," accessed April 19,
2017, http://www.icr.org/books/defenders/1288.

66. Jastrow, McCurdy, McDonald, "BA'AL AND BA'AL-WORSHIP,"
accessed April 19, 2017, Jewish Encyclopedia, http://www.
jewishencyclopedia.com/articles/2236-ba-al-and-ba-al-worship.

67. *Ba`al* (baw-al') OT:1166; a primitive root; to be master; hence, (as

denominative from OT:1167) to marry: KJV—have dominion (over), be husband, marry (-ried, wife). From OT:1166; a master; hence, a husband, or (figuratively) owner (often used with another noun in modifications of this latter sense), (Biblesoft's New Exhaustive Strong's Numbers and Concordance with Expanded Greek-Hebrew Dictionary. Copyright © 1994, 2003, 2006 Biblesoft, Inc. and International Bible Translators, Inc.)

68. Howard E. Vos, "An Introduction to Bible Archaeology" Revised ed. (Chicago: Moody Press, 1953) pp. 17–19.

69. Swartz, Glenn, "Sacred Killing: The Archaeology of Sacrifice in the Ancient Near East," 2012, accessed April 19, 2017, http://www.academia.edu/1651773/Sacred_Killing_The_Archaeology_of_Sacrifice_in_the_Ancient_Near_East.

70. "Who was Beelzebub?" GotQuestions.org, accessed April 19, 2017, https://www.gotquestions.org/who-Beelzebub.html.

71. Feraro, Shai. "The Return of Baal to the Holy Land: Canaanite Reconstructionism among Contemporary Israeli Pagans," University of California Press, Nova Religio: The Journal of Alternative and Emergent Religions, Vol. 20 No. 2, November 2016; (pp. 59-81) DOI: 10.1525/nr.2016.20.2.59, accessed April 19, 2017, http://nr.ucpress.edu/content/20/2/59.

72. Barber, Matt. "Today's Baal Worshippers," BARBWIRE, Feb. 14, 2014, http://barbwire.com/2014/02/14/todays-baal-worshipers/.

73. NCFIC, "Modern Baal Worship in Theaters, Stadiums and Living Rooms," accessed April 19, 2017, https://ncfic.org/blog/posts/modern_baal_worship_in_theaters_stadiums_and_living_rooms.

74. "Spiritual Progress Hard to Find in 2003," Barna, 12-22-03, https://www.barna.com/research/spiritual-progress-hard-to-find-in-2003/#.

75. "America's Changing Religious Landscape" Pew Research Center: Religion & Public Life. May 12, 2015, http://www.pewforum.org/2015/05/12/americas-changing-religious-landscape.

76. WND.com, "Only 17% of Christians Have a Biblical Worldview," 5-12-27, http://www.wnd.com/2017/05/only-17-of-christians-have-biblical-worldview.

Chapter 13—Baal Takes a Victory Tour

77. Ingersoll, Robert G., "Some Mistakes of Moses," accessed April 19, 2017, http://www.goodreads.com/quotes/tag/baal.

78. Tharoormarch, Kanishk, "Life Among the Ruins," NYtimes.com, 3-19-16, https://www.nytimes.com/2016/03/20/opinion/sunday/life-among-the-ruins.html?_r=0.

79. Berkowitz, Adam Eliyahu, "Temple of Ba'al Replica Arrives in London Just in Time for Ancient Pagan Festival," 4/7/16, Breaking Israel News, https://www.breakingisraelnews.com/65175/temple-baal-replica-arrives-london-just-time-ancient-pagan-festival-middle-east/#KJfdEZkpsg6J2htS.97.

80. Ronzino, Andrew, "The Truth of Halloween," The Paradigm, accessed April 19, 2017, https://greaterthanknowledge.wordpress.com/tag/baal-worship/.

81. Healy Consultants, PLC, "Doing Business in Dubai," accessed April 19, 2017, http://www.healyconsultants.com/dubai-company-registration.

82. Snyder, Michael, "The 'Arch of Baal' Was on Display for the Third Time in Honor of the 'World Government Summit,'" 2-17-17, http://www.charismanews.com/opinion/63105-the-arch-of-baal-was-displayed-for-the-third-time-in-honor-of-the-world-government-summit.

83. Ewalt, David M. "The World's Most Powerful People," Forbes, December 14, 2016, https://www.forbes.com/sites/davidewalt/2016/12/14/the-worlds-most-powerful-people-2016/#1460faf81b4c.

84. World Government Summit, "Partners 2016," accessed April 19, 2017, https://worldgovernmentsummit.org/summit/partners-2016.

85. Wam, "It's 'World Government Summit': 150 governments in Dubai from Feb. 8–10," 1-6-16, Emirates 24/7 News, http://www.emirates247.com/news/government/it-s-world-government-summit-150-governments-in-dubai-from-feb-8-10-2016-01-06-1.616141.

86. WND.com, "Major pagan god of Bible honored by world government," 2-20-17, http://www.wnd.com/2017/02/major-pagan-god-of-bible-honored-by-world-government/.

87. Ibid.

88. Berkowitz, Adam Eliyahu. "Arch of Ba'al, With Shadowy Ties to New World Order, May Be Messiah's End-of-Days Gateway: Rabbi," Breaking Israel News, 5-29-17, https://www.breakingisraelnews.com/88858/rabbi-warns-pagan-arch-end-days-gateway-will-walk/#S2sGqetylTfB8cxd.97.

Chapter 14—The Lawless One

89. Prendergast, Bill, "Bachmann update: Still a hero to millions," Daily Kos, 9-4-12, http://www.dailykos.com/story/2012/09/04/1127667/-Bachmann-update-still-a-hero-to-millions.

90. "Image," NT:1504, eikon (i-kone'); from NT:1503; a likeness, i.e. (literally) statue, profile, or (figuratively) representation, resemblance, (Biblesoft's New Exhaustive Strong's Numbers and Concordance with Expanded Greek-Hebrew Dictionary. Copyright © 1994, 2003, 2006 Biblesoft, Inc. and International Bible Translators, Inc.).

Chapter 15—The Coming Rebellion

91. Marilyn Manson Images, accessed April 19, 2017, http://www.marilynmansonimages.com/marilyn-manson5.htm.

92. Daniel 11:36, from Jamieson, Fausset, and Brown Commentary, Electronic Database. Copyright © 1997, 2003, 2005, 2006 by Biblesoft, Inc. All rights reserved.

93. Pink, Arthur W., "The Antichrist Will be the Son of Satan," Biblehub.com, accessed April 19, 2017, http://biblehub.com/library/pink/the_antichrist/ii_the_antichrist_will_be.htm.

94. Gallups, Carl, "When the Lion Roars: Understanding the Implication of Ancient Prophecies for Our Time," Oct. 2015, WND Books – Washington D.C., (The Solution To Everything): 91–98

95. Gallups, Carl, "When the Lion Roars: Understanding the Implication of Ancient Prophecies For Our Time," Oct. 2015, WND Books— Washington D.C.

Chapter 16—Let's Make a Man!

96. Dr. Michael Heiser, in his book "The Unseen Realm" uses a similar illustration from which I was inspired to construct the one I used in this chapter. See: Heiser, Michael. "The Unseen Realm: Recovering the Supernatural Worldview of the Bible," Lexham Press (September 1, 2015): 39.

97. Genesis 1:26, Cambridge Bible for Schools and Colleges, Biblehub.com, http://biblehub.com/commentaries/genesis/1-26.htm.

98. Genesis 1:26, Ellicott's Commentary for English Readers, Biblehub.com,

http://biblehub.com/commentaries/genesis/1-26.htm.

99. Gods ('elohim; theoi), Super Human Beings: Gods and Angels, International Standard Bible Encyclopedia Online, accessed April 19, 2017, http://www.internationalstandardbible.com/G/gods.html.

Chapter 17—Heaven's Witnesses

100. Genesis 3:22, Cambridge Bible for Schools and Colleges, Biblehub.com, http://biblehub.com/commentaries/genesis/3-22.htm.

101. Genesis 3:22, Matthew Poole's Commentary, Biblehub.com, http://biblehub.com/commentaries/genesis/3-22.htm.

102. See primarily: Heiser, Michael S. "Deuteronomy 32:8–9 and the Old Testament Worldview," accessed May 12, 2017, http://www.thedivinecouncil.com/Deuteronomy32OTWorldview.pdf.
See also: Schalk and Elsa, "The spiritual impact of Babel," *Set Apart People*, 10-29-15, http://www.setapartpeople.com/the-spiritual-impact-of-babel.
See also: "The Gods of the Nations," *Here a Little, There a Little*, accessed May 12, 2017, http://www.herealittletherealittle.net/index.cfm?page_name=gods-of-the-nations.

103. Genesis 11:7, Cambridge Bible for Schools and Colleges, Biblehub.com, http://biblehub.com/commentaries/genesis/11-7.htm.

104. Isaiah 6:8, Cambridge Bible for Schools and Colleges, Biblehub.com, http://biblehub.com/commentaries/isaiah/6-8.htm.

105. Isaiah 6:8, Ellicott's Commentary for English Readers, Biblehub.com, http://biblehub.com/commentaries/isaiah/6-8.htm.

106. Isaiah 6:8, Barnes' Notes on the Bible, Biblehub.com, http://biblehub.com/commentaries/isaiah/6-8.htm.

107. Schaeffer, Francis A., "How Should We Then Live? The Rise and Decline of Western Thought and Culture," accessed April 19, 2017, http://www.goodreads.com/work/quotes/522965-how-should-we-then-live-the-rise-and-decline-of-western-thought-and-cul.
Full quote: "The ironic fact is that humanism which began with man's being central eventually had no real meaning for people. On the other hand, if one begins with the Bible's position that man is created by God and in the image of God, there is a basis for that person's dignity."

108. Colossians 1:15, Ellicott's Commentary for English Readers, Biblehub.com, http://biblehub.com/commentaries/colossians/1-15.htm.

109. Brown, Jessica. "Talking to your dog is a sign of intelligence," Indy100.com, 4-4-17, https://www.indy100.com/article/talking-pets-more-intelligent-dog-cat-objects-7666431.

110. Gregg, Justin. "Is Your Toddler Really Smarter than a Chimpanzee?" BBC, 10-12-14, http://www.bbc.com/earth/story/20141012-are-toddlers-smarter-than-chimps.

111. Ibid, Schaeffer, "How Should We Then Live?"

112. Hebrew words *Tselem* and *Demuwth*, Strongs' #6754 and #1823, (Biblesoft's New Exhaustive Strong's Numbers and Concordance with Expanded Greek-Hebrew Dictionary. Copyright © 1994, 2003, 2006 Biblesoft, Inc. and International Bible Translators, Inc.).

113. Hodge, Bodie, "Were Angels Created in the Image of God?" 6-8-10, Answers in Genesis, https://answersingenesis.org/angels-and-demons/were-angels-created-in-the-image-of-god/.

Chapter 19—The Angel of the Lord

114. Genesis 16:9-10, Barnes' Notes on the Bible, Biblehub.com, http://www.biblehub.com/commentaries/genesis/16-10.html.

115. Genesis 16:13, Ellicott's Commentary for English Readers, Biblehub.com, http://www.biblehub.com/commentaries/genesis/16-13.html.

116. . Genesis 16:13, Cambridge Bible for Schools and Colleges, Biblehub.com, http://www.biblehub.com/commentaries/genesis/16-13.html.

117. Dr. Dickason, C. Fred, "Names of Angels," (Chapter—The Angel of Jehovah: His Identity), Moody Press, August 1, 1997, copyright by C. Fred Dickason. All rights reserved.

118. Ibid.

119. Colossians 1:1-3, Barnes' Notes on the Bible, Biblehub.com, http://biblehub.com/commentaries/colossians/1-16.htm.

Chapter 20—I Will Sit Enthroned

120. *Mashal*, Strong's OT # 4912. Biblehub.com, http://biblehub.com/hebrew/4912.htm.

121. Isaiah 14:4, Barnes' Notes on the Bible, (from Barnes' Notes, Electronic Database Copyright © 1997, 2003, 2005, 2006 by Biblesoft, Inc. All rights reserved.).

122. Isaiah 14, "The Bible Exposition Commentary: Old Testament," (from
     The Bible Exposition Commentary: Old Testament © 2001-2004 by
     Warren W. Wiersbe. All rights reserved.), accessed April 19, 2017, https://
     books.google.com/books?id=Hg444gp41loC&pg=PA24&lpg=PA24&dq=
     The+Bible+Exposition+Commentary+This+highest+of+God%27s+angels+
     tried+to+usurp&source=bl&ots=Rvy9Q4Zhpx&sig=q4TRkgV4yB-bKac0
     gB0aZFR4EOg&hl=en&sa=X&ved=0ahUKEwjU4cii9vHSAhVBC2MK
     HYglAgoQ6AEIGjAA#v=onepage&q=The%20Bible%20Exposition%20
     Commentary%20This%20highest%20of%20God's%20angels%20
     tried%20to%20usurp&f=false.
123. Delitzsch, Franz, "Biblical Commentary on the Prophecies of Isaiah,"
     accessed April 19, 2017, [Edinburgh: T. & T. Clark, 1875], 1:312.

Chapter 21—Beauty Beyond Compare

124. Tolstoy, Leo, "The Kreutzer Sonata Quotes," accessed March 11, 2017,
     http://www.goodreads.com/work/quotes/2266654.
125. Garland, Tony, "Q85: Is Satan in Isaiah and Ezekiel?" accessed March 11,
     2017,http://www.spiritandtruth.org/questions/85.htm?x=x.
126. Ezekiel 28:13, "Verse by Verse Bible Commentary," Expository Notes of
     Dr. Thomas Constable" accessed March 11, 2017, https://www.studylight.
     org/commentary/ezekiel/28-13.html.
127. Ezekiel 28:13, "Verse by Verse Bible Commentary," E.W. Bullinger's
     Companion Bible Notes, accessed March 11, 2017, https://www.
     studylight.org/commentary/ezekiel/28-13.html.
128. Robert Jamieson, A. R. Fausset and David Brown, "Commentary Critical
     and Explanatory on the Whole Bible," (Ezekiel 28), 1871, http://www.
     biblestudytools.com/commentaries/jamieson-fausset-brown/ezekiel/
     ezekiel-28.html.
129. Stewart, Don. "Is Ezekiel Speaking of Satan or the King of Tyre?" Blue
     Letter Bible, accessed May 2, 2017, https://www.blueletterbible.org/faq/
     don_stewart/don_stewart_82.cfm.
130. Jude 1:6, Jamieson-Fausset-Brown Bible Commentary, Biblehub.com,
     Biblehub.com, http://biblehub.com/commentaries/jude/1-6.htm.
131. Genesis 3:22, Keil and Delitzsch Biblical Commentary on the Old
     Testament, Biblehub.com, http://biblehub.com/commentaries/
     genesis/3-22.htm.

Chapter 22—Evil in the Garden

132. Genesis 2:8. For scholarly attestation of Adam having been created somewhere outside of the Garden of Eden, see the commentary entries for: Barnes' Notes on the Bible, Matthew Poole's Commentary, and Gill's Exposition of the Entire Bible, at Biblehub.com, http://biblehub.com/commentaries/genesis/2-8.htm.

133. For further reading on the potential that the earthly meeting place of the divine council was actually in the Garden of Eden see:
    a. "The Meeting Place of the Divine Council," accessed March 11, 2017, http://www.goldenageproject.org.uk/downloads/meeting_place_of_the_divine_council_eden.pdf.
    b. Heiser, Dr. Michael, "The Divine Council," accessed March 11, 2017, http://www.thedivinecouncil.com/HeiserIVPDC.pdf.

134. *Ophis*, Strong's Greek #3789, Biblehub.com, http://biblehub.com/greek/3789.htm.

135. *Nachash*, Strong's Hebrew #5175, Biblehub.com, http://biblehub.com/hebrew/5172.htm.

Chapter 23—The Forbidden Fruit

136. Lewis, C. S., "On Stories: And Other Essays on Literature," Harvest Books: Oct. 28, 2002: 111.

137. Got Questions? "What is the dispensation of Innocence?" Gotquestions.org, accessed March 11, 2017, https://www.gotquestions.org/dispensation-of-Innocence.html.

138. Augustine, "Against Two Letters of the Pelagians 1.31-32," accessed March 11, 2017, http://www.thebodyissacred.org/origin-st-augustine-sexuality-sin-sex-pleasure/.

139. Genesis 3:7, "Gill's Exposition of the Bible," Biblestudytools.com, http://www.biblestudytools.com/commentaries/gills-exposition-of-the-bible/genesis-3-7.html.

140. Ibid.

141. Genesis 3:7, "Guzik Commentary," (Man's Temptation and Fall), Blueletterbible.org, https://www.blueletterbible.org/Comm/guzik_david/StudyGuide_Gen/Gen_3.cfm.

142. Genesis 2:9, Cambridge Bible for Schools and Colleges, Biblehub.com, http://biblehub.com/commentaries/genesis/2-9.htm.

143. Genesis 2:9, Pulpit Commentary, Biblehub.com, http://biblehub.com/commentaries/genesis/2-9.htm.

144. Genesis 2:9, Commentaries, (See: Gill's, Poole's and Ellicott's commentary entries), Biblehub.com, http://biblehub.com/commentaries/genesis/2-9.htm.

145. *Ednah*, O.T. #5730, Strong's Exhaustive Concordance, Biblehub.com, http://biblehub.com/hebrew/5730.htm.

146. *Naga*, O.T. #5060, Strong's Exhaustive Concordance, Biblehub.com, http://biblehub.com/hebrew/5060.htm.

147. Genesis 3:13, Parallel Bible Translation, Biblehub.com, http://biblehub.com/genesis/3-13.htm.

148. *Nasha*, O.T. #5377, "Strong's Exhaustive Concordance," Biblehub.com, http://biblehub.com/hebrew/5377.htm

149. *Seduction*, "Definition of Seduction," Merriam-Webster Dictionary, accessed May 13, 2017, https://www.merriam-webster.com/dictionary/seduction.

150. *Chalal*, O.T. #2490, Strong's Exhaustive Concordance, Biblehub.com, http://biblehub.com/hebrew/2490.htm.

Chapter 24—The Corruption of God's Gift

151. Fitzgerald, F. Scott, "This Side of Paradise," Chapter 1, accessed March 11, 2017, https://ebooks.adelaide.edu.au/f/fitzgerald/f_scott/paradise/chapter1.html.

152. Kaufmann Kohler and Emil G. Hirsch, "Fall of Man," Jewish Encyclopedia: The unedited full-text of the 1906 Jewish Encyclopedia, accessed March 11, 2017, http://www.jewishencyclopedia.com/articles/5999-fall-of-man.

153. New World Encyclopedia, "Human Fall," (The Forbidden Fruit), accessed March 11, 2017, http://www.newworldencyclopedia.org/entry/Human_Fall.

154. Ibid.

155. John R. Levison (General Editor), "With Letters of Light: Studies in the Dead Sea Scrolls, Early Jewish Apocalypticism, Magic, and Mysticism (Ekstasis: Religious Experience from Antiquity to the Middle Ages) 1st Edition," De Gruyter; 1 edition (November 26, 2010): 95, http://www.

michaelsheiser.com/PaleoBabble/Minov%20Serpentine%20Eve%20
in%20Syriac%20Christian%20Literature%20of%20Late%20Antiquity.
pdf.

156. Genesis Chapter 3, "Commentary on the Bible by Adam Clarke," (Genesis 3:7, [Let us now examine the effects – paragraph 4]), http://www.sacred-texts.com/bib/cmt/clarke/gen003.htm.

157. Genesis 3: 22, Cambridge Bible for Schools and Colleges, Biblehub.com, http://biblehub.com/commentaries/genesis/3-22.htm.

158. (See the Benson Commentary, the Pulpit Commentary, and the Jamieson-Fausset-Brown Bible Commentary entries for this verse as additional examples of my assertion regarding the comparison of I John 2:16 with Genesis 3:6), Biblehub.com, http://biblehub.com/commentaries/genesis/3-6.htm.

159. *Phthora*, Strong's NT #5356, Biblehub.com, http://biblehub.com/greek/5356.htm.

160. *Epithumia*, Strong's NT #1939, Biblehub.com, http://biblehub.com/greek/1939.htm

161. 2 Peter 1:4, Jamieson-Fausset-Brown Bible Commentary, http://biblehub.com/commentaries/2_peter/1-4.htm.

162. . 2 Peter 1:4, "Clarke's Commentary on 2-Peter 1:4," Godvine.com, accessed 5-12-17, http://www.godvine.com/bible/2-peter/1-4.

163. 2 Peter 1:4, "John Gill's Exposition of the Scripture," Bible Study Tools, accessed 5-12-17, http://www.biblestudytools.com/commentaries/gills-exposition-of-the-bible/2-peter-1-4.html.

Chapter 25—The Corruption of All Flesh

164. *Basar*, OT #1320. Biblehub.com, http://biblehub.com/hebrew/1320.htm.

165. *Nephilim*, OT# 5303. Biblehub.com, http://biblehub.com/hebrew/5303.htm.

166. *Gibbon*, OT #1368. (See Strong's Concordance), Biblehub.com, http://biblehub.com/hebrew/1368.htm.

167. Genesis 6:2, Parallel Translations, Biblehub.com, http://biblehub.com/genesis/6-2.htm.

168. Genesis 6:2, Cambridge Bible for Schools and Colleges, Biblehub.com, http://biblehub.com/commentaries/genesis/6-2.htm.

Chapter 26—Chains of Darkness

169. Genesis 6:4, Cambridge Bible for Schools and Colleges, Biblehub.com, http://biblehub.com/commentaries/genesis/6-4.htm.

170. Genesis 6:4, Jamieson-Fausset-Brown Bible Commentary, (from Jamieson, Fausset, and Brown Commentary, Electronic Database. Copyright © 1997, 2003, 2005, 2006 by Biblesoft, Inc. All rights reserved.).

171. Genesis 6:1-2, Biblical Commentary on the Old Testament, by Carl Friedrich Keil and Franz Delitzsch, [1857-78], sacred-texts.com, http://biblehub.com/commentaries/genesis/6-4.htm.

172. For an understanding of the Book of Enoch referred to by Keil and Delitzsch, see this reference: Translated by R. H. Charles, "The Book of Enoch," 1917, accessed March 11, 2017, http://www.sacred-texts.com/bib/boe/index.htm.

173. Wayne, Jackson, "Did Jude Quote from the Book of Enoch?" Christian Courier, accessed March 11, 2017, https://www.christiancourier.com/articles/562-did-jude-quote-from-the-book-of-enoch.

174. Genesis 6:1–2, Biblical Commentary on the Old Testament, by Carl Friedrich Keil and Franz Delitzsch, accessed March 11, 2017, https://www.studylight.org/commentaries/kdo/genesis-6.html9.

175. Dickason, C. Fred, Th.D., "Names of Angels," (Chapter: Sons of God), Moody Press, August 1, 1997, copyright by C. Fred Dickason. All rights reserved: "Close inspection of the passages usually listed (Deut. 14:1; Hos 1:10; 11:1) will show that the exact term is not bene elohim."

176. Genesis 6, Guzik Bible Commentary, Biblehub.com, http://biblehub.com/commentaries/guzik/genesis/6.htm.

177. Dickason, C. Fred, Th.D., "Names of Angels," (Chapter: Sons of God), Moody Press, August 1, 1997, copyright by C. Fred Dickason. All rights reserved.

178. "Is there any evidence for the giants mentioned in the Bible?" accessed March 11, 2017, gotquestions.org, https://www.gotquestions.org/giants-in-the-Bible.html

179. Got Questions? "Could an alien deception be part of the end times?" https://www.gotquestions.org/alien-deception.html.

180. Heiser, Michael S. Ph.D., "The Unseen Realm: Recovering the Supernatural World View of the Bible," Lexham Press, September 1, 2015, p. 101.

181. "Bio for Michael Heiser, Ph.D.," LOGOS, https://www.logos.com/academic/bio/heiser.

182. Genesis 6:2, (See these commentary entries as examples of the multiple sources with the same basic message), See: Matthew Henry's Concise Commentary, Barnes' Notes on the Bible, and Jamieson-Fausset-Brown Bible Commentary, http://biblehub.com/commentaries/genesis/6-2.htm.

Chapter 27—Like the Angels in Heaven

183. Author's Note: As an example of an opposing argument see: Howe, Thomas A., "Who Were the Sons of God in Genesis 6?" (Article ID: JAG062), http://www.equip.org/article/who-were-the-sons-of-god-in-genesis-6/.

184. Matthew 22:28, Expositor's Greek New Testament, http://biblehub.com/commentaries/matthew/22-30.htm.Chapter 28—Something Wicked

185. Leonard, Tom, "Apocalypse Island: Tech billionaires are building boltholes in New Zealand because they now fear social collapse or nuclear war. So what do they know that we don't?" 2-3-17, http://www.dailymail.co.uk/news/article-4190322/Tech-billionaires-building-boltholes-New-Zealand.html.

186. "'Pandora's Box': Tech Fueling Urge to Be 'Gods on Earth'—Pastor: 'There's really no way to go back if something goes wrong'," WND.com, 2-4-17, http://www.wnd.com/2017/02/pandoras-box-tech-fueling-urge-to-be-gods-on-earth/#VP8UC4XIBL5stIxE.99.

187. Martin, Sean. "NASA astronaut claims aliens DO exist—and humanity doesn't have long left," Express U.K, 9-20-16, http://www.express.co.uk/news/weird/712596/Nasa-astronaut-aliens-exist-humanity-long-left.

188. Dowd, Maureen. "Elon Musk's Billion-Dollar Crusade to Stop the A.I. Apocalypse," Vanity Fair, (April 2017), http://www.vanityfair.com/news/2017/03/elon-musk-billion-dollar-crusade-to-stop-ai-space-x.

189. Griffin, Andrew, "Stephen Hawking: Artificial intelligence could wipe out humanity when it gets too clever as humans will be like ants," Independent, 10-8-15, http://www.independent.co.uk/life-style/gadgets-and-tech/news/stephen-hawking-artificial-intelligence-could-wipe-out-humanity-when-it-gets-too-clever-as-humans-a6686496.html

190. Batts, Vicki, "Chimera: Scientists have grown a Pig-Human hybrid creature

in a lab," Natural News, 2-6-17, http://naturalnews.com/2017-02-06-chimera-scientists-have-grown-a-pig-human-hybrid-creature-in-a-lab-for-study.html.

191. Martin, Sean, "Scientists take a step closer to ETERNAL LIFE as they PRESERVE and REVIVE brain," Express UK, 2-15-16, http://www.express.co.uk/news/science/643538/Scientists-take-a-step-closer-to-ETERNAL-LIFE-as-they-PRESERVE-and-REVIVE-brain.

192. Gray, Richard, "Could this creepy robot be the answer to eternal life? Technology used to make Bina 48 could one day let us upload our minds to computers," 2-6-15, Daily Mail UK, http://www.dailymail.co.uk/sciencetech/article-2942582/Could-creepy-robot-answer-eternal-life-Technology-allow-people-upload-minds-computers.html#ixzz4agPeBEd1.

193. Hamill, Jasper, "WHO'S THE DADDY NOW? Men could have babies WITHOUT women by creating artificial eggs from skin cells," The Sun, 9-13-16, https://www.thesun.co.uk/news/1776276/men-could-have-babies-without-women-by-creating-artificial-eggs-from-skin-cells/.

194. Fernandez, Colin, "A human-pig hybrid embryo has been created in a world first: Breakthrough could open up the possibility for 'designer' animal organs to be used in people," Daily Mail, 1-26-17, http://www.dailymail.co.uk/sciencetech/article-4161022/Human-animal-hybrid-embryo-created-time.html.

195. Dormehl, Luke, "Realdoll builds artificially intelligent sex robots with programmable personalities," Fox News, 2-6-17, http://www.foxnews.com/tech/2017/02/06/realdoll-builds-artificially-intelligent-sex-robots-with-programmable-personalities.html.

196. Bonasio, Alice, "Sex in Virtual Reality Is Getting Even More Immersive in 2017," 1-21-17, https://uploadvr.com/porn-teledildonics-2017/.

197. Waddell, Lily, "Sex robot theme parks 'better than Disney World' to offer raunchy getaways," Daily Star, 3-11-17, http://www.dailystar.co.uk/news/latest-news/593296/HBO-Westworld-sex-robots-Disney-World-theme-park-Las-Vegas-Bangkok-orgies.

198. McCrum, Kirstie, "Virtual reality 'sex suit' lets men experience realistic intercourse all on their own," Mirror, 4-6-16, http://www.mirror.co.uk/news/world-news/virtual-reality-sex-suit-lets-7698685.

199. O'Neill, Sean, "The human universe: Could we become gods?"

New Scientist, 4-29-15, https://www.newscientist.com/article/
mg22630191-100-the-human-universe-could-we-become-gods/.

200. "Ray Kurzweil on How We Will Become God-Like," 33rd Square, 1-2-14,
http://www.33rdsquare.com/2014/01/ray-kurzweil-on-how-we-will-
become-god.html.

201. Weston, Phoebe, "Super humans who are sexier, stronger and smarter
will arrive by 2029 as brains begin to fuse with machines, Google expert
claims," accessed March 11, 2017, Daily Mail, http://www.dailymail.co.uk/
sciencetech/article-4319436/Singularity-create-super-humans-Google-
expert-claims.html.

Chapter 29—Just Like This

202. "Exorcism Thriving in U.S., Say Experts," ABC News, accessed March 11,
2017, http://abcnews.go.com/US/story?id=92541.

203. Gallagher, Richard, "As a psychiatrist, I diagnose mental illness. Also, I
help spot demonic possession," Washington Post, 7-1-16, https://www.
washingtonpost.com/posteverything/wp/2016/07/01/as-a-psychiatrist-i-
diagnose-mental-illness-and-sometimes-demonic-possession/?utm_term=.
a32aab7dec7f.

204. Day, Michael, "Global demonic possessions are reaching
'emergency levels', exorcism expert warns Pope," Express UK,
10-28-14, http://www.express.co.uk/news/weird/528622/
Devil-Woman-Demonic-Possession-Pope-Francis.

205. Evans, Ruth, 'Witchcraft' abuse cases on the rise," BBC, 10-11-15, http://
www.bbc.com/news/uk-34475424.

206. In March of 2017, the same group said that they would repeat
the ritual on March 26 and on every crescent moon "until
Donald Trump is removed from office," according to the
group's Facebook page. See: http://www.wnd.com/2017/03/
witches-to-cast-spell-on-trump-again/#55O8Q1ACy7rk9WVZ.99.

207. Boland, Barbara, "FBI: 'Epidemic' levels of pedophilia,
child sex trafficking," Washington Examiner,
7-30-15, http://www.washingtonexaminer.com/
fbi-epidemic-levels-of-pedophilia-child-sex-trafficking/article/2569241.

208. Howard, Jacqueline, "STD rates reach record high in United

States," CNN, 10-20-16, http://www.cnn.com/2016/10/20/health/std-statistics-record-high/.

209. Miksche, Mike, America May Be Heading into an STD Epidemic—and Gay and Bi Men Are Going to Be the Hardest Hit," Slate.com, January 16, 2017, http://www.slate.com/blogs/outward/2017/01/16/stds_are_on_the_rise_among_gay_and_bi_msm_is_an_epidemic_on_the_horizon.html.

210. UNAIDS, "UNAIDS report on the global AIDS epidemic 2013," World Health Organization, September 2013, http://www.who.int/hiv/pub/me/unaids_global_report/en/.

211. Bakalara, Nicholas. "Close to Half of American Adults Infected With HPV, Survey Finds," New York Times, 4-6-17, https://www.nytimes.com/2017/04/06/health/hpv-virus-survey-united-states.html.

212. Bellevue, Donna, "Resurrecting Dead People Using Stem Cells Given the Green Light," ITechPost.com, March 11, 2017, http://www.itechpost.com/articles/90865/20170310/resurrecting-dead-people-using-stem-cells-given-permission-in-the-us.htm.

213. Falk, Dan. "Godlike 'Homo Deus' Could Replace Humans as Tech Evolves," NBC News *Mach*, Updated May.31.2017, https://www.nbcnews.com/mach/mach/godlike-homo-deus-could-replace-humans-tech-evolves-n757971.

Chapter 30—Contact

214. Hollingham, Richard, "The Gaming Tech That May Help Find Alien Life," BBC, 1-23-17, http://www.bbc.com/future/story/20170123-the-gaming-tech-that-may-help-find-alien-life.

215. Szarek, Rob, "Are Ancient Aliens Really Futuristic Human Time Travelers?" The Huffington Post (The Blog), 12-3-13, http://www.huffingtonpost.com/rob-szarek/are-ancient-aliens-really_b_4380799.html.

216. Click, "Hacker fears 'UFO cover-up'," BBC, 5-5-06, http://news.bbc.co.uk/2/hi/programmes/click_online/4977134.stm.

217. Wright, Robert, "Can Evolution Have a Higher Purpose?" 12-12-16, New York Times, https://www.nytimes.com/2016/12/12/opinion/can-evolution-have-a-higher-purpose.html.

218. Chozick, Amy, "Hillary Clinton Gives U.F.O. Buffs Hope She Will Open the X-Files," New York Times, May 10, 2016, https://www.nytimes.com/2016/05/11/us/politics/hillary-clinton-aliens.html.

219. Watkins, Eli, "Clinton campaign chair: 'The American people can handle the truth' on UFOs," CNN, 4-7-16, http://www.cnn.com/2016/04/07/politics/john-podesta-hillary-clinton-ufo/.

220. Speigel, Lee, "Leaked Emails Reveal Former Astronaut Wanted to Meet With Obama Official About Alien Life." 10/12/2016, https://www.msn.com/en-us/news/us/leaked-emails-reveal-former-astronaut-wanted-to-meet-with-obama-official-about-alien-life/ar-BBxjm4K.

221. Ibid.

222. "Ronald Reagan: The Alien Threat," Accessed on April 4, 2017, http://www.bibliotecapleyades.net/exopolitica/exopolitics_reagan03.htm. Watch President Reagan make "alien threats" statements in several public appearances: https://www.youtube.com/watch?v=iQxzWpy7PKg. President Reagan's speech to the U.N. can be viewed here: https://www.youtube.com/watch?v=j5uzdWqhY8s.

223. Ibid.

224. (YouTube Video) "Are UFOs Real: President Bill Clinton UFO Speech," uploaded March 29, 2015, (starting at about the 2:15 mark), accessed March 11, 2017, https://www.youtube.com/watch?v=gZqLlHRepSo.

Chapter 31—Mainstream Mind Control

225. Hamill, Jasper. "Houston, We Have an Admission: Meet the NASA astronauts who believe aliens are visiting Earth and communicating with humanity," U.K. Sun, 4-6-17, https://www.thesun.co.uk/tech/3268325/meet-the-nasa-astronauts-who-believe-aliens-are-visiting-earth-and-communicating-with-humanity.

226. Wall, Mike, "Could Mysterious Cosmic Light Flashes Be Powering Alien Spacecraft?" Science.com, 3-9-17, http://www.space.com/35996-fast-radio-bursts-powering-alien-spacecraft.html.

227. Fox News, "Apollo 14 astronaut claims peace-loving aliens prevented 'nuclear war' on Earth," Foxnews.com, 8-15-15, http://www.foxnews.com/science/2015/08/14/apollo-14-astronaut-claims-peace-loving-aliens-prevented-nuclear-war-on-earth.html.

228. Speigel, Lee. "WikiLeaks Documents Reveal United Nations Interest in UFOs," Huffington Post, 10-29-16, http://www.huffingtonpost.com/entry/wikileaks-ufos-united-nations_us_5813aa17e4b0390e69d0322e.

229. Hamill, Jasper. "Houston, We Have an Admission: Meet the NASA astronauts who believe aliens are visiting Earth and communicating with humanity," U.K. Sun, 4-6-17, https://www.thesun.co.uk/tech/3268325/meet-the-nasa-astronauts-who-believe-aliens-are-visiting-earth-and-communicating-with-humanity.

230. Pettit, Harry. "Billionaire Bigelow space mogul says he is 'absolutely convinced' there are aliens on Earth," Daily Mail, 5-30-17, http://www.dailymail.co.uk/sciencetech/article-4554970/Robert-Bigelow-absolutely-convinced-aliens-Earth.html.

231. Oberth, Prof. Herman. "Flying Saucers Come from a Distant World," Cleveland Plain Dealer, Section: The American Weekly, 1954 October 24, Page 4, Quote Page 4, Column 1, Cleveland, Ohio. (Genealogy Bank), accessed March 11, 2017, Verified here: http://quoteinvestigator.com/2016/11/14/flying-saucer/#note-14829-2.

232. "Could an alien deception be part of the end times?" GotQuestions.org, accessed March 11, 2017, https://www.gotquestions.org/alien-deception.html

233. Keel, John. "Operation Trojan Horse" (Lilburn, GA: Illuminet Press, 1996): p. 266, accessed March 11, 2017, Cited here: http://creation.com/ufos-not-extraterrestrial.

234. Story, Ronald, The Mammoth Encyclopedia of Extraterrestrial Encounters, in an article by Jacques Vallée, pp. 753–754. accessed March 11, 2017, This article was a summary of his conclusions in his 1977 book Unidentified Flying Objects: The Psychic Solution. Cited here: http://creation.com/ufos-not-extraterrestrial.

235. Bates, Gary, "UFOs are not extraterrestrial! Modern secular researchers are getting closer to the truth," Creation.com, 7-5-16, http://creation.com/ufos-not-extraterrestrial.

236. Drooby, Emily. "UFO sightings have reached an all-time high," AOL.com, 2-24-17, https://www.aol.com/article/news/2017/02/24/ufo-sightings-have-reached-an-all-time-high/21721159/.

Chapter 32—A New Age Dawning

237. Carnegie Endowment for International Peace, "The Imperial Japanese Mission to the United States, 1917: Chapter X, New York - II,"

Washington D.C. 1918, Accessed on April 4, 2017, https://net.lib.byu. edu/estu/wwi/comment/japanvisit/JapanC10.htm.

238. Elgot, Jessica. "Stephen Hawking: Jeremy Corbyn is a disaster for Labour" The Guardian, March 7, 2107, https://www.theguardian.com/politics/2017/mar/07/ stephen-hawking-jeremy-corbyn-disastrous-labour-resign.

239. Wikipedia, "New World Order (conspiracy theory)," accessed March 11, 2017, https://en.wikipedia.org/wiki/New_World_Order_ (conspiracy_theory).

240. Farah, Joseph, "Meet the Real Walter Cronkite: 'Most trusted' newsman pushed radical agenda." WND.com, 7-18-2009, http://www.wnd.com /2009/07/104399/#ybYg7vLB8efQPVrt.99.Hear and watch Walter Cronkite speak these words at this video: https://www.youtube.com/ watch?v=gqceRP3LiMw.

241. February 17, 1950, appearance before the U.S. Senate Committee on Foreign Relations Senate Report (Senate Foreign Relations Committee) (1950). Revision of the United Nations Charter: Hearings Before a Subcommittee of the Committee on Foreign Relations, Eighty-First Congress. United States Government Printing Office. p. 494. accessed March 11, 2017, Testimony on Wikisource: https://en.wikisource.org/ wiki/James_Warburg_before_the_Subcommittee_on_Revision_of_the_ United_Nations_Charter#We_shall_have_world_government.

242. Jasper, William F., "TPP—Trilateralist Power Politics," The New American, 4-25-16, https://www.thenewamerican.com/world-news/ item/23032-tpp-trilateralist-power-politics.

243. Ibid.

244. Ibid.

245. Grove, Richard. "Researching the Infamous Quotations Attributed to Zbigniew Brzezinski," May 1, 2013…citing this source: Zbigniew Brzezi ski, "Between Two Ages: America's Role in the Technetronic Era," pp.252-253: https://tragedyandhope.com/ researching-the-infamous-quotations-attributed-to-zbigniew-brzezinski/.

246. Grove, Richard. "Researching the Infamous Quotations Attributed to Zbigniew Brzezinski," May 1, 2013… citing this source: Zbigniew Brzezi ski, "America in the

Technetronic Age", (appeared in the now-defunct journal Encounter), January 1968. p.21: https://tragedyandhope.com/researching-the-infamous-quotations-attributed-to-zbigniew-brzezinski/.

247. Talbott, Strobe. "America Abroad: The Birth of the Global Nation." July 20, 1992, TIME.com., http://content.time.com/time/magazine/article/0,9171,976015,00.html#ixzz2dz1q6axw.

248. Bell, Larry. "In Their Own Words: Climate Alarmists Debunk Their 'Science'," Forbes, 2-5-13, https://www.forbes.com/sites/larrybell/2013/02/05/in-their-own-words-climate-alarmists-debunk-their-science/#2f0b86768a37.

249. Ibid.

250. The Holy See, "ENCYCLICAL LETTER LAUDATO SI' OF THE HOLY FATHER FRANCIS ON CARE FOR OUR COMMON HOME," 5-24-15, (p. 51), accessed March 11, 2017, http://w2.vatican.va/content/francesco/en/encyclicals/documents/papa-francesco_20150524_enciclica-laudato-si.pdf.

251. Wam, "It's 'World Government Summit': 150 governments in Dubai from Feb. 8-10," Emirates 24/7 News, January 06, 2016, http://www.emirates247.com/news/government/it-s-world-government-summit-150-governments-in-dubai-from-feb-8-10-2016-01-06-1.616141.

252. Snyder, Michael, "12 Times Pope Francis Has Openly Promoted a One World Religion or a New World Order," Charisma News, accessed March 11, 2017, http://www.charismanews.com/opinion/58963-12-times-pope-francis-has-openly-promoted-a-one-world-religion-or-a-new-world-order.

253. "Vatican calls for 'central World Bank' and 'global authority,'" Mirror Spectrum, January 3, 2017, http://mirrorspectrum.com/spectrum/vatican-calls-for-central-world-bank-and-global-authority#.

254. Sinclair, Timothy J., "Global Governance," Polity; 1 edition (October 8, 2012), accessed March 11, 2017, https://books.google.com/books?id=Dh6neRbMuEcC&pg=PT147&lpg=PT147&dq=aliens+from+another+planet+Global+governance&source=bl&ots=8qUZcG8mSd&sig=9tNdtEfbVDIjO3-h9RYr6y8OsPI&hl=en&sa=X&ved=0ahUKEwjZka_u083SAhUp4YMKHaK4B_sQ6AEIIzAC#v=onepage&q=aliens%20from%20another%20planet%20Global%20governance&f=false.

255. Ibid.

256. Pierre Teilhard de Chardin, "The Phenomenon of Man," (Harper Perennial, 1955): 244–245.

257. Pierre Teilhard de Chardin, "The Future of Mankind," (Harper & Row, 1955): 182.

258. Robert Muller, "Most of All They Taught Me Happiness," (Garden City, NY: Image Book, 1985): 116–117.

259. Maynard, Elliott and Sharon, "A Proper Earth Government—A Framework & How to Create It," Robert Muller—Contributor, Humanitad, (copyright 2015), accessed March 11, 2017, http://www.humanitad.org/team/23/.

260. Ibid.

261. Hensch, Mark, "Bill Clinton: Nationalism taking us to 'the edge of our destruction'," The Hill, 3-9-17, http://thehill.com/homenews/news/323259-bill-clinton-nationalism-the-edge-of-our-destruction.

Chapter 33—Reversing the Curse

262. Luke 4:1, Matthew 4:1. (Regarding the location of Jesus' temptation experience),

Cambridge Bible for Schools and Colleges:

"The scene of the temptation is supposed to be the mountain near Jericho, thence called Quarantania. The tradition is not ancient, but the site is very probable, being rocky, bleak, and repellent …" http://biblehub.com/commentaries/luke/4-1.htm.

Pulpit Commentary:

"Tradition has fixed upon a hill district bordering on the road which leads up from Jericho to Jerusalem, as the scene of the temptation. The hill itself, from being the supposed spot where the Lord spent these forty days, is named Quarantania. The rocks in this neighborhood contain many caves." http://biblehub.com/commentaries/luke/4-1.htm.

Ellicott's Commentary for English Readers:

"The scene of the Temptation was probably not far from that of the Baptism, probably, too, as it implies solitude, on the eastern rather than the western side of the Jordan. The traditional Desert of Quarantania (the name referring to the forty days' fast) is in the neighbourhood of Jericho." http://biblehub.com/commentaries/matthew/4-1.htm.

Meyer's New Testament Commentary:

The same wilderness of Judea spoken of in ch. 3. According to the tradition, we are to think of the very rugged wilderness of Quarantania (wilderness of Jericho, Joshua 16:1). http://biblehub.com/commentaries/matthew/4-1.htm.

263. Colossians 2:15, "Ellicott's Commentary for English Readers," Biblehub.com, http://biblehub.com/commentaries/colossians/2-15.htm.

264. Colossians 2:15, "Barnes' Notes on the Bible," Biblehub.com, http://biblehub.com/commentaries/colossians/2-15.htm.

265. Colossians 2:15, "Barnes' Notes on the Bible," Biblehub.com, http://biblehub.com/commentaries/colossians/2-15.htm.

266. 2 Corinthians 2:14, "Vincent's Word Study," Biblehub.com, http://biblehub.com/commentaries/2_corinthians/2-14.htm.

267. Ephesians 4:8, "Ellicott's Commentary for English Readers," Biblehub.com, http://biblehub.com/commentaries/ephesians/4-8.htm.

268. Acts 1:4, Biblehub.com, "Meyer's NT Commentary":

"The ascension took place on the Mount of Olives. ... It is not the distance of the place of the ascension, but of the Mount of Olives, on which it occurred, that is meant. Luke here supposes that more precisely defined locality as already known; but if he had had any particular design in naming the Mount of Olives (Baumgarten, p. 28 f.: that he wished to lead their thoughts to the future, according to Ezekiel 11:23; Zechariah 14:6), he must have said so, and could least of all presume that Theophilus would understand such a tacit prophetic allusion, especially as the Mount of Olives was already sufficiently known to him from the Gospel, Acts 19:29, Acts 21:37, without any such latent reference." (Author's note: Most scholarly commentaries are in agreement that Acts 1:4 is a literal reference to the exact place of Jesus' ascension as being the Mount of Olives, although there are other arguments for a different location.), http://biblehub.com/commentaries/acts/1-12.htm.

Chapter 34—Eternal Destiny

269. Dr. Willard, Dallas, "Your Place in This World," LifeWay Christian Resources, transcribed and published from Dr. Willard's commencement address at Greenville College in May 2004. Transcribed and edited by Steve

Bond of Holman Bible Publishers. accessed March 11, 2017, http://www.dwillard.org/articles/artview.asp?artID=109.

270. 2 Peter 1:4, MacLaren's Expositions, Biblehub.com, http://biblehub.com/commentaries/2_peter/1-4.htm.

271. 2 Peter 1:4, Matthew Poole's Commentary, Biblehub.com, http://biblehub.com/commentaries/2_peter/1-4.htm.

272. The Church of Jesus Christ of Latter-Day Saints, "Becoming Like God," accessed March 11, 2017, https://www.lds.org/topics/becoming-like-god?lang=eng&old=true.From the website's article:
"When asked about this topic [Of God having once been a "man"], Church President Gordon B. Hinckley told a reporter in 1997, "That gets into some pretty deep theology that we don't know very much about." When asked about the belief in humans' divine potential, President Hinckley responded, "Well, as God is, man may become. We believe in eternal progression. Very strongly."

273. Reed, Elizabeth Armstrong. "Primitive Buddhism: Its Origin and Teachings," Forgotten Books (May 20, 2012), accessed March 11, 2017, https://books.google.com/books?id=-P0WAAAAYAAJ&pg=PA132&lpg=PA132&dq=into+the+%E2%80%9Cdivine+essence,+buddhists&source=bl&ots=q-M-hh8FJK&sig=mu3Brqba8eoACb880RZVzEVieDY&hl=en&sa=X&ved=0ahUKEwiwlMXU2fLSAhUEOCYKHdqRDssQ6AEILjAE#v=onepage&q=into%20the%20%E2%80%9Cdivine%20essence%2C%20buddhists&f=false.

Chapter 35—Our Higher Calling

274. Revelation 20:4, "Barnes' Notes on the Bible," (Commentaries), [See also Gill's Exposition of the Scriptures, the Cambridge Bible for Schools and Colleges, Vincent's Word Studies, and the Pulpit Commentary at the same page for further affirmation of this proposition] http://biblehub.com/commentaries/jude/1-14.htm.

275. Psalm 149:6-9, "Matthew Henry's Concise Commentary," Biblehub.com, http://biblehub.com/commentaries/jude/1-14.htm.

276. Jude 1:14, "Barnes' Notes on the Bible," (Commentaries), [See also Matthew Poole's Commentary at the same page for further affirmation of this proposition], Biblehub.com, http://biblehub.com/commentaries/jude/1-14.htm.

Chapter 37—Just Down the Road

277. Luke 12:8–9, Pulpit Commentary, Biblehub.com, http://biblehub.com/commentaries/luke/12-8.htm.